THE GROLIER LIBRARY
OF
SCIENCE BIOGRAPHIES

VOLUME 3

D'Abano–Flamsteed

Grolier Educational
Sherman Turnpike, Danbury, Connecticut 06816

Published 1997 by
Grolier Educational
Danbury Connecticut 06816

Copyright © 1996 by Market House Books Ltd.
Published for the School and Library market exclusively
by Grolier Educational, 1997

Compiled and Typeset by Market House Books Ltd, Aylesbury, UK.

General Editors
    John Daintith BSc, PhD
    Derek Gjertsen BA

Market House Editors
    Elizabeth Martin MA
    Anne Stibbs BA
    Fran Alexander BA
    Jonathan Law BA
    Peter Lewis BA, DPhil
    Mark Salad

Picture Research
    Linda Wells

Contributors
    Eve Daintith BSc
    Rosalind Dunning BA
    Garry Hammond BSc
    Robert Hine BSc, MSc
    Valerie Illingworth BSc, MPhil
    Sarah Mitchell BA
    Susan O'Neill BSc
    W. J. Palmer MSc
    Roger F. Picken BSc, PhD
    Carol Russell BSc
    W. J. Sherratt BSc, MSc, PhD
    Jackie Smith BA
    B. D. Sorsby BSc, PhD
    Elizabeth Tootill BSc, MSc
    P. Welch DPhil
    Anthony Wootton

Published by arrangement with
The Institute of Physics Publishing
Bristol BS1 6NX
UK

ISBN   Volume 3   0-7172-7629-5
            Ten-Volume Set   0-7172-7626-0
Library of Congress Catalog Number: 96-31474
Cataloging Information to be obtained directly from Grolier Educational.
First Edition
Printed in the United States of America

CONTENTS

PREFACE

ABOUT THE GROLIER LIBRARY OF SCIENCE BIOGRAPHIES

The 19th-century poet and essayist Oliver Wendell Holmes wrote:

> Science is a first-rate piece of furniture for a man's upper chamber, if he has common sense on the ground floor.
>
> *The Poet at the Breakfast-Table* (1872)

While it has been fashionable in this century to assume that science is capable of solving all human problems, we should, perhaps, pause to reflect on Holmes's comment. Scientific knowledge can only be of value to the human race if it is made use of wisely by the men and women who have control of our lives.

If this is true, all thinking people need a solid piece of scientific furniture in their upper chambers. For this reason the editors and publishers of this series of books have set out to say as much about science itself as about the scientists who have created it.

All the entries contain basic biographical data – place and date of birth, posts held, etc. – but do not give exhaustive personal details about the subject's family, prizes, honorary degrees, etc. Most of the space has been devoted to their main scientific achievements and the nature and importance of these achievements. This has not always been easy; in particular, it has not always been possible to explain in relatively simple terms work in the higher reaches of abstract mathematics or modern theoretical physics.

Perhaps the most difficult problem was compiling the entry list. We have attempted to include people who have produced major advances in theory or have made influential or well-known discoveries. A particular difficulty has been the selection of contemporary scientists, in view of the fact that of all scientists who have ever lived, the vast majority are still alive. In this we have been guided by lists of prizes and awards made by scientific societies. We realize that there are dangers in this – the method would not, for instance, catch an unknown physicist working out a revolutionary new system of mechanics in the seclusion of the Bern patent office. It does, however, have the advantage that it is based on the judgments of other scientists. We have to a great extent concentrated on what might be called the "traditional" pure sciences – physics, chemistry, biology, astronomy, and the earth sciences. We also give a more limited coverage of medicine and mathematics and have included a selection of people who have made important contributions to engineering and technology. A few of the entries cover workers in such fields as anthropology and psychology, and a small number of philosophers are represented.

A version of this book was published in 1993 by the Institute of Physics, to whom we are grateful for permission to reuse the material in this set. Apart from adding a number of new biographies to the Institute of Physics text, we have enhanced the work with some 1,500 photographs and a large number of quotations by or about the scientists themselves. We have also added a simple pronunciation guide (the key to which will be found on the back of this page) to provide readers with a way of knowing how to pronounce the more difficult and unfamiliar names.

Each volume in this set has a large biographical section. The scientists are arranged in strict alphabetical order according to surname. The entry for a scientist is given under the name by which he or she is most commonly known. Thus the American astrophysicist James Van Allen is generally known as Van Allen (not Allen) and is entered under V. The German chemist Justus von Liebig is commonly referred to as Liebig and is entered under L. In addition, each volume contains a section on "Sources and Further Reading" for important entries, a glossary of useful definitions of technical words, and an index of the whole set. The index lists all the scientists who have entries, indicating the volume number and the page on which the entry will be found. In addition scientists are grouped together in the index by country (naturalized nationality if it is not their country of origin) and by scientific discipline. Volume 10 contains a chronological list of scientific discoveries and publications arranged under year and subject. It is intended to be used for tracing the development of a subject or for relating advances in one branch of science to those in another branch. Additional information can be obtained by referring to the biographical section of the book.

JD
DG 1996

PRONUNCIATION GUIDE

A guide to pronunciation is given for foreign names and names of foreign origin; it appears in brackets after the first mention of the name in the main text of the article. Names of two or more syllables are broken up into small units, each of one syllable, separated by hyphens. The stressed syllable in a word of two or more syllables is shown in **bold** type.

We have used a simple pronunciation system based on the phonetic respelling of names, which avoids the use of unfamiliar symbols. The sounds represented are as follows (the phonetic respelling is given in brackets after the example word, if this is not pronounced as it is spelled):

a *as in* bat
ah *as in* palm (pahm)
air *as in* dare (dair), pear (pair)
ar *as in* tar
aw *as in* jaw, ball (bawl)
ay *as in* gray, ale (ayl)
ch *as in* chin
e *as in* red
ee *as in* see, me (mee)
eer *as in* ear (eer)
er *as in* fern, layer
f *as in* fat, phase (fayz)
g *as in* gag
i *as in* pit
I *as in* mile (mIl), by (bI)
j *as in* jaw, age (ayj), gem (jem)
k *as in* keep, cactus (**kak**-tus), quite (kwIt)
ks *as in* ox (oks)
ng *as in* hang, rank (rangk)
o *as in* pot

oh *as in* home (hohm), post (pohst)
oi *as in* boil, toy (toi)
oo *as in* food, fluke (flook)
or *as in* organ, quarter (**kwor**-ter)
ow *as in* powder, loud (lowd)
s *as in* skin, cell (sel)
sh *as in* shall
th *as in* bath
th as in feather (**fe*th***-er)
ts *as in* quartz (kworts)
u *as in* buck (buk), blood (blud), one (wun)
u(r) *as in* urn (but without sounding the "r")
uu *as in* book (buuk)
v *as in* van, of (ov)
y *as in* yet, menu (**men**-yoo), onion (**un**-yon)
z *as in* zoo, lose (looz)
zh *as in* treasure (**tre**-zher)

The consonants b, d, h, l, m, n, p, r, t, and w have their normal sounds and are not listed in the table.

In our pronunciation guide a consonant is occasionally doubled to avoid confusing the syllable with a familiar word, for example, -iss rather than -is (which is normally pronounced -iz); -off rather than -of (which is normally pronounced -ov).

d'Abano, Pietro

(*c.* 1250–1316)

ITALIAN PHYSICIAN AND PHILOSOPHER

D'Abano (**dah**-bah-noh) was born at Abano near Padua in Italy and studied in Greece and Constantinople before learning medicine in Paris. He became professor of medicine at Padua University in 1306 and soon became a celebrated teacher and physician.

His knowledge of Greek enabled him to study the texts of the ancient scholars and physicians and to attempt to reconcile medicine and philosophy in his most famous book known as the *Conciliator*. This rationalist stance together with his interest in astrology brought d'Abano into conflict with the Catholic Church. In 1315 he was accused of being a heretic and was twice brought before the Inquisition. Acquitted the first time, he died before a second trial was completed and his body was hidden by friends. He was nevertheless found guilty and the Inquisition ordered that his effigy be burned instead.

Daguerre, Louis-Jacques-Mandé

(1789–1851)

FRENCH PHYSICIST, INVENTOR, AND PAINTER

Daguerre (da-**gair**), the inventor of the daguerreotype (the first practical photograph), first became interested in the effect of light on films from the artistic point of view. Born in Cormeilles near Paris, France, he worked first as a tax officer, later becoming a painter of opera scenery. Working with Charles-Marie Bouton he invented the diorama – a display of paintings on semitransparent linen that transmitted and reflected light – and opened a diorama in Paris (1822).

From 1826 Daguerre turned his attention to heliography (photographing the sun) and he was partnered in this by Joseph-Nicéphore Niepce until Niepce's death in 1833. Daguerre continued his work and in 1839 presented to the French Academy of Sciences the daguerreotype, which needed only about 25-minutes exposure time to produce an image, compared with over eight hours for Niepce's previous attempts. In the daguerreotype a photographic image was obtained on a copper plate coated with a light-sensitive layer of silver iodide and bromide.

d'Ailly, Pierre

(1350–1420)

FRENCH GEOGRAPHER,
COSMOLOGIST, AND THEOLOGIAN

D'Ailly (da-**yee**), who was born in Compiègne, France, studied at the University of Paris, serving as its chancellor from 1389 until 1395. He then became a bishop, first of Le Puy and subsequently of Cambrai. He became a cardinal in 1411.

Primarily concerned with church affairs, in which he advocated reform, d'Ailly was also interested in science and was the leading geographical theorist of his time. He was the author of the influential work *Imago mundi* (Image of the World), which was completed by 1410 and printed in about 1483. This was a summary of the classical and Arabian geographers, typical of the medieval period, and was influenced by Roger Bacon. D'Ailly's underestimate of the Earth's circumference and exaggeration of the size of Asia may well have influenced Columbus, whose copy of d'Ailly's work, with his marginal annotations, still survives.

D'Ailly's work had been written without the benefit of Ptolemy's *Geography*, which only became available in a Latin version shortly afterward. He produced, in 1413, the *Compendium cosmographiae* (Compendium of Cosmography). This was basically a summary of Ptolemy, reviving uncritically the full fabric of Ptolemaic geography, which was already being dismantled by such travelers as Marco Polo.

Daimler, Gottlieb Wilhelm

(1834–1900)

GERMAN ENGINEER AND
INVENTOR

Daimler (**dIm**-ler or daym-ler), who was born in Schorndorf, Germany, became a gunsmith's apprentice in 1848. He studied at Stuttgart technical school, worked for a period at an engineering plant, and completed his education at Stuttgart Polytechnic. After traveling in England and France, he worked from 1863 in German engineering companies, beginning work on an internal-combustion engine in 1872.

In 1885 Daimler set up a company with Wilhelm Maybach and in 1883 and 1885 designs for an internal-combustion engine suitable for light vehicles were patented. In 1890 he founded the Daimler-Motoren-Gesellschaft company, which, in 1899, built the first Mercedes car.

Dainton, Frederick Sydney

(1914–   )

BRITISH PHYSICAL CHEMIST AND
SCIENTIFIC ADMINISTRATOR

Perhaps science will only regain its lost primacy as peoples and governments begin to recognize that sound scientific work is the only secure basis for the construction of policies to ensure the survival of mankind without irreversible damage to Planet Earth.

—*New Scientist*, 3 March 1990

Born in the English industrial city of Sheffield, Dainton was educated at the universities of Oxford and Cambridge. After World War II he remained in Cambridge until 1950, when he moved to the University of Leeds as professor of physical chemistry. In 1965 Dainton was appointed vice-chancellor of the University of Nottingham. He returned to chemistry in 1970, when he was elected professor of chemistry at Oxford. Soon after, in 1973, he was made chairman of the University Grants Committee, a post he held until his retirement in 1978.

Dainton's early work in physical chemistry was on the kinetics and thermodynamics of polymerization reactions. From about 1945 he turned his attention to studies of radiolysis – i.e., chemical changes produced by high-energy radiation (alpha, beta, or gamma rays). In particular, he has studied the properties and reactions of hydrated electrons in liquids.

From 1965 he was a member of the Council for Scientific Policy and was its chairman from 1969 to 1973. While holding this office he was influential in decisions made about the way British academic research is financed. He was raised to the British peerage, as Baron Dainton of Hallam Moors, in 1986.

Dale, Sir Henry Hallett

(1875–1968)

BRITISH PHYSIOLOGIST

Educated at Cambridge University and St. Bartholomew's Hospital in his native city of London, Dale became, in 1904, director of the Wellcome Physiological Research Laboratories. His work there over the next ten years included the isolation (with Arthur Ewins) from ergot fungi of a pharmacologically active extract – acetylcholine – which he found had similar effects to the parasympathetic nervous system on various organs. It was later shown by Otto Loewi that a substance released by electrical stimulation of the vagus nerve was responsible for effecting changes in heartbeat. Following up this work, Dale showed that the substance is in fact acetylcholine, thus establishing that chemical as well as electrical stimuli are involved in nerve action. For this research Dale and Loewi shared the 1936 Nobel Prize for physiology or medicine. Dale also worked on the properties of histamine and related substances, including their actions in allergic and anaphylactic conditions. He was the chairman of an international committee responsible for the standardization of biological preparations, and from 1928 to 1942 was director of the National Institute for Medical Research.

d'Alembert, Jean Le Rond

(1717–1783)

FRENCH MATHEMATICIAN,
ENCYCLOPEDIST, AND
PHILOSOPHER

> Push on, and faith will catch up with you.
> —Advice to people unable to accept the
> methods of the calculus

D'Alembert (da-lahm-**bair**) was the illegitimate son of a Parisian society hostess, Mme de Tenzin, and was abandoned on the steps of a Paris church, from which he was named. He was brought up by a glazier and his wife, and his father, the chevalier Destouches, made sufficient money available to ensure that d'Alembert received a good education although he never acknowledged that d'Alembert was his son. He graduated from Mazarin College in 1735 and was admitted to the Academy of Sciences in 1741.

D'Alembert's mathematical work was chiefly in various fields of applied mathematics, in particular dynamics. In 1743 he published his *Traité de dynamique* (Treatise on Dynamics), in which the famous *d'Alembert principle* is enunciated. This principle is a generalization of Newton's third law of motion, and it states that Newton's law holds not only for fixed bodies but also for those that are free to move. D'Alembert wrote numerous other mathematical works on such subjects as fluid dynamics, the theory of winds, and the properties of vibrating strings. His most significant purely mathematical innovation was his invention and development of the theory of partial differential equations. Between 1761 and 1780 he published eight volumes of mathematical studies.

Apart from his mathematical work he is perhaps more widely known for his work on Denis Diderot's *Encyclopédie* (Encyclopedia) as editor of the mathematical and scientific articles, and his association with the philosophes. D'Alembert was a friend of Voltaire's and he had a lively interest in theater and music, which led him to conduct experiments on the properties of sound and to write a number of theoretical treatises on such matters as harmony. He was elected to the French Academy in 1754 and became its permanent secretary in 1772 but he refused the presidency of the Berlin Academy.

Dalén, Nils Gustaf

(1869–1937)

SWEDISH ENGINEER

Born in Stenstorp, Sweden, Dalén (da-**layn**) graduated in mechanical engineering in 1896 from the Chalmers Institute at Göteborg and then spent a year at the Swiss Federal Institute of Technology at Zurich. For several years he researched and improved hot-air turbines, compressors, and air pumps and from 1900 to 1905 worked with an engineering firm, Dalén and Alsing. He then became plant manager for the Swedish Carbide and Acetylene Company, which in 1909 became the Swedish Gas Accumulator Company with Dalén as managing director.

Dalén is remembered principally for his inventions relating to acetylene lighting for lighthouses and other navigational aids, and in particular an automatic light-controlled valve, for which he received the 1912 Nobel Prize for physics. The valve, known as "Solventil," used the difference in heat-absorbing properties between a dull black surface and a highly polished one to produce differential expansion of gases, and thus to regulate the main gas valve of an acetylene-burning lamp. The lamp could thus be automatically dimmed or extinguished in daylight, and this allowed buoys and lighthouses to be left unattended and less gas to be used. The system soon came into widespread use and is still in use today.

Another invention of Dalén's was a porous filler for acetylene tanks, "Agamassan," that prevented explosions. It was ironic that in 1912 he was himself blinded by an explosion during the course of an experiment. This did not, however, deter him from continuing his experimental work up to his death.

Dalton, John

(1766–1844)

BRITISH CHEMIST AND PHYSICIST

> An enquiry into the relative weights of the ultimate particles of bodies is a subject, as far as I know, entirely new; I have lately been prosecuting this enquiry with remarkable success.
> —*On the Absorption of Gases by Water*
> (1802)

The son of a hand-loom weaver from Eaglesfield in the northwest of England, Dalton was born into the nonconformist tradition of the region and remained a Quaker all his life. He was educated at the village school until the age of 11, and received tuition from Elihu Robinson, a wealthy Quaker, meteorologist, and instrument maker, who first encouraged Dalton's interest in meteorology. At the age of only 12, Dalton himself was teaching in the village. He then worked on the land for two years before moving to Kendal with his brother to teach (1781). In 1793 he moved to Manchester where he first taught at the Manchester New College, a Presbyterian institute. In 1794 he was elected to the Manchester Literary and Philosophical Society at which most of his papers were read.

From 1787 until his death Dalton maintained a diary of meteorological observations of the Lake District where he lived. His first published work, *Meteorological Observations and Essays* (1793), contained the first of his laws concerning the behavior of compound atmospheres: that the same weight of water vapor is taken up by a given space in air and in a vacuum. Both Dalton and his brother were color blind and he was the first to describe the condition, sometimes known as daltonism, in his work *Extraordinary Facts Relating to the Vision of Colours* (1794).

In 1801 Dalton read four important papers to the Manchester Philosophical Society. *On the Constitution of Mixed Gases* contains what is now known as the law of partial pressures and asserts that air is a mixture, not a compound, in which the various gases exert pressure on the walls of a vessel independently of each other. *On the Force of Steam* includes the first explanation of the dew point and hence the founding of exact hygrometry. It also demonstrates that water vapor behaves like any other gas. The third paper, *On Evaporation*, shows that the quantity of water evaporated is proportional to the vapor pressure. *On the Expan-*

sion of Gases by Heat contains the important conclusion that all gases expand equally by heat. This law had been discovered by Jacques Charles in 1787 but Dalton was the first to publish.

During this time, Dalton was developing his atomic theory, for which he is best known. A physical clue to the theory was provided by the solubility of gases in water. Dalton expected to find that all gases had the same solubility in water but the fact that they did not helped to confirm his idea that the atoms of different gases had different weights. The first table of atomic weights was appended to the paper *On the Absorption of Gases by Water*, read in 1802 but not printed until 1805. In another paper read in 1802 and printed in 1805 he showed that when nitric oxide is used to absorb oxygen in a eudiometer they combine in two definite ratios depending on the method of mixing. This was the beginning of the law of multiple proportions and led Dalton to much work on the oxides of nitrogen and the hydrocarbons methane and ethylene to confirm the law.

The atomic theory was first explicitly stated by Dalton at a Royal Institution lecture in December 1803 and first appeared in print in Thomas Thomson's *System of Chemistry* (1807). Dalton's own full exposition appeared in *A New System of Chemical Philosophy* (1808), with further volumes in 1810 and 1827. The basic postulates of the theory are that matter consists of atoms; that atoms can neither be created nor destroyed; that all atoms of the same element are identical, and different elements have different types of atoms; that chemical reactions take place by a rearrangement of atoms; and that compounds consist of "compound atoms" formed from atoms of the constituent elements.

Using this theory, Dalton was able to rationalize the various laws of chemical combination (conservation of mass, definite proportions, multiple proportions) and show how they followed from the theory. He did, however, make the mistake of assuming "greatest simplicity": i.e., that the simplest compound of two elements must be binary (e.g., water was HO). His system of atomic weights was not very accurate (e.g., he gave oxygen an atomic weight of seven rather than eight). Dalton's theory remained open to dispute until 1858 when Stanislao Cannizzaro's

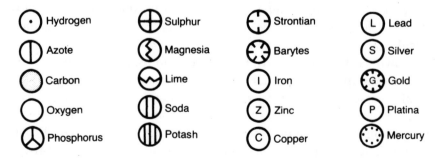

CHEMICAL ELEMENTS   *The symbols for the chemical elements used by John Dalton.*

rediscovery of Amedeo Avogadro's work removed the last objections to the theory. Dalton's symbols for atoms and molecules were spherical and he used wooden molecular models similar to the modern version.

Dam, Carl Peter Henrik

(1895–1976)

DANISH BIOCHEMIST

Dam was born in Copenhagen and educated at the polytechnic and the university there, obtaining his doctorate in 1934. He taught at the university from 1923 until 1941, when – although stranded in America because of the war – he was appointed professor of biochemistry at the Copenhagen Polytechnic. From 1956 until 1963 Dam served as director of the Biochemical Division of the Danish Fat Research Institute.

From 1928 to 1930 Dam worked on the problem of cholesterol metabolism in chickens. Cholesterol, first analyzed by Heinrich Wieland, is a sterol with an important role in mammalian physiology. It was known that many mammals could readily synthesize it, but it was assumed that chickens lacked this ability. To test this assumption Dam began to rear chickens on a cholesterol-free diet enriched with vitamins A and D.

As it turned out he found that chickens could synthesize cholesterol but, more importantly, he also found that if kept on such a diet for two to three weeks the chickens developed hemorrhages under the skin, and blood removed for examination showed delayed coagulation. Supplementing the diet with fat, vitamin C, and cholesterol made no appreciable difference, so Dam concluded that the condition was due to lack of a hitherto unrecognized factor in the diet.

The missing factor, found to be present in green leaves and pig liver, was designated vitamin K by Dam in 1935 (K being the initial letter of "koagulation," the Scandinavian and German form of the word). Using ether, Dam went on to extract the fat-soluble vitamin K from such sources as alfalfa, and in 1939 succeeded, with Paul Karrer, in isolating it. It was for this work that Dam shared the 1943 Nobel Prize for physiology or medicine with Edward Doisy.

Dana, James Dwight

(1813–1895)

AMERICAN GEOLOGIST,
MINERALOGIST, AND ZOOLOGIST

> We should give a high place in our estimate to
> all investigation tending to evaluate the vari-
> ation of permanence of species, their muta-
> bility or immutability.
> —*Thoughts on Species* (1856)

Dana was born at Utica in New York State and educated at Yale (1830–33) where he became interested in geology. He worked initially as assistant to Benjamin Silliman and published, in 1837, *A System of Mineralogy*, one of the major textbooks on the subject.

He sailed as geologist and naturalist on the Wilkes expedition (1838–42) visiting the Antarctic and Pacific. On his return, Dana published a series of research reports on the voyage during the period 1844–54, which established his reputation as an important scientist. These included *Zoophytes* (1846), *Geology* (1849), and *Crustacea* (1852).

In 1847 Dana formulated his geosynclinal theory of the origin of mountains. He introduced the term geosyncline to refer to troughs or dips in the Earth's surface that became filled with sediment. These huge deposits of sediment could then, Dana proposed, be compressed and folded into mountain chains.

He was appointed to the chair of natural history at Yale in 1856 and in 1864 to the chair of geology and mineralogy where he remained until his retirement in 1890. He published several important books while at Yale, including his most notable textbook, *Manual of Geology* (1863), and the synthesis of his work on coral reefs in *Corals and Coral Islands* (1872). In agreement with Charles Darwin's ideas, published in 1842, Dana argued that coral islands are the result of subsidence of the island together with the upward growth of corals.

Daniell, John Frederic

(1790–1845)

BRITISH CHEMIST AND
METEOROLOGIST

> His extensive intercourse with men in general added to his natural perspicacity,
> gave him a clear insight into character, and conferred on him advantages which
> men of science in general do not possess.
>
> —Obituary notice of Daniell (1845)

Daniell was the son of a London lawyer. He started work in the sugar-refining factory of a relative and, on the basis of early researches, he was elected to the Royal Society at the age of 23. He was appointed as first professor of chemistry at the newly opened King's College, London, in 1831.

Daniell invented a number of scientific instruments, including a hygrometer (1820) to measure humidity in the atmosphere. His theories on the atmosphere and wind movements were published in *Meteorological Essays and Observations* (1823). He also stressed the importance of moisture in hothouse management.

Daniell is best remembered for his introduction in 1836 of a new type of electric cell. The voltaic cell, introduced by Alessandro Volta in 1797, lost power once the current was drawn. This was due to bubbles of hydrogen collecting on the copper plate and producing resistance to the free flow of the circuit (polarization). With the growth of telegraphy there was a real need for a cell that could deliver a constant current over a long period of time. In the *Daniell cell* a zinc rod is immersed in a dilute solution of sulfuric acid contained in a porous pot, which stands in a solution of copper sulfate surrounded by copper. Hydrogen reacts with the copper sulfate. The porous pot prevents the two electrolytes from mixing, and at the positive (copper) electrode, copper is deposited from the copper sulfate. Thus no hydrogen bubbles can form on this electrode.

Daniels, Farrington

(1889–1972)

AMERICAN CHEMIST

Born in Minneapolis in Minnesota, Daniels was educated at the University of Minnesota and at Harvard, where he obtained his PhD in 1914. He moved to the University of Wisconsin in 1920, spending his whole career there and serving as professor of chemistry from 1928 until his retirement in 1959.

Daniels worked on a wide variety of chemical problems. In addition to a textbook, *Outlines of Physical Chemistry* (1931), he wrote on photochemistry, nitrogen fixation, and thermoluminescence.

He was also interested in the utilization of solar energy, publishing a book on the subject, *Direct Use of the Sun's Energy* (1964), and organizing a symposium on it in 1954, many years before the discussion of solar energy had become fashionable.

Dansgaard, Willi

(1922–   )

DANISH METEOROLOGIST

Dansgaard (**dans**-gord) was born in the Danish capital of Copenhagen and educated at the university there, obtaining his PhD in 1961. He has studied the applications of environmental isotopes to meteorological, hydrological, and glaciological problems, and in particular to the climate of the last 100,000 years. Oxygen is present in two stable isotopes – the normal oxygen–16 and a much smaller proportion of oxygen–18 with two extra neutrons in its nucleus. In 1947 Harold Urey demonstrated that the variation of the two isotopes in sea water depended on temperature, i.e., the colder the temperature the smaller the oxygen–18 content of the seas. He had further established that a slight change of temperature would produce a measurable alteration in oxygen–18 levels.

In the early 1960s the U.S. army drilled down into the Greenland icecap, producing an ice core 4,600 feet (1,400 m) long and with a 100,000-year history. Dansgaard realized that by making careful measurement of the core's varying oxygen–18 level he should be able to reconstruct the climatic history of the last 100,000 years. The most recent ice age, ending 10,000 years ago, was clearly marked, as was evidence of a weather cycle during the last 1,000 years.

Darby, Abraham

(*c.* 1678–1717)

BRITISH METALLURGIST

Darby, who was born in Dudley, England, developed the first successful method of smelting iron ore with coke, and in doing so made possible the large-scale production of good quality iron castings. Previously only wood charcoal had been used but supplies of this were depleted and there were insufficient fuel supplies to provide the growing volume of iron. Attempts to use coal were unsuccessful because the sulfur impurities it contained spoiled the iron. By coking the coal the sulfur could be removed. Darby, who had experience in smelting copper with coke, founded a factory at Coalbrookdale to smelt iron using coke, achieving success in 1709. Abundant coal supplies and Darby's process meant that brass could be replaced by iron from large furnaces. Thomas Newcomen's new steam engine (1712) needed hard-wearing metal parts for cylinders, etc. The iron castings introduced by Darby soon became an integral part of the industrial developments of the day.

Darby's grandson, also named Abraham, built the world's first iron bridge at Coalbrookdale (1779).

Darlington, Cyril Dean

(1903–1981)

BRITISH GENETICIST

> Mankind...will not willingly admit that its destiny can be revealed by the breeding of flies or the counting of chiasmata.
> —Royal Society Tercentenary Lecture, 1960

Born at Chorley in Lancashire, England, Darlington graduated in agriculture from Wye College, London, in 1923 and joined the John Innes Horticultural Institution, which was then under the directorship of William Bateson. He studied nuclear division, comparing mitosis (normal cell division) with meiosis (the reduction division that halves the chromosome number prior to gamete formation). He demonstrated that the chromosomes have already replicated by the first stage of mitosis whereas the chromosomes are still single in the earliest stage of meiosis, a discovery basic to nuclear cytology.

Darlington was also extremely interested in the crossing over of chromosomes that occurs at meiosis. He saw it as a mechanism that not only allows for recombination of genes between chromosomes; it is also able to account for the complete succession of meiotic events.

Darlington became director of the John Innes Institute in 1939 and presided over the move of the Institute from Merton to Bayfordbury in 1949. He became professor of botany at Oxford in 1953 and became emeritus professor in 1971. Darlington wrote a number of books on genetics, including *Evolution of Genetic Systems* (1939). With Ronald Fisher, he founded the journal *Heredity* in 1947.

Dart, Raymond Arthur

(1893–1988)

AUSTRALIAN ANATOMIST

> The loathsome cruelty of mankind to man forms one of his inescapable, characteristic, and differentiative features; it is explicable only in terms of his cannibalistic origins.
> —Quoted by Richard Leakey in *The Making of Mankind* (1981)

Born in Toowong, Australia, Dart was educated at the universities of Queensland and Sydney where he qualified as a physician in 1917. After a short period (1919–22) at University College, London, Dart moved to South Africa to serve as professor of anatomy at the University of the Witwatersrand, Johannesburg, a post he held until his retirement in 1958.

In 1924 Dart was privileged to make one of the great paleontological discoveries of the century, the Taung skull. For this he was indebted to his student Josephine Salmons who brought him in the summer of 1924 a fossil collected from a mine at Taung, Bechuanaland. Dart named it *Australopithecus africanus*, meaning southern African ape, and declared it to be intermediate between anthropoids and man. Such a claim was far from acceptable to many scholars at the time who, like Arthur Keith, dismissed the skull as that of a young anthropoid. Other and older australopithecine remains were later discovered by Robert Broom in South Africa, East Africa, and Asia, making it clear that they were in fact hominid. It is still however a matter of controversy whether *Australopithecus* lies in the direct line of descent to *Homo sapiens* or whether it represents a quite separate and unsuccessful evolutionary sideline.

Darwin, Charles Robert

(1809–1882)

BRITISH NATURALIST

> We must, however, acknowledge, as it seems to me, that man with all his noble qualities…still bears in his bodily frame the indelible stamp of his lowly origin.
> —*The Descent of Man* (1871)

> The preservation of favourable variations and the rejection of injurious variations, I call Natural Selection, or Survival of the Fittest.
> —*On the Origin of Species* (1859)

Darwin, who was born in Shrewsbury in England, began his university education by studying medicine at Edinburgh (1825), but finding he had no taste for the subject he entered Cambridge University to prepare for the Church. At Cambridge his interest in natural history, first stimulated by the geologist Adam Sedgwick, was encouraged by the professor of botany John Henslow. Their friendship led to Henslow's recommending Darwin to the admiralty for the position of naturalist on HMS *Beagle*, which was preparing to survey the coast of South America and the Pacific.

The *Beagle* sailed in 1831 and Darwin, armed with a copy of Charles Lyell's *Principles of Geology*, initially concerned himself more with the geological aspects of his work. However, his observations of animal species – particularly the way in which they gradually change from region to region – also led him to speculate on the development of life. He was particularly struck by the variation found in the finches of the Galápagos Islands, where he recorded some 14 different species, each thriving in a particular region of the islands. Darwin reasoned that it was highly unlikely that each species was individually created; more probably they had evolved from a parent species of finch on mainland Ecuador. Further considerations, back in England, as to the mechanism that brought this about resulted in probably the most important book in the history of biology.

On returning to England in 1836, Darwin first concerned himself with recording his travels in *A Naturalist's Voyage on the Beagle* (1839), which received the acclaim of Alexander von Humboldt. His interest in geology was reflected in *Structure and Distribution of Coral Reefs* (1842) and *Geological Observations on Volcanic Islands* (1844). These early works, which established his name in the scientific community and won the respect of Lyell, were fundamental to the development of his theories on evolution.

Early on Darwin had perceived that many questions in animal geography, comparative anatomy, and paleontology could only be answered by disregarding the theory of the immutability of the species (an idea widely held at the time) and accepting that one species evolved from another. The idea was not original but Darwin's contribution was to propose a means by which evolution could have occurred and to present his case clearly, backed up by a wealth of evidence. In 1838 he read Thomas Malthus's *An Essay on the Principle of Population* and quickly saw that Malthus's argument could be extended from man to all other forms of life. Thus environmental pressures, particularly the availability of food, act to select better adapted individuals, which survive to pass on their traits to subsequent generations. Valuable characteristics that arise through natural variability are therefore preserved while others with no survival value die out. If environmental conditions change, the population itself will gradually change as it adapts to the new conditions, and with time this will lead to the formation of new species. Darwin spent over 20 years amassing evidence in support of this theory of evolution by natural selection, so as to provide a buffer against the inevitable uproar that would greet his work on publication. In this period the nature of his studies was divulged only to close friends, such as Joseph Hooker, T. H. Huxley, and Charles Lyell.

The stimulus to publish came in June 1858 when Darwin received, quite unexpectedly, a communication from Alfred Russel Wallace that was effectively a synopsis of his own ideas. The question of priority was resolved through the action of Lyell and Hooker, who arranged for a joint paper to be read to the Linnean Society in July 1858. This consisted of Wallace's essay and a letter, dated 1857, from Darwin to the American botanist Asa Gray outlining Darwin's theories. Darwin later prepared an "abstract" of his work, published in November 1859 as *On the Origin of Species by Means of Natural Selection.*

As expected the work made him many enemies among orthodox scientists and churchmen since beliefs in the Creation and divine guidance were threatened by Darwin's revelations. Darwin, a retiring man, chose not to defend his views publicly – a task left to (and seemingly immensely enjoyed by) Huxley, "Darwin's bulldog," notably at the famous Oxford debate in 1860. Darwin continued quietly with his work, publishing books that extended and amplified his theories. One of these was *The Descent of Man* (1871), in which he applied his theory to the evolution of man from subhuman creatures. Many of his books are seen as pioneering works in various fields of biology, such as ecology and ethology.

Darwin was, however, troubled by one flaw in his theory – if inheritance were blending, i.e., if offspring received an average of the features of their parents (the then-held view of heredity), then how could the variation, so essential for natural selection to act on, come about? This problem was put in a nutshell by Fleeming Jenkin, professor of engineering at University College, London, who wrote a review of the *Origin* in 1867. In this Jenkin pointed out that any individual with a useful trait, assuming it mated with a normal partner, would pass on only 50% of the character to its children, 25% to its grandchildren, 12½% to its greatgrandchildren, and so on until the useful feature disappeared. The logic of this drove Darwin to resort to Lamarckian ideas of inheritance (of acquired characteristics) as elaborated in his theory of pangenesis in the sixth edition of the *Origin*. The question was not resolved until the rediscovery, nearly 20 years after Darwin's death, of Gregor Mendel's work, which demonstrated the particulate nature of inheritance, i.e., that hereditary characteristics are transmitted from parents to offspring by discrete entities later known as genes.

Darwin was troubled through most of his life by continuous illness, which most probably was due to infection by the trypanosome parasite causing Chagas's disease, contracted during his travels on the *Beagle*. On his death he was buried, despite his agnosticism, in Westminster Abbey.

Darwin, Erasmus

(1731–1802)

BRITISH PHYSICIAN

> Soon shall thy arm, unconquer'd steam, afar
> Drag the slow barge, or drive the rapid car;
> Or on wide-waving wings expanded bear
> The flying chariot through the field of air.
> —Predicting the uses of steam power.
> *The Botanic Garden* (1791)

Darwin was born at Elston in England. He studied medicine at the universities of Cambridge and Edinburgh, obtaining his MB from Cambridge in 1755. Darwin set up practice in Lichfield, where he soon established a reputation such that George III asked him to move to London to become his personal physician – an offer Darwin declined. He remained in Lichfield and founded, with friends, the Lunar Society of Birmingham – so called because of the monthly meetings held at members' houses. It included such eminent men as Joseph Priestley, Josiah Wedgwood, James Watt, and Matthew Boulton.

Darwin was something of an inventor, but is best remembered for his scientific writings, which often appeared in verse form. These were generally well received until the politician George Canning produced a very damaging parody of his work. This was part of a general campaign by the government against the Lunar Society for its support of the French and American revolutions and its denouncement of slavery.

In his work *Zoonomia* (1794–96), Darwin advanced an evolutionary theory stating that changes in an organism are caused by the direct influence of the environment, a proposal similar to that put forward by Jean Baptiste Lamarck some 15 years later.

Darwin was the grandfather, by his first wife, of Charles Robert Darwin and, by his second wife, of Francis Galton.

Darwin, Sir George Howard

(1845–1912)

BRITISH ASTRONOMER AND GEOPHYSICIST

> I appeal...for mercy to the applied mathematician...If our methods are often wanting in elegance and do but little to satisfy that aesthetic sense of which I spoke before, yet they constitute honest attempts to unravel the secrets of the universe in which we live.
> —Speech to the Fifth International Congress of Mathematicians, 1912

Darwin, the second son of the famous biologist Charles Darwin, was born at Down in England. He was educated at Clapham Grammar School, where the astronomer Charles Pritchard was headmaster, and Cambridge University. He became a fellow in 1868 and, in 1883, Plumian Professor of Astronomy, a post he held until his death. He was knighted in 1905.

His most significant work was on the evolution of the Earth–Moon system. His basic premise was that the effect of the tides has been to slow the Earth's rotation thus lengthening the day and to cause the Moon to recede from the Earth. He gave a mathematical analysis of the consequences of this, extrapolating into both the future and the past. He argued that some 4.5 billion years ago the Moon and the Earth would have been very close, with a day being less than five hours. Before this time the two bodies would actually have been one, with the Moon residing in what is now the Pacific Ocean. The Moon would have been torn away from the Earth by powerful solar tides that would have deformed the Earth every 2.5 hours.

Darwin's theory, worked out in collaboration with Osmond Fisher in 1879, explains both the low density of the Moon as being a part of the Earth's mantle, and also the absence of a granite layer on the Pacific floor. However, the theory is not widely accepted by astronomers. It runs against the Roche limit, which claims that no satellite can come closer than 2.44 times the planet's radius without breaking up; there are also problems with angular momentum. Astronomers today favor the view that the Moon has formed by processes of condensation and accretion. Whatever its faults, Darwin's theory is important as being the first real attempt to work out a cosmology on the principles of mathematical physics.

Daubrée, Gabriel Auguste

(1814–1896)

FRENCH GEOLOGIST

Daubrée (doh-**bray**), who was born at Metz in France, was educated at the University of Strasbourg. After investigating the tin mines of England he was employed, in 1838, as an engineer for Bas-Rhin and prepared a geological map of the area (1840–48). He was then appointed professor of geology at the University of Strasbourg, becoming professor of geology at the Museum of Natural History, Paris, in 1861. Finally, in 1862 he became director of the Imperial School of Mines.

Daubrée was a pioneer of experimental geology, publishing his research in his most significant work, *Etudes synthétiques de géologie expérimentale* (1879; Synthesis Studies on Experimental Geology), in which he tried to show that an understanding of geochemical processes can be attained by reproducing them in the laboratory. In particular he worked on the effect that heating water at great depths in the Earth would have on the production of metamorphic rocks.

Daubrée also built up an extensive collection of meteorites and published his findings in *Météorites et la constitution géologique du globe* (1886; Meteorites and the Geological Constitution of the World). He concluded from his study of the composition of meteorites that the Earth has an iron core.

Dausset, Jean

(1916–   )

FRENCH PHYSICIAN AND
IMMUNOLOGIST

Dausset (doh-**say**), the son of a doctor from Toulouse in southern France, gained his MD from the University of Paris in 1945 following wartime service in the blood transfusion unit. He was professor of hematology at the University of Paris from 1958 and professor of immunohematology from 1968. He was professor of experimental medicine at the Collège de France from 1977 to 1987.

Dausset's war experience stimulated his interest in transfusion reactions, and in 1951 he showed that the blood of certain universal donors (those of blood group O), which had been assumed safe to use in all transfusions, could nonetheless be dangerous. This was because of the presence of strong immune antibodies in their plasma, which develop following antidiphtheria and antitetanus injections. Donor blood is now systematically tested for such antibodies.

In the 1950s Dausset noticed a peculiar feature in the histories of patients who had received a number of blood transfusions: they developed a low white blood cell (leukocyte) count. He suspected that the blood transfused could well have contained antigens that stimulated the production of antibodies against the leukocytes. With insight and considerable courage Dausset went on to claim that the antigen on the blood cells, soon to be known as the HLA or human lymphocyte antigen, was the equivalent of the mouse H-2 system, described by George Snell.

The significance of Dausset's work was enormous. It meant that tissues could be typed quickly and cheaply by simple blood agglutination tests as opposed to the complicated and lengthy procedure of seeing if skin grafts would take. Such work made the technically feasible operation of kidney transplantation a practical medical option, for at last the danger of rejection could be minimized by rapid, simple, and accurate tissue typing. Further confirmation of Dausset's work was obtained when the specific regions of the HLA gene complex were later identified by J. van Rood and R. Ceppellini as a single locus on human chromosome 6.

Dausset later shared the 1980 Nobel Prize for physiology or medicine with Snell and Baruj Benacerraf.

Davaine, Casimir Joseph

(1812–1882)

FRENCH PHYSICIAN

> I congratulate myself on having often carried on your clever researches.
> —Louis Pasteur, letter to Davaine (1879)

Born in St. Amand-les-Eaux, France, Davaine (da-**ven**) studied medicine and worked for most of his life in general practice in Paris. Around 1850 he began studying anthrax in cattle and became, arguably, the first scientist to recognize the role of a specific bacteria as the causal agent of an identifiable disease.

The rodlike organisms of anthrax were first described by Franz Pollender in 1849. Pollender found these organisms in the blood of cattle killed by anthrax but was unsure whether they were the cause or consequence of the disease. In 1863 Davaine took the crucial step of demonstrating that the disease could be transmitted to other cattle by inoculating them with the blood of diseased animals. However, if the blood was heated the disease could no longer be transmitted. Further, Davaine found, if the blood was mixed with water and the mixture allowed to stand then fluid taken from the top of the vessel proved harmless but anthrax could still be transmitted with a sample from the bottom. Such was the evidence assembled by Davaine to support the existence of disease transmitting "bactéridies."

His theory, however, did not explain the well-established fact that anthrax could break out in apparently uncontaminated areas. It was only when Robert Koch was able to show in 1876 that the bacillus formed spores, which could exist unchanged in the soil, that the full force of Davaine's work became clear.

Davenport, Charles Benedict

(1866–1944)

AMERICAN ZOOLOGIST AND GENETICIST

Davenport, who was born in Stamford, Connecticut, obtained a zoology doctorate at Harvard in 1892, where he taught until 1899. From 1901 until 1904 he was curator of the Zoological Museum at the University of Chicago, and from 1904 until 1934 was director of the Carnegie Institution's Department of Genetics at Cold Spring Harbor. In 1910 Davenport founded the Eugenics Record Office, directing it until 1934.

Davenport's early studies of animal genetics, using chickens and canaries, were carried out at the turn of the century, and he was among the first to accept Gregor Mendel's rediscovered theory of heredity. He later turned his attention to man, and in *Heredity in Relation to Eugenics* (1912) offered evidence for the inheritance of particular human traits, suggesting that the application of genetic principles to human breeding might improve the race (eugenics). From 1898 Davenport was assistant editor of the *Journal of Experimental Zoology*; he was also editor of both *Genetics* and the *Journal of Physical Anthropology*.

Davis, Raymond

(1914–   )

AMERICAN CHEMIST

Born in Washington DC, Davis was educated at the universities of Maryland and Yale where he obtained his PhD in 1942. After serving four years in the U.S.A.A.F., Davis took the post of senior chemist at the Brookhaven National Lab, New York, and remained there until his retirement in 1984. He has continued to work, however, as a research professor in the astronomy department of the University of Pennsylvania, Philadelphia.

For many years Davis, an experimentalist, has worked on the detection of neutrinos emitted by the Sun. In working out the reactions that power the Sun, theorists, such as John Bahcall, predict that a certain number of neutrinos should be produced, and that a measurable number should be detectable on Earth.

The problem is that neutrinos have a very low probability of interaction with matter. Millions of them pass unimpeded through the Earth every second. The average time lapse for an interaction of a neutrino with an atom is 10^{36} seconds. To increase the probability of detecting a neutrino it was necessary to use a detector containing a large number of atoms. The result was a 100,000-gallon tank of cleaning fluid (tetrachloroethene), containing about 10^{30} atoms. To exclude confusing interactions with cosmic rays Davis deposited his tank in 1969 at the bottom of the one-mile-deep Homestake Mine at Lead, South Dakota.

Davis was looking for a specific reaction. Neutrinos can react with the isotope chlorine-37 (about a quarter of chlorine atoms) converting it into the radioactive argon-37. The argon atoms could be removed at regular intervals and counted. Theory predicted that Davis should observe 7.9±2.6 solar neutrinos per second, otherwise known as solar neutrino units (SNUs). Actually Davis began by observing about 2 SNUs, and after twenty years of continuous observation he is still observing no more than 2 SNUs.

Davis has sought to eliminate the possibility that the anomalous results are the products of a faulty experimental design. After twenty years spent refining his work, he remains convinced that any errors are unlikely to be traced to the experiment. Further, other workers have produced very similar results. This discrepancy between theory and experiment constitutes the *solar neutrino problem*.

Davis, William Morris

(1850–1934)

AMERICAN PHYSICAL GEOGRAPHER

> No one now regards a river and its valley as ready-made features of the earth's surface. All are convinced that rivers have come to be what they are by slow processes of natural development...
> —*National Geographic Magazine* (1889)

Davis, who was born in Philadelphia, Pennsylvania, was educated at Harvard. He returned to teach there in 1877 after a period as a meteorologist in Argentina and as an assistant with the North Pacific Survey. He became professor of physical geography in 1890 and of geology in 1898.

Davis is acknowledged as the founder of the science of geomorphology, the study of landforms. In his *The Rivers and Valleys of Pennsylvania* (1889) he first introduced what later became known as the *Davisian systems* of landscape analysis. His aim was to provide an explanatory description of how landforms change in an ideal situation and his most important contribution to this was his introduction of the "cycle of erosion" into geographical thought.

He proposed a complete cycle of youth, maturity, and old age to describe the evolution of a landscape. In youth rivers occupy steep V-shaped valleys while in old age the valleys are broad. The end product would be a flat featureless plain he called a "peneplain." This was an ideal cycle but in practice the cycle would invariably be interrupted by Earth movements. It was, nevertheless, strongly attacked by German geographers, who objected to it on the grounds that it neglected such vital factors as weathering and climate in transforming the landscape. They also believed him to be undermining their argument that landforms could only be discovered by local fieldwork and the production of regional monographs.

Davis also produced an influential work, *Elementary Meteorology* (1894), which was used as a textbook for over 30 years, and, in 1928, published *The Coral Reef Problem.*

Davisson, Clinton Joseph

(1881–1958)

AMERICAN PHYSICIST

Davisson, who was born in Bloomington, Illinois, was educated at the University of Chicago and at Princeton, where he obtained his PhD in 1911. After working for a short period at the Carnegie Institute of Technology, Pittsburgh, Davisson joined the Bell Telephone Laboratory (then Western Electric) in 1917 and remained there until his retirement in 1946.

Davisson began his work by investigating the emission of electrons from a platinum oxide surface under bombardment by positive ions. He moved from this to studying the effect of electron bombardment on surfaces, and observed (1925) the angle of reflection could depend on crystal orientation. Following Louis de Broglie's theory of the wave nature of particles, he realized that his results could be due to diffraction of electrons by the pattern of atoms on the crystal surface.

In 1927 he performed a classic experiment with Lester Germer in which a beam of electrons of known momentum (p) was directed at an angle onto a nickel surface. The angles of reflected (diffracted) electrons were measured and the results were in agreement with de Broglie's equation for the electron wavelength ($\lambda = h/p$). In 1937 he shared the Nobel Prize for physics with George Thomson for "their experimental discovery of the diffraction of electrons by crystals."

Davy, Sir Humphry

(1778–1829)

BRITISH CHEMIST

> Sir Humphrey Davy
> Abominated gravy.
> He lived in the odium
> Of having discovered sodium.
> —Edmund Clerihew Bentley, *Biography for Beginners* (1905)

The progression of physical science is much more connected with your prosperity than is usually imagined. You owe to experimental philosophy some of the most important and peculiar of your advantages. It is not by foreign conquests chiefly that you are become great, but by a conquest of nature in your own country.

—Lecture at the Royal Institution (1809)

The son of a small landowner and wood-carver, Davy went to school in his native town of Penzance and in Truro. At the age of 17 he was apprenticed to an apothecary and surgeon with a view to qualifying in medicine. He was self-reliant and inquisitive from an early age and taught himself chemistry from textbooks. In 1798 he was appointed to Thomas Beddoes's Pneumatic Institute at Clifton, Bristol, to investigate the medicinal properties of gases. Davy's first papers were published by Beddoes in 1799. In one he concluded, independently of Count Rumford, that heat was a form of motion; the other contained some fanciful speculations on oxygen, which he called phosoxygen. Davy soon discovered the inebriating effect of nitrous oxide and his paper *Researches, Chemical and Philosophical; chiefly concerning Nitrous Oxide* (1800), and the subsequent fashion for taking the "airs," made him famous. At Clifton he met many eminent people, including the poets William Wordsworth, Samuel Taylor Coleridge, and Robert Southey (Davy was himself a Romantic poet), and his flirtation with fashionable society began.

In 1801 Davy moved to London, to the Royal Institution, where his lectures were spectacularly successful. At Clifton he had begun to experiment in electrochemistry, following William Nicholson's electrolysis of water, and this was to prove his most fruitful field. In the early years at the Royal Institution, however, he did much work of an applied nature, for example on tanning and on agricultural chemistry. In his 1806 Bakerian Lecture to the Royal Society he predicted that electricity would be capable of resolving compounds into their elements and in the following year he was able to announce the isolation of potassium and sodium from potash and soda. This result cast doubts on Antoine Lavoisier's oxygen theory of acidity. Davy was essentially a speculative and manipulative chemist, not a theorist, and he reasoned incorrectly that ammonia (because of its alkaline properties), and hence nitrogen, might contain oxygen. He remained skeptical about the elementary nature of bodies for many years and tried to show that sulfur and phosphorus contained hydrogen.

Davy's work in the years immediately following the discovery of sodium was hindered by his social success and competition for priority with the French chemists Joseph Gay-Lussac and Louis Thenard. He prepared boron, calcium, barium, and strontium by electrolysis but his priority was disputed. In 1810 he published a paper on chlorine, which established that it contained no oxygen – another blow against the oxygen theory of acidity – and was in fact an element. The name "chlorine" was proposed by Davy.

In 1812 Davy was knighted, married a wealthy widow, and published his book *Elements of Chemical Philosophy*. In 1813 he appointed Michael Faraday as his assistant and the Davys and Faraday visited France. Working in Michel Chevreul's laboratory, he established that iodine, discovered two years before by Bernard Courtois, was an element similar in many properties to but heavier than chlorine. On his return to England, Davy was commissioned to investigate the problem of firedamp (methane) explosions in mines. In 1816, only six months after beginning the investigation, he produced the famous safety lamp, the *Davy lamp*, in which the flame was surrounded by a wire gauze.

Davy became president of the Royal Society in 1820 and the rest of his life was much taken up by traveling on the Continent. Despite his successes there is something incomplete about his life. He never accepted the atomic theory of Dalton, his great contemporary. He had in fact more in common with his Romantic poet friends than he did with Dalton. Jöns Berzelius said of him that his work consisted of "brilliant fragments."

Dawes, William Rutter

(1799–1868)

BRITISH ASTRONOMER

Dawes's father was an astronomer, often on colonial service, and later taught mathematics in a London school. Dawes, who was born in London, was originally intended for the Church but finding the views of the established church uncongenial, studied medicine at St. Bartholomew's Hospital, London instead. He practiced for some time in Berkshire and in 1826 went to Liverpool where he was persuaded to exchange medicine for the post of a Dissenting minister in Ormskirk, Lancashire.

It was in Ormskirk that Dawes took up the serious study of astronomy in 1829. He built his own observatory and equipped it with a Dollond refractor. In 1839 Dawes moved to London to take charge of George Bishop's observatory in Regent's Park. Bishop had made a fortune in the wine trade and hoped to gain recognition by sponsoring some important discovery in his observatory. A second marriage to a wealthy widow in 1842 allowed Dawes to leave the somewhat disagreeable service of Bishop in 1844 and, despite persistent ill health, to devote himself to his own private astronomical researches first in Kent at Cranbrook and Maidstone and after 1857 at Haddenham in Buckinghamshire.

Dawes, the keenest of observers, worked for many years on double stars. During his Ormskirk period he published details on over 200 of them. Basic data on a further 250 were published in 1852 in Bishop's *Astronomical Observations at South Villa*. In November 1850 he narrowly missed an important discovery when he reported that while observing Saturn's rings he noted in the ansa, that part visible at the side of the planet and sticking out like a handle, "a light ... at both ends." Dawes had in fact observed the faint inner "crepe ring" of Saturn, Ring C, but had been narrowly anticipated in this by the American astronomer William C. Bond.

Dawkins, Richard

(1941–   )

BRITISH ETHOLOGIST

> We are survival machines – robot vehicles
> blindly programmed to preserve the selfish
> molecules known as genes. This is a truth
> which still fills me with astonishment.
> —*The Selfish Gene* (1976)

Dawkins was educated at Oxford University where he worked for his doctorate under Niko Tinbergen. He initially taught at the University of California, Berkeley, before returning to Oxford in 1970 as lecturer in animal behavior. He was appointed reader in zoology in 1989 and professor of public understanding of science in 1995.

In *The Selfish Gene* (1976) Dawkins did much to introduce the work of such scholars as William Hamilton, Robert L. Trivers, and John Maynard Smith to a wider public. He tried to show that such apparently altruistic behavior as birds risking their lives to warn the flock of an approaching predator can be seen as the "selfish" gene ensuring its own survival (by ensuring the survival of the descendents and relatives of the "heroic" bird) – indeed that such behavior is as relentlessly under the control of the selfish gene as the compulsive rutting of the dominant stag. The work was immensely successful, being translated into eleven languages and selling 150,000 copies in English alone.

In 1986 Dawkins published another successful work, *The Blind Watchmaker*. The title refers to the image used by William Paley in his *Natural Theology* (1802). If anyone were to find a watch he would be able to infer from its mechanism that it had a maker; equally with nature, where the mechanisms of hand, eye, heart, and brain demand the existence of a designer just as strongly. Dawkins accepted the argument but insisted that the watchmaker was merely the operation of natural selection. In case after case he argued that the same effects could be produced by natural selection a good deal more plausibly than by a divine watchmaker.

One of the most original features of Dawkins's work was his demonstration that with few simple recursive rules, and some very simple starting points, various complex life forms or biomorphs were produced on his computer screen. And, he emphasized, the biomorphs were produced not by Dawkins as designer (he was as surprised as anyone else by the outcome) but by the application of simple rules to a large number of apparently random initial positions.

Dawkins has continued to write on evolutionary theory, most notably in his *Climbing Mount Improbable* (1996), where he shows how such unlikely candidates as a spider's web and the vertebrate eye can have evolved under the guiding power of natural selection.

In 1993 he introduced the notion of a "mental virus" to explain how certain cultural practices can spread.

Day, David Talbot

(1859–1925)

AMERICAN CHEMIST

Day was born in East Rockport, Ohio, and educated at Johns Hopkins University, gaining his PhD in 1884. He started his career as a demonstrator in chemistry at the University of Maryland but left to become head of the Mineral Resources Division of the U.S. Geological Survey in 1886.

Day investigated the reasons for the differences found in the composition of various petroleum deposits and concluded that percolation through mineral deposits affected the nature of the underlying petroleum. His experiments, in which he ran crude petroleum through fuller's earth, anticipated the later development of adsorption chromatography by Mikhail Tsvet.

Day did much to stimulate the growth of the petroleum industry and in 1922 produced one of its basic texts, *Handbook of the Petroleum Industry*. From 1914 to 1920 he was a consultant chemist with the Bureau of Mines.

Deacon, Henry

(1822–1876)

BRITISH INDUSTRIAL CHEMIST

Deacon, a Londoner, started his career as an apprentice with an engineering firm at the age of 14. He later joined the firm of Nasmyth and Gaskell, near Manchester, before joining Pilkington's glassworks at St. Helens. There he introduced, in 1844, a new method for grinding and smoothing glass. Leaving the glassworks in 1851, Deacon went into partnership with the younger William Pilkington in 1853 to manufacture alkali at Widnes.

Deacon made a significant improvement in the Leblanc process for producing alkali, using one of its by-products, hydrochloric acid, to produce chlorine. William Gossage had introduced his tower to condense and collect the toxic hydrochloric acid fumes in 1836. In 1870 Deacon patented his method where the hydrochloric acid was passed over clay balls soaked in copper chloride, which, in air, oxidized the acid, yielding chlorine. The chlorine was used in making bleaching powder for the textiles industry. The process was supplanted by an alternative method of converting the hydrochloric acid into chlorine introduced by Walter Weldon (1866–69).

de Bary, Heinrich Anton

(1831–1888)

GERMAN BOTANIST

De Bary (de bah-**ree**), who was born in Frankfurt am Main in Germany, gained his medical degree from Berlin in 1853 and practiced briefly in Frankfurt before devoting all his time to botany. He became

Privatdozent (nonstipendiary lecturer) in botany at Tübingen and then professor of botany, first at Freiburg im Breisgau (1855), then Halle (1867), and finally Strassburg (1872), where he remained until his death.

When de Bary began working on fungi some people still believed in the spontaneous generation of fungi, and the general ignorance of fungal life cycles severely impeded the development of intelligent control measures against fungal epidemics of crops. De Bary's first mycological publication, *Researches on Fungal Blights* (1853), dealt with the rust and smut diseases of plants and maintained that fungi are the cause, and not the effect, of these diseases. In 1865 he demonstrated that the fungus that causes stem rust of wheat, *Puccinia graminis*, needs two hosts – wheat and barberry – to complete its life cycle. De Bary showed in 1866 that individual lichens consist of a fungus and an alga in intimate association and in 1879 he introduced the term "symbiosis" to describe mutually advantageous partnerships between dissimilar organisms.

De Bary's work was instrumental in encouraging a more developmental approach to mycology and his research on host–parasite interactions greatly helped in the fight against plant diseases.

De Beer, Sir Gavin Rylands

(1899–1972)

BRITISH ZOOLOGIST

Born in London, De Beer graduated from Oxford University, where he was a fellow from 1923 to 1938. He served in both World Wars; during World War II he landed in Normandy in 1944, where he was in charge of psychological warfare. He was professor of embryology at University College, London, 1945–50, and then director of the British Museum (Natural History) in London (1950–60).

In an early publication, *Introduction to Experimental Biology* (1926), de Beer finally disproved the germ-layer theory. Embryological investigations had indicated that vertebrate structures such as cartilage and certain bone cells were formed from the ectoderm, or outer layer of the embryo, and not, as was previously thought, from the mesoderm. As this goes against the germ-layer theory, orthodox embryologists argued that the experimental manipulations involved in such work altered the normal course of development. De Beer's contribution was to find a system that does not involve such manipulations so establishing the validity of earlier work.

De Beer has also done work to show that adult animals retain some of the juvenile characters of their evolutionary ancestors (*pedomorphosis*), thus refuting Ernst Haeckel's theory of recapitulation. He has suggested that gaps in the evolutionary development of animals may be accounted for by the impermanence of the soft tissues of young ancestors. Studies of *Archeopteryx*, the earliest known bird, led him to propose piecemeal evolutionary changes in such animals, thus explaining the combination of reptilian and avian characters (e.g., teeth and feathers). De Beer also carried out research into the functions of the pituitary gland. In the field of ancient history, de Beer applied scientific methods to various problems, for example, the origin of the Etruscans and Hannibal's journey across the Alps. His other books include *Embryology and Evolution of Chordate Animals* (1962, with Julian Huxley), *The Elements of Experimental Embryology* (1962), and a biography of Charles Darwin (1961). He was knighted in 1954.

Debierne, André Louis

(1874–1949)

FRENCH CHEMIST

Born in Paris, France, Debierne (de-**byairn**) was educated at the Ecole de Physique et Chemie. After graduation he worked at the Sorbonne and as an assistant to Pierre and Marie Curie, finally succeeding the latter as director of the Radium Institute. On his retirement in 1949 he in turn was succeeded by Marie Curie's daughter, Irène Joliot-Curie.

Debierne was principally a radiochemist; his first triumph came in 1900 with the discovery of a new radioactive element, actinium, which he isolated while working with pitchblende. In 1905 he went on to show that actinium, like radium, formed helium. This was of some significance in helping Ernest Rutherford to appreciate that some radioactive elements decay by emitting an alpha particle (or, as it turned out to be, the nucleus of a helium atom). In 1910, in collaboration with Marie Curie, he isolated pure metallic radium.

de Broglie, Prince Louis Victor Pierre Raymond

(1892–1987)

FRENCH PHYSICIST

De Broglie (de broh-**glee**) was descended from a French family ennobled by Louis XIV. He was born in Dieppe, France, and educated at the Sorbonne. Originally a historian, he became interested in science in World War I when he was posted to the Eiffel Tower as a member of a signals unit. He pursued this interest after the war and finally obtained his doctorate in physics from the Sorbonne in 1924. He taught there from 1926, serving as professor of theoretical physics at the newly founded Henri Poincaré Institute (1928–62).

De Broglie is famous for his theory that particles (matter) can have wavelike properties. At the start of the 20th century physicists explained phenomena in terms of particles (such as the electron or proton) and electromagnetic radiation (light, ultraviolet radiation, etc.). Particles were "matter" – conceived as discrete entities forming atoms and molecules; electromagnetic radiation was a wave motion involving changing electric and magnetic fields.

In 1905 two papers by Albert Einstein began a change in this conventional view of the physical world. His work on the special theory of relativity led to the idea that matter is itself a form of energy. More specifically he explained the photoelectric effect by the concept that electromagnetic radiation (a wave) can also behave as particles (photons). Later, in 1923, Arthur Compton produced further evidence for this view in explaining the scattering of x-rays by electrons.

In 1924 de Broglie, influenced by Einstein's work, put forward the converse idea – that just as waves can behave as particles, particles can also behave as waves. He proposed that an electron, for instance, can behave as if it were a wave motion (a *de Broglie wave*) with wavelength h/p, where p is the momentum of the electron and h is Planck's constant. This revolutionary theory was put forward in de Broglie's doctoral thesis. Experimental support for it was obtained independently by George Thomson and by Clinton J. Davisson and the wavelike behavior of particles was used by Erwin Schrödinger in his formulation of wave mechanics.

The fact that particles can behave as waves, and vice versa, is known as wave–particle duality and has caused intense debate as to the "real" nature of particles and electromagnetic radiation. De Broglie took the view that there is a true deterministic physical process underlying quantum mechanics – i.e., that the current indeterminate approach in terms of probability can be replaced by a more fundamental theory. He based his ideas on the concept of particles that are concentrations of energy guided through space by a real wave and exchanging energy with a "subquantum medium."

De Broglie received the 1929 Nobel Prize for physics for his "discovery of the wave nature of the electron."

Debye, Peter Joseph William

(1884–1966)

DUTCH–AMERICAN PHYSICIST AND PHYSICAL CHEMIST

Only experiments can decide...
—*Notes on Magnetization at Low Temperatures* (1926)

Born at Maastricht in the Netherlands, Debye (de-**bI**) studied electrical engineering at Aachen and gained his PhD at Munich in 1910. He held chairs of physics at Zurich (1911–12 and 1919–27), Utrecht (1912–14), Göttingen (1914–19), and Leipzig. He was director of the Kaiser Wilhelm Institute for Theoretical Physics (1935–40) before emigrating to America where he was professor of chemistry at Cornell (1940–50).

Debye was essentially a theoretician and most of his work, although varied, had a common theme: the application of physical methods to problems of molecular structure. An early work was the derivation of a relation governing the change of the specific heat capacity of solids with temperature. In 1915 he gave a theoretical treatment of electron diffraction by gases, not realized in practice until 1930. At Göttingen, Debye and P. Scherrer discovered a method of producing x-ray diffraction patterns from powders. This was later extended to the production of diffraction patterns from simple molecules such as CCl_4 (1928).

A major part of Debye's work was devoted to dipole moments, beginning in 1912. He used these to determine the degree of polarity of covalent bonds and to determine bond angles. Together with his x-ray work and results from rotational spectra, this enabled the precise spatial configuration of small molecules to be deduced. For example, the planarity of the benzene molecule was confirmed by dipole moment measurements. Debye is probably better known, however, for the *Debye–Hückel theory* of electrolytes (1923). This was a theory that could be applied to concentrated solutions of ionic compounds, and was a great advance on the theories of the time, which applied only to very dilute solutions. The Debye–Hückel theory takes account of the fact that an ion in solution tends to attract other ions of opposite charge.

Dedekind, (Julius Wilhelm) Richard

(1831–1916)

GERMAN MATHEMATICIAN

For what I have accomplished and what I have become, I have to thank my…indefatigable working rather than any outstanding talent.
    —Quoted by Hans Zincke in *Richard Dedekind Recalled* (1916)

The son of an academic lawyer from Braunschweig, Germany, Dedekind (**day**-de-kint) was educated at the Caroline College there and at Göttingen, where he gained his doctorate in 1852. After four years spent teaching at Göttingen, he was appointed professor of mathematics at the Zurich Polytechnic. In 1862 he returned to Braunschweig to the Technical High School where he remained until his retirement in 1912.

In 1872 Dedekind published his most important work *Stetigkeit und Irrationale Zahlen* (Continuity and Irrational Numbers) in which he provided a rigorous definition of the irrational numbers. He began by "cutting" or dividing the rational numbers into two nonempty disjoint sets *A* and *B* such that if *x* belongs to *A* and *y* to *B*, then $x < y$. If *A* has a greatest member *A'* then *A'* is a rational number; if *B* has a smallest number *B'* then *B'* will also be a rational number. But if *A* has no greatest number and *B* no smallest, then the cut defines an irrational number.

In the same work Dedekind gave the first precise definition of an infinite set. A set is infinite, he argued, when it is "similar to a proper part of itself." Thus the set *N* of natural numbers can be shown to be "similar," that is, matched or put into a one-to-one correspondence with a proper part, in this case 2*N*:

N	1	2	3	4	5	6	7	8	9 ...
	↓	↓	↓	↓	↓	↓	↓	↓	↓
2*N*	2	4	6	8	10	12	14	16	18...

Whereas the only thing a finite set can be matched with is the set itself.

In a later work, *Was sind und was sollen die Zahlen?* (What Numbers Are and Should Be, 1888) Dedekind demonstrated how arithmetic could be derived from a set of axioms. A simpler but equivalent version, formulated by Peano in 1889, is much better known.

de Duve, Christian René

(1917–)

BELGIAN BIOCHEMIST

De Duve (de **doo**-ve) was born at Thames Ditton in southern England and educated at the Catholic University of Louvain where he obtained his MD in 1941. After holding brief appointments at the Nobel Institute in Stockholm and at Washington University he returned to Louvain in 1947 and was appointed professor of biochemistry in 1951. From 1962 to 1988 he held a similar appointment at Rockefeller University in New York.

In 1949 de Duve was working on the metabolism of carbohydrates in the liver of the rat. By using centrifugal fractionation techniques to separate the contents of the cell, he was able to show that the enzyme glucose-6-phosphatase is associated with the microsomes – organelles whose role was only speculative until de Duve began this work. He also noted that the process of homogenization led to the release of the enzyme acid phosphatase, the amount of which seemed to vary with the degree of damage inflicted on the cells. This suggested to de Duve that the enzyme in the cell was normally enclosed by some kind of membrane. If true, the supposition would remove a problem that had long troubled cytologists – namely how it was that such powerful enzymes did not attack the normal molecules of the cell. This question could now be answered by proposing a self-contained organelle, which neatly isolated the digestive enzymes. Confirmation for this view came in 1955 with the identification of such a body with the aid of the electron microscope. As its role is digestive or lytic, de Duve proposed the name *lysosome*. The peroxisomes (organelles containing hydrogen peroxide in which oxidation reactions take place) were also discovered in de Duve's laboratory.

For such discoveries de Duve shared the 1974 Nobel Prize for physiology or medicine with Albert Claude and George Palade.

De Forest, Lee

(1873–1961)

AMERICAN PHYSICIST AND INVENTOR

The radio was conceived as a potent instrumentality for culture, fine music, the uplifting of America's mass intelligence. You have debased this child, you have sent him out in the street in rags of ragtime, tatters of jive and boogie-woogie, to collect money from all and sundry.
　　　—Complaining to radio executives about the quality of broadcasting

De Forest, who was born in Council Bluffs, Iowa, was interested in science from the age of 13. His father, a congregational minister, wanted him to study for the Church, but De Forest refused, going instead, in 1893, to the Sheffield Scientific School at Yale University. His PhD thesis, *Hertzian Waves from the Ends of Parallel Wires* (1899), was probably the first PhD thesis on radio in America, and drew on the work of Heinrich Hertz and Guglielmo Marconi. While working for the Western Electric Company in Chicago, he developed an electrolytic detector and an alternating-current transmitter.

In 1907 De Forest patented the Audion tube, a thermionic grid-triode vacuum tube that was a very sensitive receiver of electrical signals. This invention was crucial to the development of telecommunications equipment. In 1912 he had the idea of "cascading" these to amplify high-frequency radio signals, making possible the powerful signals needed for long-distance telephones and for radio broadcasting. His invention formed the basis of radio, radar, telephones, and computers until the advent of solid-state electronics.

Throughout his career De Forest pushed for the acceptance of radio broadcasting. He was not a very good business manager, however, and had to sell many of his patents. Later he worked on a sound film system that was similar to the one eventually adopted. In the 1930s he designed Audion diathermy machines for medical use and during World War II he worked on military research at the Bell Telephone Laboratories.

De Geer, Charles

(1720–1778)

SWEDISH ENTOMOLOGIST

De Geer (de yayr) was born in Finspang, Sweden, and educated in the classics at the University of Utrecht; he then studied under Linnaeus at Uppsala. His extensive *Mémoires pour servir à l'histoire des insectes* (7 vols., 1752–78; Contributory Notes on the History of Insects) include excellent drawings and probably the earliest published accounts of the maternal instinct in such nonsocial insects as the earwig *Forficula auriculara* and the shield bug *Elasmucha griseus*. He also initiated a system of insect classification based on the wings and mouthparts.

Dehmelt, Hans Georg

(1922–   )

AMERICAN PHYSICIST

Born at Gorlitz in Germany, Dehmelt (**day**-melt) left the Berlin Gymnasium in 1940 to join the German army. He was allowed for a time to study physics at Breslau University but, in 1945, he was taken prisoner by the Americans at Bastogne, Belgium. After the war he continued his education at Göttingen, gaining his PhD there in 1950. He went to America in 1952 as a postdoctoral student at Duke University, North Carolina, and remained there until 1955. He then moved to the University of Washington, Seattle, where he was appointed professor of physics in 1961, the same year he became a naturalized American citizen.

Dehmelt has worked for many years on the seemingly impossible task of imprisoning a single electron for an extended period in a suitable container. In this manner Dehmelt hoped to measure more accurately the magnetic moment (g) of the electron. Earlier experiments by H. R. Crane at Michigan University had involved passing a beam of electrons through a magnetic field. But the evidence gathered in this manner necessarily involves the interactions of other electrons.

In 1955 Dehmelt began work on what later become known as a *Penning trap*. In 1973 he succeeded in isolating a single electron and went on to show (1975) how accuracy could be further improved by "cooling" the

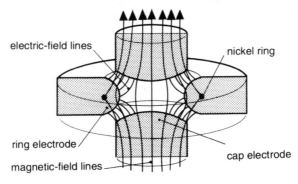

ELECTRON TRAP   The arrangement of electrodes used by Dehmelt in his electron trap.

electron (i.e., decreasing its kinetic energy). In this way it proved possible to measure g with an accuracy of 4 parts in a trillion.

The Penning trap operates with a combination of electrical and magnetic fields. An electron in a uniform magnetic field cannot move across the field lines, but is able to escape by moving parallel to the field. To avoid this, an electric field is imposed upon the magnetic field. This field is produced by three electrodes – two negatively charged end traps and a positively charged encircling nickel ring.

For his work in this area Dehmelt shared the 1989 Nobel Prize for physics with Wolfgang Paul and Norman Ramsey.

De la Beche, Sir Henry Thomas

(1796–1855)

BRITISH GEOLOGIST

De la Beche (de la besh) entered the army but at the end of the Napoleonic Wars he chose to devote himself to geology instead. After traveling extensively in Europe and Jamaica on his own research work, he became, in 1835, director of the Geological Survey of Great Britain, which had been recently formed largely on his initiative. He was also instrumental in setting up the Royal School of Mines in 1851, of which he was the first principal.

He wrote extensively on the geology of southwest England and Jamaica, publishing the first account of the geology of Jamaica in 1827 and his report on the geology of Devon during the period 1832–35.

In 1834, while working in Devon, he made his most significant discovery. He observed that some rock strata contained fossil plants similar to those of the Carboniferous system, discovered by William Conybeare in 1822, but did not contain any of the fossils of the preceding Silurian system, recently discovered by Roderick Murchison. The Silurian was believed to merge directly into the Carboniferous and De la Beche assumed the strata he had discovered came before the Silurian. However, William Lonsdale, librarian of the Geological Society, convincingly argued for a system, later named the Devonian, which overlay the Silurian and underlay the Carboniferous.

De la Beche wrote extensively on geology; his *A Geological Manual* (1831), *How to Observe* (1835), and *Geological Observer* (1851) were in part aimed at satisfying the growing popular interest in geology.

Delambre, Jean Baptiste Joseph

(1749–1822)

FRENCH ASTRONOMER AND MATHEMATICIAN

Born in Amiens in northern France, Delambre (de-**lahm**-bre) was most unusual for a mathematician and astronomer in that he did not begin the serious study of his subject until he was well over 30 years old. As a student he had been interested in the classics and only turned to the exact sciences when he was 36. He published tables of Jupiter and Saturn in 1789 and of Uranus in 1792. He also measured an arc of the meridian between Dunkirk and Barcelona to establish a basis for the new metric system. He succeeded Joseph de Lalande as professor of astronomy at the Collège de France in 1795. In his later years he devoted himself to a monumental six-volume *Histoire de l'astronomie* (1817–27; History of Astronomy).

De la Rue, Warren

(1815–1889)

BRITISH ASTRONOMER

Born in Guernsey, in the Channel Islands, De la Rue was the son of a printer and worked most of his life in his father's business. He was educated in Paris and studied science privately. He was initially interested in chemistry, being a friend of and working with August Hofmann, but later, at the suggestion of James Nasmyth, he took up astronomy, building a small observatory for himself.

De la Rue devoted himself to problems of photographic astronomy. He was the first to apply the collodion process (invented by Frederick Archer in 1851) to photographing the Moon. In 1852 he took some photographs that were sharper than any previously produced and that could be enlarged without blurring. Ten years later he was producing photographs that could show as much as could be seen through any telescope. In 1854 he designed the photoheliograph, a device for taking telescopic photographs of the Sun. In 1860 he used it to take dramatic photographs of prominences during the total eclipse in Spain, proving that they were solar (and not, as had been thought, lunar) in origin.

De la Rue gave up active astronomical investigation in 1873, donating his telescope to the observatory at Oxford and devoting the rest of his life to his business and to his chemical researches.

Delbrück, Max

(1906–1981)

GERMAN-BORN AMERICAN
PHYSICIST AND MOLECULAR
BIOLOGIST

While the artist's communication is linked forever with its original form, that of the scientist is modified, amplified, fused with the ideas and results of others.
—*The Eighth Day of Creation*

The son of a history professor, Delbrück (**del**-bruuk) trained as a physicist first in his native city of Berlin, and then at Tübingen, Bonn, and Göttingen, where he completed his doctorate in 1930. After spending the period from 1931 to 1933 in Copenhagen, Delbrück was appointed to the Kaiser Wilhelm Institute for Chemistry, Berlin. He left Germany for America in 1937, working first at the California Institute of Technology and from 1940 until 1947 at Vanderbilt University, Nashville. Delbrück returned to Cal Tech in 1947 and remained there as professor of biology until his retirement in 1976. He became a naturalized American citizen in 1945.

While at Copenhagen, under the influence of Niels Bohr, Delbrück's interest was diverted from atomic physics to questions about the nature of life. In the late 1930s he began to work with bacteriophages, the viruses discovered by D'Hérelle that infect and destroy bacteria. They were relatively simple, reproduced quickly, and were easy to handle; an ideal organism, Delbrück argued, in which to study the mechanisms of replication and development.

In 1939, with E. Ellis, he first demonstrated the phenomenon of "one-step growth." Working with the phage T4 he found that "a virus particle enters a bacterial cell and after a certain period (between 13 and 40 minutes, depending on the virus, on the dot for any particular type), the bacterial cell is lysed and 100 particles are liberated." How can one particle, Delbrück asked, become 100 in a mere 20 minutes?

Soon after he began to collaborate with Salvador Luria. In 1943 they published a paper, *Mutations of Bacteria from Virus Sensitivity to Virus Resistance.* How, they asked, do bacteria acquire resistance to lethal phage? Is it induced by contact, or does it arise from a fortunate mutation? Luria and Delbrück realized that the dynamics of bacterial growth would differ in each case. The number of resistant strains found in bacterial colonies exposed to phage should fluctuate more than if the resistance was induced. Delbrück worked out the statistics and Luria performed the experiment; the results clearly revealed that bacteria underwent mutations.

Delbrück went on to show in 1945, in collaboration with W. Bailey, that phage can reproduce sexually. They were working with the two viruses T2 and T4r, both of which could be bred in bacterium B. They found that:

T2 formed small colonies and attacked bacterium A.

T4r formed large colonies and attacked bacterium C.

When both T2 and T4r were bred together in B, the parent types produced two new strains:

Strain 1: formed small colonies and attacked bacterium C.

Strain 2: formed large colonies and attacked bacterium A.

Obviously, Delbrück concluded, "the parents had got together and exchanged something."

By this time Delbrück had begun to be recognized as the leader of what became known as "the phage group." From 1945 onwards he ran an annual summer phage course at Cold Spring Harbor Laboratory, New York, which was attended over the years by most of the leading molecular biologists of the following decade. For Delbrück himself, however, the mid-1950s seemed to be a good time to move on. He turned to the study of sensory mechanisms in the fungus *Phycomyces*. It grew towards the light, against gravity, and into the wind. How did it sense these stimuli? What range of light did it respond to? These and other questions were tackled by Delbrück and his coworkers in what was soon called "the Phycomyces group." His last published paper in 1981 was in this field and proposed that the chemical photoreceptor of *Phycomyces* was a flavin and not, as had been supposed, a carotene.

For his earlier work with the phage group Delbrück shared the 1969 Nobel Prize for physiology or medicine with Salvador Luria and Alfred Hershey

D'Elhuyar, Don Fausto

(1755–1833)

SPANISH CHEMIST AND MINERALOGIST

No city on the New Continent, not even in the United States, offers scientific establishments so vast and so solid as does the capital of Mexico. It is enough to cite here the School of Mines, of which the scholar D'Elhuyar is director.
—Alexander von Humboldt, *Political Essay on the Kingdom of New Spain* (1826)

Born in Logroño, Spain, D'Elhuyar (**del**-yoo-ar) studied mineralogy with his brother, Juan José, at the Freiberg Mining Academy under Abraham Werner. He then studied chemistry in Paris (1772–77). He returned to Spain shortly after and was sent to Mexico in 1788 to supervise mining operations. On his return to Spain in 1821 he was made director general of mines.

The D'Elhuyar brothers working together in 1783 discovered the element tungsten (formerly also known as wolfram). Two very dense minerals were known to chemists in the 18th century: "tungsten" (Swedish meaning "heavy stone") and wolframite. In 1781 Carl Scheele had discovered that "tungsten" (now known as scheelite) contained tungstic acid. The brothers proved that the same acid is present in wolframite, from which mineral they succeeded in isolating the element tungsten.

DeLisi, Charles

(1941–   )

AMERICAN BIOPHYSICIST

DeLisi (de-**lee**-see) was educated at City College, in his native New York, and at New York University, where he completed his PhD in 1969. After periods at Yale and Los Alamos, he moved, in 1975, to the National Institute of Health, Bethesda, Maryland as head of mathematical biology. In 1985, he moved to Washington to head the Office of Health and Environmental Research (O.H.E.R.), a part of the U.S. Department of Energy. DeLisi returned to academic life in 1988 and since 1990 he has been professor of biomedical engineering at Boston University.

While at O.H.E.R. DeLisi was concerned with the health effects of radiation. Some people, he realized, were genetically disposed to develop cancer when exposed to low levels of radiation. But, before one could spot such tendencies in any individual, it would first be necessary to know more about the human genome. As a physicist DeLisi was used to thinking in terms of large expensive projects and consequently began to consider the possibility of mapping the entire human genome. He soon heard that similar ideas has been canvassed by Robert Sinsheimer, a molecular biologist at the University of California, at a small conference in 1985 at Santa Cruz.

DeLisi set about organizing a similar meeting in 1986 in Santa Fe, New Mexico. That the project was accepted so readily was largely due to DeLisi. He arranged for the O.H.E.R. to make $4.5 million available and proposed that a five-year plan of research be drawn up. DeLisi went on to initiate the Human Genome Project by setting up research centers at three national laboratories, namely, Los Alamos, Livermore, and Lawrence.

Del Rio, Andrès Manuel

(1764–1849)

SPANISH MINERALOGIST

Del Rio (del-**ree**-oh) was born in the Spanish capital Madrid and graduated in Spain in 1781 before going on to study in France, England, and Germany, where he was a pupil of Abraham Werner at the Freiberg Mining Academy. He had been chosen by Charles III to develop and modernize the mining industry in the Spanish empire. Consequently he was sent to Mexico City to become, in 1794, professor of mineralogy at the School of Mines set up by Fausto D'Elhuyar. While in Mexico he published the *Elementos de orictognosia* (1795; Principles of the Science of Mining), possibly the first mineralogical textbook published in the Americas. He was forced into exile in the period 1829–34 after Mexico's war of independence but on his return he tried to reestablish the scientific tradition he had first introduced.

As a scientist he is best remembered for his independent discovery of the element vanadium in 1801. He had found what he took to be a new metal in some lead ore from the Mexican mines and named it "erythronium" (from the Greek *erythros*, red) as its salts turned red when ignited. However, he failed to press his claim, being persuaded by other scientists that it was probably a compound of lead and chromium. Nils Gabriel Sefström rediscovered the metal in 1830 and named it vanadium. Its identity with Del Rio's erythronium was demonstrated by Friedrich Wöhler in 1831.

De Luc, Jean André

(1727–1817)

SWISS GEOLOGIST AND METEOROLOGIST

> [De Luc] was probably one of the most accurate observers of nature that ever existed.
> —John Frederic Daniell, *Meteorological Essays and Observations* (1823)

De Luc (de look) came from an Italian family, which had moved to Switzerland from Tuscany in the 15th century; he was born in the Swiss lakeside city of Geneva. He initially concentrated on commercial activities with science as a side line but, in 1773, after the collapse of his business, he moved to England where he devoted himself to science. He was appointed as reader to Queen Charlotte, retaining that post until his death.

In a series of letters *Sur l'histoire de la terre* (On the History of the Earth) addressed to Queen Charlotte in 1779, James Hutton in 1790, and Johann Blumenbach in 1798, De Luc, following in the tradition of Thomas Burnet, tried to write a history of the Earth that took account of the advances in geology yet was still compatible with the Creation as described in Genesis.

De Luc proposed that the Earth itself was old though the flood was recent. The flood was caused by a collapse of the existing lands causing their inundation by the oceans and the emergence of the present continents. As these had been the predivial ocean floor it was only reasonable to suppose that they should contain marine fossils. De Luc thus explained one of the puzzles facing early geologists – the presence of marine fossils in the center of continents.

De Luc opposed Hutton's fluvial theory that such major terrestrial features as valleys are the result of the still continuing action of the rivers. He pointed out that many valleys contain no rivers, that rivers far from eroding actually deposit material, and that there seems to be no relation between the size of the river and the valley it is supposed to have created. His main objection was over downstream lakes, for in this case, when the enormous amount of material eroded from the valley is considered, De Luc argued that the lake should have been filled in long before. Hutton's unsatisfactory answer was that such infilling does take place but that the lakes are much younger than the rivers. This issue was not finally resolved until the crucial role of glaciation was established by Louis Agassiz some fifty years later.

De Luc was also a major figure in meteorological research. His two works, *Recherches sur la modification de l'atmosphère* (1772; Studies on Atmospheric Change) and *Idées sur la météorologie* (1786–87; Thoughts on Meteorology), made important suggestions for advances in instrumental design. His most important achievement was his formula, in 1791, for converting barometric readings into height, which provided the first accurate measurements of mountain heights.

Demarçay, Eugene Anatole

(1852–1904)

FRENCH CHEMIST

Born in Paris, France, Demarçay (de-mar-**say**) was a research chemist who also maintained his own private laboratory in the city. In 1901, while working with a sample of the newly discovered element samarium (discovered by Paul Lecoq de Boisbaudran in 1879) he found traces of an additional element, europium. More dramatic, however, was his earlier work with the Curies in 1898. They had discovered one new radioactive element, polonium, early in the year. But they found further radioactivity in their sample of pitchblende after the removal of polonium. They took the small sample they had extracted to Demarçay, an expert spectroscopist, who was able to find a new line in the spectrum. This enabled the Curies to announce the existence of a much more strongly radioactive element, radium.

Demerec, Milislav

(1895–1966)

CROATIAN–AMERICAN GENETICIST

Demerec (**dem**-er-ek) was born in Kostajnica in Croatia and graduated from the College of Agriculture in Krizevci in 1916. After a few years' work at the Krizevci Experimental Station, he moved to America. He gained his PhD in genetics from Cornell University in 1923 and then worked at the Carnegie Institution, Cold Spring Harbor, where he remained for most of his career, becoming director in 1943.

Demerec was concerned with gene structure and function, especially the effect of mutations. He found that certain unstable genes are more likely to mutate than others and that the rate of mutation is affected by various biological factors, such as the stage in the life cycle. He also demonstrated that chromosome segments that break away and rejoin in the wrong place may cause suppression of genes near the new region of attachment. This lent additional support to the idea of the "position effect," first demonstrated by Alfred Sturtevant.

Demerec's work with the bacterium *Salmonella* revealed that genes controlling related functions are grouped together on the chromosome rather than being randomly distributed through the chromosome complement. Such units were later termed "operons." His radiation treatment of the fungus *Penicillium* yielded a mutant strain producing much larger quantities of penicillin – a discovery of great use in World War II. He showed that antibiotics should be administered initially in large doses, so that resistant mutations do not develop, and should be given in combinations, because any bacterium resistant to one is most unlikely to have resistance to both.

Demerec greatly increased the reputation of Cold Spring Harbor while director there and also served on many important committees. He founded the journal *Advances in Genetics* and wrote some 200 scientific articles.

Democritus of Abdera

(C. 460 BC–C. 370 BC)

GREEK PHILOSOPHER

Everything existing in the Universe is the fruit of chance and necessity.
—Quoted by Diogenes Laertius
(3rd century)

Democritus (de-**mok**-ri-tus) was reputedly a prolific author but only fragments of his work still exist and little is known about his life. He is believed to have been born a wealthy citizen of Abdera and to have traveled in Egypt and Persia. He wrote on many subjects, and was reputedly the most learned man of his time.

Democritus is best known for his atomic theory. Despite the fact that Leucippus is generally regarded as the originator of the atomic theory, and the difficulty in separating Democritus's contribution from that of the later Epicurus and Lucretius, Democritus was acknowledged by Aristotle (the principle source for Democritus's ideas) to be the leading exponent of the theory. In the "classical" atomic theory, coming into being and dissolution were explained by the linking and flying apart of small hard indestructible particles. Conservation of matter was recognized ("nothing is created out of nothing") and the important doctrine of primary and secondary qualities (later taken up by Galileo and John Locke) was enunciated by Democritus in the memorable aphorism: "Ostensibly there are sweet and bitter, hot and cold, and color; in reality only atoms and the void." The primary qualities were size, shape, and position. Whether or not Democritus attributed weight to atoms is controversial. The theory was deterministic in that the atomic interactions were thought to be ordered by "necessity." Atomism was ignored from the time of Aristotle until the mid-17th century when it was reintroduced by Pierre Gassendi and Galileo.

De Moivre, Abraham

(1667–1754)

FRENCH MATHEMATICIAN

The manner of his [De Moivre's] death has a certain interest for psychologists. Shortly before it he declared that it was necessary for him to sleep some ten minutes or quarter of an hour longer each day than the preceding one. The day after he had thus reached a total of something over twenty-three hours he slept up to the limit of twenty-four hours, and then died in his sleep.
—W. W. Rouse Ball, *A Short Account of the History of Mathematics*

Although born at Vitry in France, as a Huguenot De Moivre (de **mwah-vre**) was forced to flee to England to escape the religious persecution that flared up in 1685 after the revocation of the Edict of Nantes. In England he came to know both Isaac Newton and Edmond Halley, eventually becoming a fellow of the Royal Society of London himself in 1697.

De Moivre made important contributions to mathematics in the fields of probability and trigonometry. His interest in probability was no doubt stimulated by the fact that despite his abilities he was unable to find a permanent post as a mathematician and so was forced to earn his living by, among other things, gambling. De Moivre was the first to define the concept of statistical independence and to introduce analytical techniques into probability. His work on this was published in *The Doctrine of Chances* (1718), later followed by *Miscellanea analytica* (1730; Analytical Miscellany). De Moivre also introduced the use of complex numbers into trigonometry. *De Moivre's theorem* is the relationship

$(\cos A + i \sin A)^n = \cos nA + i \sin nA$.

Dempster, Arthur Jeffrey

(1886–1950)

CANADIAN–AMERICAN PHYSICIST

Dempster was born in Toronto, Ontario, in Canada and educated at the university there. He emigrated to America in 1914, attended the University of Chicago, obtained his PhD in 1916, and began teaching in 1919. In 1927, he was made professor of physics.

He is noted for his early developments of and work with the mass spectrograph (invented by Francis W. Aston). In 1935, he was able to show that uranium did not consist solely of the isotope uranium–238, for seven out of every thousand uranium atoms were in fact uranium–235. It was this isotope, ^{235}U, that was later predicted by Niels Bohr to be capable of sustaining a chain reaction that could release large amounts of atomic fission energy.

Derham, William

(1657–1735)

BRITISH PHYSICIST

Let us ransack all the globe, let us with the greatest accuracy inspect every part thereof, search out the innermost secrets of any of the creatures; let us examine them with all our gauges...pry into them with all our microscopes and most exquisite instruments, till we find them to bear testimony to their infinite workman.

—*Physico-theology* (1713)

Born at Stoughton in Worcestershire, England, and educated at Trinity College, Oxford, Derham was ordained in 1682. He was appointed to the living of Upminister where he remained for the rest of his life.

Derham is best known for his attempt to measure the speed of sound. Martin Mersenne in 1640 had claimed a value of 1,038 feet per second while Newton, in the first edition of *Principia* (1687), had calculated it to be 968 feet per second. In 1705 Derham observed from the tower of his Upminiser church the flash of cannons being fired 12 miles away across the Thames at Blackheath. By timing the interval between the flash and roar of the cannon he was able to calculate the speed of sound to be 1,142 feet per second, a result in good agreement with the 1,130 feet per second at 20°C given in modern textbooks. In the second edition of his *Principia* (1713), Newton revised his calculation in the light of Derham's published results.

Derham was also the author of two immensely popular works: *Physico-theology* (1713) and *Astro-theology* (1715). Based on his Boyle lectures, they set out to show that the basic facts of Newtonian mechanics and cosmology were convincing evidence for the "being and attributes of God."

Also known as an editor, Derham published a number of posthumous works of John Ray as well as *The Philosophical Experiments* (1726) of Robert Hooke.

Desaguliers, John Theophilus

(1683–1744)

FRENCH–ENGLISH PHYSICIST

Desaguliers (day-sa-goo-**lyay**) was born into a Huguenot family in La Rochelle, France. The family was forced by religious persecution to flee to England; John began giving popular lectures on science and its applications in Oxford in 1710. In 1713 he moved to London where he continued to lecture and became experimental assistant to Isaac Newton until Newton's death in 1727. He is important in spreading Newtonian theory both in England and on the Continent. He was also an experimenter – particularly on the flow of electricity, being the first to use the terms "conductor" and "insulator" – and an inventor, improving the design of Thomas Savery's steam engine by adding a safety valve and an internal water jet.

Desargues, Girard

(1591–1661)

FRENCH MATHEMATICIAN AND ENGINEER

Little is known of the early life of Desargues (day-**zarg**) except that he was born in Lyons in France. He did serve as an engineer at the siege of La Rochelle (1628) and later became a technical adviser to Cardinal de Richelieu and the French government. He is said to have known René Descartes.

Around 1630 Desargues joined a group of mathematicians in Paris and concentrated on geometry. In his most famous work, *Brouillon projet d'une atteinte aux événements des rencontres d'une cône avec un plan*

(1639; Proposed Draft of an Attempt to Deal with the Events of the Meeting of a Cone with a Plane), he applied projective geometry to conic sections. *Desargues's theorem* states that if the corresponding points of two triangles in nonparallel planes in space are joined by three lines that intersect at a single point, then the pairs of lines that are the extensions of corresponding sides will each intersect on the same line. Blaise Pascal was greatly influenced by Desargues, whose contribution to projective geometry was not recognized until a handwritten copy of his work was found in 1845. This oversight probably arose because he used obscure botanical symbols instead of the better-known Cartesian symbolism.

Descartes, René du Perron

(1596–1650)

FRENCH MATHEMATICIAN, PHILOSOPHER, AND SCIENTIST

Cogito, ergo sum. (I think, therefore I am.)
　　　　　　　　—*Discours de la méthode* (1637; Discourse on Method)

It is contrary to reason to say that there is a vacuum or space in which there is absolutely nothing.
　　　　　　　　—*Principia philosophiae* (1644; Principles of Philosophy)

Descartes (day-**kart**) was the son of a counselor of the Britanny *parlement*; his mother, who died shortly after his birth, left him sufficient funds to make him financially independent. Born at La Haye in France, he was educated by the Jesuits of La Flèche (1604–12) and at the University of Poitiers, where he graduated in law in 1616. For the next decade Descartes spent much of his time in travel throughout Europe and in military service, first with the army of the Prince of Orange, Maurice of Nassau, and later with the Duke of Bavaria, Maximilian, with whom he was present at the battle of the White Mountain outside Prague in 1620. In the years 1628–49 Descartes settled in the freer atmosphere of Holland. There, living quietly, he worked on the exposition and development of his system. Somewhat unwisely, he allowed himself to be enticed into the personal service of Queen Christina of Sweden in Stockholm in 1649. Forced to indulge the Queen's passion for philosophy by holding tutorials with her at 5 a.m. on icy Swedish mornings Descartes, who normally loved to lie thinking in a warm bed, died within a year from pneumonia and the copious bleeding inflicted by the enthusiastic Swedish doctors.

Descartes is in many ways, in mathematics, philosophy, and science, the first of the moderns. The moment of modernity can be dated precisely to 10 November 1619, when, as later described in his *Discours de la méthode* (1637; Discourse on Method), he spent the whole day in seclusion in a *poêle* (an overheated room). He began systematically to doubt all supposed knowledge and resolved to accept only "what was presented to my mind so clearly and distinctly as to exclude all ground of doubt."

Descartes thus managed to pose in a single night the problem whose solution would obsess philosophers for the next 300 years. The same night also provided him with one of the basic insights of modern mathematics – that the position of a point can be uniquely defined by coordinates locating its distance from a fixed point in the direction of two or more straight lines. This was revealed in his *La Geométrie* (1637; Geometry), published as an appendix to his *Discourse*, and describing the invention of analytic or coordinate geometry, by which the geometric properties of curves and figures could be written as and investigated by algebraic equations. The system is known as a *Cartesian coordinate* system.

His theories on physics were published in his *Principia philosophiae* (1644; Principles of Philosophy). "Give me matter and motion and I will construct the universe," Descartes had proclaimed. The difficulty for him arose from his account of matter which, on metaphysical grounds, he argued, "does not at all consist in hardness, or gravity or color or that which is sensible in another manner, but alone in length, width, and depth," or, in other words, extension. From this initial handicap Descartes was forced to deny the existence of the void and face such apparently intractable problems as how bodies of the same extension could possess different weights. With such restrictions he was led to describe the universe as a system of vortices. Matter came in three forms – ordinary matter opaque to light, the ether of the heavens transmitting light, and the subtle particles of light itself. With considerable ingenuity and precious little concern for reality Descartes used such a framework within which he was able to deal with the basic phenomena of light, heat, and motion. Despite its initial difficulties it was developed by a generation of Cartesian disciples to pose as a viable alternative to the mechanics worked out later in the century by Newton. Unlike many less radical thinkers Descartes did not shrink from applying his mechanical principles to physiology, seeing the human body purely in terms of a physicomechanical system with the mind as a separate entity interacting with the body via the pineal gland – the supposed seat of the soul.

The fundamental impact of Descartes's work was basically one of demystification. Apart from the residual enigma of the precise relationship between mind and body, the main areas of physics and physiology had been swept clear of such talk as that of occult powers and hidden forms.

Desch, Cyril Henry

(1874–1958)

BRITISH METALLURGIST

Desch, the son of a London surveyor, was educated at King's College, London. He taught in Glasgow from 1909 until 1920, when he took up an appointment at the University of Sheffield where he served as professor of metallurgy from 1920 to 1931. Desch then moved to the National Physical Laboratory at Teddington, Middlesex, where he was in charge of the metallurgy department until his retirement in 1939.

Desch is mainly known for his publication in 1910 of his *Textbook of Metallography*, a work that served as the standard account of the subject for the first half of the century.

de Sitter, Willem

(1872–1934)

DUTCH ASTRONOMER AND MATHEMATICIAN

De Sitter (de **sit**-er), the son of a judge from Leiden in the Netherlands, studied mathematics and physics at the University of Groningen, his interest in astronomy being aroused by Jacobus Kapteyn. After serving at the Cape Town Observatory from 1897 to 1899 and, back at Groningen, as assistant to Kapteyn from 1899 to 1908, he was appointed to the chair of astronomy at the University of Leiden. He also served as director of Leiden Observatory from 1919 to 1934.

De Sitter is remembered for his proposal in 1917 of what came to be called the "de Sitter universe" in contrast to the "Einstein universe." Einstein had solved the cosmological equations of his general relativity theory by the introduction of the cosmological constant, which yielded a static universe. But de Sitter, in 1917, showed that there was another solution to the equations that produced a static universe if no matter was present. The contrast was summarized in the statement that Einstein's universe contained matter but no motion while de Sitter's involved motion without matter.

The Russian mathematician Alexander Friedmann in 1922 and the Belgian George Lemaître independently in 1927 introduced the idea of an expanding universe that contained moving matter. It was then shown in 1928 that the de Sitter universe could be transformed mathematically into an expanding universe. This model, the "Einstein–de Sitter universe," comprised normal Euclidean space and was a simpler version of the Friedmann–Lemaître models in which space was curved.

De Sitter also spent much time trying to calculate the mass of Jupiter's satellites from the small perturbations in their orbits. The results were published in 1925 in his *New Mathematical Theory of Jupiter's Satellites*.

Desmarest, Nicolas

(1725–1815)

FRENCH GEOLOGIST

Desmarest (day-ma-**ray**) was the son of a school teacher from Soulaines-Dhuys in France. He first came to notice when he won a prize essay set by the Amiens Academy in 1751 on whether England and

France had ever been joined together. Working for a while in Paris as an editor of scholarly works, he eventually started work for the department of commerce in 1757 investigating and reporting on various trades and industries. He served as inspector-general of manufactures (1788–91).

In 1763, following the work of Jean Guettard, he noticed large basalt deposits and traced these back to ancient volcanic activity in the Auvergne region. He mapped the area and worked out the geology of the volcanoes and their eruptions in great detail, publishing his work in the *Encyclopédie* (Encyclopedia) of 1768. This work disproved the theory that all rocks were sedimentary by revealing basalt's igneous origins. He later produced an influential work, *Géographie physique* (1794; Physical Geography).

Désormes, Charles Bernard

(1777–1862)

FRENCH CHEMIST

Désormes (day-**zorm**), who was born at Dijon in France, studied at the Ecole Polytechnique and was an assistant to Guyton de Morveau until 1804. With Jacques and Joseph Montgolfier and his son-in-law, Nicolas Clément, he was coowner of a chemical factory at Verberie.

Clément and Désormes discovered carbon monoxide (1801), investigated the catalytic effect of nitric oxide in the lead-chamber process of sulfuric acid manufacture, and were involved in the early work on iodine, which was discovered by Bernard Courtois in 1811. Their most important work, however, was in physical chemistry on the specific heats of gases. In 1819 they published an important paper on the determination of the ratio of the principal specific heats (i.e., the ratio of the specific heat of a gas at constant pressure to that at constant volume).

Deville, Henri Etienne Sainte-Claire

(1818–1881)

FRENCH CHEMIST

The son of a wealthy shipowner from the West Indies island of St. Thomas, Deville (de-**veel**) studied medicine in Paris but became interested in chemistry by attending Louis Thenard's lectures. He isolated toluene and methyl benzoate from tolu balsam and investigated other natural products before turning to inorganic chemistry, following his appointment as professor of chemistry at Besançon (1845).

Deville's first major discovery was that of nitrogen pentoxide (1849). Following this success he became professor of chemistry at the Ecole Normale Supérieure (1851) and also lectured at the Sorbonne from 1853. Deville is best known for his work on the large-scale production of aluminum. This had been obtained by Kaspar Wöhler in 1827 but had been produced only in small quantities. Deville developed a commercially successful process involving reduction of aluminum chloride by sodium; the first ingot was produced in 1855. Deville was an expert on the purification of metals and produced (among others) crystalline silicon (1854) and boron (1856), pure magnesium (1857), and pure titanium (1857; with Wöhler). He did much work on the purification of platinum and in 1872 was commissioned to produce the standard kilogram.

After his work on aluminum, Deville's most important researches were those on dissociation. Working with L. J. Troost, he discovered that many molecules were dissociated at high temperature, giving rise to anomalous vapor-density results. Deville's work explained these results and helped to confirm Amedeo Avogadro's hypothesis. His other work included the production of artificial gemstones and improved furnaces.

de Vries, Hugo

(1848–1935)

DUTCH PLANT PHYSIOLOGIST AND
GENETICIST

Born the son of a politician at Haarlem in the Netherlands, de Vries (de vrees) studied botany at Leiden and Heidelberg. He became an expert on the Netherlands flora and later turned his attention from classification to physiology and evolution. He entered Julius von Sachs's laboratory at Würzburg University, where he conducted important experiments on the water of plant cells. He demonstrated that the pressure (turgor) of the cell fluid is responsible for about 10% of extension growth, and introduced the term *plasmolysis* to describe the condition in nonturgid cells in which the cell contents contract away from the cell wall. His work in this field led to Jacobus van't Hoff's theory of osmosis.

During the 1880s, de Vries became interested in heredity. In 1889 he published *Intracellular Pangenesis*, in which he critically reviewed previous research on inheritance and advanced the theory that elements in the nucleus, "pangenes," determine hereditary traits. To investigate his theories, he began breeding plants in 1892 and by 1896 had obtained clear evidence for the segregation of characters in the offspring of crosses in 3:1 ratios. He delayed publishing these results, proposing to include them in a larger book, but in 1900 he came across the work of Gregor Mendel, published 34 years earlier, and announced his own findings. This stimulated both Karl Correns and Erich von Tschermak-Seysenegg to publish their essentially similar observations.

De Vries's work on the evening primrose, *Oenothera lamarckiana*, began in 1886 when he noticed distinctly differing types within a colony of the plants. He considered these to be mutants and formulated the idea of evolution proceeding by distinct changes such as those he observed, believing also that new species could arise through a single drastic mutation. He published his observations in *The Mutation Theory* (1901–03). It was later shown that his *Oenothera* "mutants" were in fact triploids or tetraploids (i.e., they had extra sets of chromosomes) and thus gave a misleading impression of the apparent rate and magnitude of mutations. However, the theory is still important for demonstrating how variation, essential for evolution, can occur in a species.

De Vries was professor of botany at Amsterdam from 1878 to 1918 and was elected a fellow of the Royal Society in 1905.

Dewar, Sir James

(1842–1923)

BRITISH CHEMIST AND PHYSICIST

Dewar, the son of a wine merchant, was born at Kincardine-on-Forth in Scotland. He was educated at Edinburgh University where he was a pupil of Lyon Playfair. In 1869 he was appointed lecturer in chemistry at the Royal Veterinary College, Edinburgh, and from 1873 also held the post of assistant chemist to the Highland and Agricultural Society of Scotland. In 1875 Dewar became Jacksonian Professor of Experimental Philosophy at Cambridge University, England, and from 1877 he was also Fullerian Professor of Chemistry at the Royal Institution, London. He did most of his work in London where the facilities for experimental work were much better.

Dewar conducted his most important work in the field of low temperatures and the liquefaction of gases. In 1878 he demonstrated Louis Cailletet's apparatus for the liquefaction of oxygen and by 1891 he was able to produce liquid oxygen in quantity. In about 1872 he devised a double-walled flask with a vacuum between its highly reflective walls, the *Dewar flask*, and used this to store liquefied oxygen at extremely low temperatures. This vessel (the thermos flask) has come into everyday use for keeping substances either hot or cold.

Hydrogen had so far resisted liquefaction and Dewar now turned his attention to this. Using the Joule–Thomson effect together with Karl von Linde's improvements of this, he produced a machine with which he obtained temperatures as low as 14 K and he produced liquid hydrogen in

1898 and solid hydrogen in 1899. Only helium now resisted liquefaction; this was achieved by Heike Kamerlingh-Onnes in 1908.

From about 1891 Dewar also studied explosives and with Frederick Abel he developed the smokeless powder, cordite. He was knighted in 1904.

Dewar, Michael James Stuart

(1918–)

BRITISH–AMERICAN CHEMIST

Born at Ahmednagar in India, Dewar was educated at Oxford University where he obtained his DPhil in 1942. After research at Oxford he worked in industry as a physical chemist for the Courtauld company from 1945 until his appointment in 1951 as professor of chemistry at Queen Mary College, London. In 1959 Dewar moved to America and served successively as professor of chemistry at the University of Chicago and from 1963 at the University of Texas. In 1990 he was appointed graduate research professor at the University of Florida.

Dewar is noted for his contributions to theoretical chemistry. In his *Electronic Theory of Organic Chemistry* (1949) he argued strongly for the molecular-orbital theory introduced by Robert Mulliken. He did much to improve molecular-orbital calculations and by the 1960s he was able to claim that he and his colleagues could rapidly and accurately calculate a number of chemical and physical properties of molecules.

d'Hérelle, Felix

(1873–1949)

FRENCH–CANADIAN BACTERIOLOGIST

D'Hérelle (day-**rel**), the son of a Canadian father and Dutch mother, was born in Montreal, Quebec, and went to school in Paris, later studying medicine at the University of Montreal. He worked as a bacteriologist in Guatemala and Mexico from 1901 until 1909, when he returned to Europe to take up a position at the Pasteur Institute in Paris. D'Hérelle moved to the University of Leiden in 1921 but after only a short stay resigned to become director of the Egyptian Bacteriological Service (1923). Finally, in 1926, d'Hérelle was appointed to the chair of bacteriology at Yale, a position he held until his retirement in 1933.

D'Hérelle is best known for his discovery of the bacteriophage – a type of virus that destroys bacteria. This work began in 1910 in Yucatan, when he was investigating diarrhea in locusts as a means of locust control. While developing cultures of the causative agent, a coccobacillus, d'Hérelle found that occasionally there would develop on a culture a clear spot, completely free of any bacteria. The cause of these clean spots became clear to him in 1915, while investigating a more orthodox form of dysentery in a cavalry squadron in Paris. He mixed a filtrate from the clear area with a culture of the dysentery bacilli and incubated the resulting broth overnight. The next morning the culture, which had been very turbid, was perfectly clear: all the bacteria had vanished. He concluded that this was the action of "a filterable virus, but a virus parasitic on bacteria."

A similar discovery of what d'Hérelle termed a "bacteriolytic agent" was announced independently by Frederick Twort in 1915. D'Hérelle published his own account first in 1917, followed by his monograph *The Bacteriophage, Its Role in Immunity* (1921). He spent the rest of his career attempting to develop bacteriophages as therapeutic agents. Thus he tried to cure cholera in India in 1927 and bubonic plague in Egypt in 1926 by administering to the patients the appropriate phage. D'Hérelle himself claimed good results with his treatment, although in the hands of other workers the effect of phage on such diseases as cholera and plague appeared to be minimal. This conclusion d'Hérelle continued to resist until his death, claiming that no proper test using his methods had ever been carried out.

However, the importance of the bacteriophage as a research tool in molecular biology cannot be disputed. It was the so-called phage group, centered on Max Delbrück, that made many of the early advances in this discipline in the 1940s.

Dicearchus of Messina

(about 310 BC)

GREEK GEOGRAPHER AND PHILOSOPHER

Dicearchus (dI-see-**ar**-kus) was a pupil of Aristotle and spent most of his life in Sparta. As none of his works have survived it is difficult to be sure of his contributions to geography. He wrote on a large number of topics including the soul, prophecy, and political theory.

His main work in geography was entitled *Periodos ges* (Tour of the Earth) and he also wrote a history of Greek civilization entitled *Bios Hellados* (Life of Greece). As Dicearchus was writing so soon after Alexander the Great's campaigns it is assumed that his works would have contained much new information on the geography of Asia. He is variously reported to have been the first to establish lines of latitude on maps, to have included the heights of mountains, and to have made a reasonable attempt at measuring the size of the Earth using methods that Eratosthenes was later to perfect.

Dicke, Robert Henry

(1916–   )

AMERICAN PHYSICIST

Dicke, who was born in St. Louis, Missouri, graduated in 1939 from Princeton University and obtained his PhD in 1941 from the University of Rochester. He spent the war at the radiation laboratory of the Massachusetts Institute of Technology, joining the Princeton faculty in 1946. In 1957 he was appointed professor of physics and served from 1975 to 1984 as Albert Einstein Professor of Science. In 1984 he was appointed Albert Einstein Emeritus Professor of Science.

In 1964, unaware that he was repeating a line of thought pursued earlier by George Gamow, Ralph Alpher, and Robert C. Herman in 1948, Dicke began to think about the consequences of a big-bang origin of the universe. Assuming a cataclysmic explosion some 18 billion years ago with a temperature one minute after of about 10 billion degrees, then intense radiation would have been produced in addition to particles of matter. As the universe expanded this radiation would gradually lose energy. Could there still be any trace left of this "primeval fireball"? It would in fact be detected as black-body radiation, characteristic of the temperature of the black body, which is a perfect emitter of radiation. At Dicke's instigation his colleague P. J. E. Peebles made the necessary calculations and concluded that the remnant radiation should now have a temperature of only about 10 K, later corrected to about 3 K, i.e., –270°C. At this temperature a black body should radiate a weak signal at microwave wavelengths from 0.05 millimeter to 50 centimeters with a peak at about 2 millimeters. Further, the signal should be constant throughout the entire universe.

Dicke began to organize a search for such radiation and had actually begun to install an antenna on his laboratory roof when he heard from Arno Penzias and Robert Wilson that they had detected background microwave radiation at a wavelength of 7 centimeters. It was this confluence of theory, calculation, and observation that really established the big-bang theory.

Another major area of study for Dicke is gravitation. In the 1960s he carried out a major evaluation of the experiment originally performed by Roland von Eötvös to confirm that the gravitational mass of a body is equal to its inertial mass. Dicke was able to establish the accuracy of the equivalence to one part in 10^{11}. This equivalence is basic to Einstein's theory of general relativity.

In 1961, following a suggestion of Paul Dirac in 1937, Dicke and Carl Brans proposed that the gravitational constant was not in fact a constant, but slowly decreases at a rate of one part in 10^{11} per year. The resulting *Brans–Dicke theory* differs somewhat from Einstein's general relativity at a number of points. Thus while Einstein predicts that a ray of light should be deflected by the Sun's gravitational field 1.75 seconds (″) of arc, the Brans–Dicke theory leads to a figure of 1.62″; such a difference is within the range of observational error and so is not readily detectable. Again the perihelion of Mercury should advance for Einstein by 43″ per century, for Brans–Dicke a mere 39″. A value of 43″ has in fact been measured but Dicke maintains that part of this value, 4″, could be explained by the Sun's nonspherical shape. It has however been claimed that very precise measurements of radio pulses from pulsars appear to favor Einstein. The theory was concurrently and independently developed by Pascual Jordan, and is thus sometimes known as the *Brans–Dicke–Jordan theory*. The idea of a changing gravitational constant was put forward by Paul Dirac.

Diels, Otto Paul Hermann

(1876–1954)

GERMAN ORGANIC CHEMIST

The son of Hermann Diels (deelz), a famous classical scholar, Diels was born in Hamburg, Germany. He gained his doctorate under Emil Fischer in Berlin (1899), becoming professor there in 1906. From 1916 until his retirement in 1948 he was professor at Kiel. In 1906 he made an extremely unexpected discovery, that of a new oxide of carbon, carbon suboxide (C_3O_2), which he prepared by dehydrating malonic acid with phosphorus pentachloride. Diels's second major discovery was a method of removing hydrogen from steroids by means of selenium. He used this method in research on cholesterol and bile acids, obtaining aromatic hydrocarbons that enabled the structures of the steroids to be deduced.

In 1928 Diels and his assistant Kurt Alder discovered a synthetic reaction in which a diene (compound containing two double bonds) is added to a compound containing one double bond flanked by carbonyl or carboxyl groups to give a ring structure. The reaction proceeds in the mildest conditions, is of general application, and hence of great utility in synthesis. It has been used in the synthesis of natural products, such as sterols, vitamin K, and cantharides, and of synthetic polymers. For this discovery Diels and Alder were jointly awarded the Nobel Prize for chemistry in 1950.

Diesel, Rudolph Christian Carl

(1858–1913)

GERMAN ENGINEER AND
INVENTOR

Diesel (**dee**-zel), the designer of the *diesel engine*, was born to German parents in Paris and brought up there until the age of 12. He was academically talented, but his schooling was interrupted in August 1870, when the Franco-Prussian war broke out and the Diesels were deported to London. His cousin, a teacher in Augsburg, Bavaria, invited Diesel to go there to study and he later won a scholarship to the Munich Institute of Technology.

After graduating, Diesel worked as a mechanic for two years in Switzerland and then worked in Paris as a thermal engineer. He was a devout Lutheran and a dedicated pacifist, believing in international religious liberation. In the laboratory that he set up in 1885, an accident with ammonia gas gave him the idea of using chemical firework-type weapons instead of lethal bombs and bullets on the battlefields. In 1893, he demonstrated his first engine and, although the first few attempts failed, within three years he had developed a pressure-ignited heat engine with an efficiency of 75.6%. (Equivalent steam engines had an efficiency of 10%.)

By 1898 Diesel was a millionaire but his fortune soon disappeared. He toured the world giving lectures and visited America in 1912. His health was bad, he suffered from gout, and was depressed by the buildup to World War I. On the ferry returning from London in 1913, after dining apparently happily with a friend, he disappeared and was assumed to have drowned in the English Channel.

Diesenhofer, Johann

(1943–   )

GERMAN CHEMIST

Diesenhofer (**dee**-zen-hof-er), who was born in Zusamaltheim, Germany, obtained his PhD from the Max Planck Institute for Biochemistry, at Martinsried near Munich, in 1974. He remained at the Institute until 1987 when he moved to America to work at the Howard Hughes Medical Institute, Dallas, Texas.

In 1982 Hartmut Michel had succeeded in crystallizing the membrane proteins of the photosynthetic reaction center. Clearly, to understand how photosynthesis worked at the molecular level it would be necessary to determine the structure of these proteins, and Michel invited his colleague Diesenhofer to tackle the problem. By 1985, using the well-established techniques of x-ray crystallography, Diesenhofer's group had managed to locate the position of more than 10,000 atoms.

Diesenhofer's analysis revealed complex protein structures holding a molecular cluster containing four chorophyll molecules, two pheophytins (molecules resembling chlorophyll), two quinones (dehydrogenizing agents), and a single iron atom. It has been possible to show how this center can transform energy from incident photons. On absorbing a photon, one of the chlorophyll molecules releases an electron. This is transferred by the pheophytins and quinones to the membrane's outer surface. At the same time, an adjoining cytochrome molecule donates an electron to one of the chlorophyll molecules and thus gains a positive charge. In this way the photon energy has been stored in the charge separation of the negative electron and the positive cytochrome. And so begins the molecular process of photosynthesis.

For this work Diesenhofer shared the 1988 Nobel Prize for chemistry with his Institute colleagues Hartmut Michel and Robert Huber.

Diophantus of Alexandria

(about 250)

GREEK MATHEMATICIAN

> This tomb holds Diophantus. Ah, how great a marvel! The tomb tells scientifically the measure of his life. God granted him to be a boy for the sixth part of his life...five years after his marriage He granted him a son. Alas! late-born wretched child; after attaining the measure of half his father's life, chill Fate took him. After consoling his grief by this science of numbers for four years he ended his life.
>
> —*The Greek Anthology*

Diophantus (dI-oh-**fan**-tus) was one of the outstanding mathematicians of his era but almost nothing is known of his life and his writings survive only in fragmentary form. His most famous work was in the field of number theory and of the so-called *Diophantine equations* named for him. His major work, the *Arithmetica* (Arithmetic), contained many new methods and results in this field. It originally consisted of 13 books but only 6 survived to be translated by the Arabs. However Diophantus was not solely interested in equations with only integral (whole number) solutions and also considered rational solutions. Diophantus made considerable innovations in the use of symbolism in Greek mathematics – the lack of suitable symbolism had previously hampered work in algebra.

Dioscorides, Pedanius

(*c.* 40 AD–*c.* 90 AD)

GREEK PHYSICIAN

> If you have not sufficient facility in reading Greek, then you can turn to the herbal of Dioscorides, which describes and draws the herbs of the field with wonderful faithfulness.
> —Cassiodorus (6th century)

Little is known of the life of Dioscorides (dI-os-**kor**-i-deez) except that he was born in Anazarbus (now in Turkey) and became a surgeon to Emperor Nero's armies, having most probably learned his skills at Alexandria and Tarsus. Many writings are attributed to him but the only book for which his authorship is undisputed is *De materia medica* (On Medicine). This pharmacopeia remained the standard medical text until the 17th century, undergoing many revisions and additions and greatly influencing both Western and Islamic cultures. It describes animal derivatives and minerals used therapeutically but is most important for the description of over 600 plants, including notes on their habitat and the methods of preparation and medicinal use of the drugs they contain. Many of the common and scientific plant names in use today originate from Dioscorides and the yam family, Dioscoreaceae, is named for him.

Dirac, Paul Adrien Maurice

(1902–1984)

BRITISH MATHEMATICIAN AND PHYSICIST

It seems that if one is working from the point of view of getting beauty in one's equations, and if one has really a sound insight, one is on a sure line of progress.
—*Scientific American*, May 1963

Dirac (di-**rak**), whose father was Swiss, was born in Bristol in the west of England. After graduating in 1921 in electrical engineering at Bristol University, Dirac went on to study mathematics at Cambridge University, where he obtained his PhD in 1926. After several years spent lecturing in America, he was appointed (1932) to the Lucasian Professorship of Mathematics at Cambridge, a post he held until his retirement in 1969. In 1971 he became professor of physics at Florida State University.

Dirac is acknowledged as one of the most creative of the theoreticians of the early 20th century. In 1926, slightly later than Max Born and Pascual Jordan in Germany, he developed a general formalism for quantum mechanics. In 1928 he produced his relativistic theory to describe the properties of the electron. The wave equations developed by Erwin Schrödinger to describe the behavior of electrons were nonrelativistic. A significant deficiency in the Schrödinger equation was its failure to account for the electron spin discovered in 1925 by Samuel Goudsmit and George Uhlenbeck. Dirac's rewriting of the equations to incorporate relativity had considerable value for it not only predicted the correct energy levels of the hydrogen atom but also revealed that some of those levels were no longer single but could be split into two. It is just such a splitting of spectral lines that is characteristic of a spinning electron.

Dirac also predicted from these equations that there must be states of negative energy for the electron. In 1930 he proposed a theory to account for this that was soon to receive dramatic confirmation. He began by taking negative energy states to refer to those energy states below the lowest positive energy state, the ground state. If there were a lower energy state for the electron below the ground state then, the question arises, why do some electrons not fall into it? Dirac's answer was that such states have already been filled with other electrons and he conjured up a picture in which space is not really empty but full of particles of negative energy. If one of these particles were to collide with a sufficiently energetic photon it would acquire positive energy and be observable as a normal electron, apparently appearing from nowhere. But it would not appear alone for it would leave behind an empty hole, which was really an absence of a negatively charged particle or, in other words, the presence of a positively charged particle. Further, if the electron were to fall back into the empty hole it would once more disappear, appearing to be annihilated together with the positively charged particle, or positron as it was later called.

Out of this theory there emerged three predictions. Firstly, that there was a positively charged electron, secondly, that it could only appear in conjunction with a normal electron, and, finally, that a collision between them resulted in their total common annihilation. Such predictions were soon confirmed following the discovery of the positron by Carl Anderson in 1932. Dirac had in fact added a new dimension of matter to the universe, namely antimatter. It was soon appreciated that Dirac's argument was sufficiently general to apply to all particles.

In 1937 Dirac published a paper entitled *The Cosmological Constants* in which he considered "large-number coincidences," i.e., certain relationships that appear to exist between the numerical properties of some natural constants. An example is to compare the force of electrostatic attraction between an electron and a proton with the gravitational attraction due to their masses. The ratio of these is about $10^{40}:1$. Similarly, it is also found that the characteristic "radius" of the universe is 10^{40} times as large as the characteristic radius of an electron. Moreover, 10^{40} is approximately the square root of the number of particles in the universe.

These coincidences are remarkable and many physicists have speculated that these apparently unrelated things may be connected in some way. The ratios were first considered in the 1930s by Arthur Eddington, who believed that he could calculate such constants and that they arose from the way in which physics observes and interprets nature. Dirac used the 10^{40} number above in a model of the universe. He argued that there was a connection between the force ratio and the radius ratio. Since the radius of the universe increased with age the gravitational "constant," on which the force ratio depends, may decrease with time.

Above all else however Dirac was a quantum theorist. In 1930 he published the first edition of his classic work *The Principles of Quantum Mechanics*. In 1933 he shared the Nobel Prize for physics with Schrödinger.

Dirichlet, (Peter Gustav) Lejeune

(1805–1859)

GERMAN MATHEMATICIAN

In mathematics as in other fields, to find oneself lost in wonder at some manifestation is frequently the half of a new discovery.

—*Works*, Vol. II

Born in Düren (now in Germany), Dirichlet (dee-ri-**klay**) studied mathematics at Göttingen where he was a pupil of Karl Gauss and Karl Jacobi. He also studied briefly in Paris where he met Joseph Fourier, who stimulated his interest in trigonometric series. In 1826 he returned to Germany and taught at Breslau and later at the Military Academy in Berlin. He then moved to the University of Berlin, which he only left 27 years later when he returned to Göttingen to fill the chair left vacant by Gauss's death.

Dirichlet's work in number theory was very much inspired by Gauss's great work in that field, and Dirichlet's own book, the *Vorlesungen über Zahlentheorie* (1863; Lectures on Number Theory), is of comparable historical importance to Gauss's *Disquisitiones*. He made many very significant discoveries in the field and his work on a problem connected with primes led him to make the fundamentally important innovation of using analytical techniques to obtain results in number theory.

His stay in Paris had stimulated Dirichlet's interest in Fourier series and in 1829 he was able to solve the outstanding problem of stating the conditions sufficient for a Fourier series to converge. (The other problem of giving necessary conditions is still unsolved.) Fourier also gave the young Dirichlet an interest in mathematical physics, which led him to important work on multiple integrals and the boundary-value problem, now known as the *Dirichlet problem*, concerning the formulation and solution of those partial differential equations occurring in the study of heat flow and electrostatics. These are of great importance in many other areas of physics. The growth of a more rigorous understanding of analysis owes to Dirichlet what is essentially the modern definition of the concept of a function.

Djerassi, Carl

(1923–　)

AMERICAN CHEMIST

Djerassi (jer-**as**-i) was born in the Austrian capital of Vienna, the son of a Bulgarian physician and an Austrian mother. As both parents were Jewish, Djerassi emigrated to America in 1939. He was educated at Kenyon College, Ohio, and at the University of Wisconsin, where he completed his PhD in 1945, the same year in which he became an American citizen. From 1945 to 1949 he worked for the pharmaceutical company CIBA in Summit, New Jersey, as a research chemist. In 1949 Djerassi decided to join a new pharmaceutical company, Syntex, in Mexico City, to work on the extraction of cortisone from plants. At that time it was being produced from cattle bile at a cost of $200 a gram.

Despite competition from other leading laboratories, Syntex were the first to extract cortisone ($C_{21}H_{28}O_5$) from a vegetable source, namely diosgenin ($C_{27}H_{42}O_3$), a steroid derived from a variety of wild Mexican yam.

Following their initial success Djerassi and his team turned their attention to the steroid hormone progesterone. Known as "nature's contraceptive," the hormone inhibits ovulation. Why, then, could it not be taken as a simple, natural contraceptive? The difficulty was that taken orally it lost most of its activity. Further, as hormones were extracted from such animal sources as human urine, bull's testicles, and sow's ovaries where they occur in small amounts, they tended to be very expensive. The first step was to produce progesterone synthetically. This was achieved at Syntex by Djerassi and others in the early 1950s, the price of progesterone dropped dramatically and it became available in large quantities.

Chemists were inhibited by the belief that steroid hormones were structure-specific; change the structure, the claim went, and the potency is lost. Djerassi was aware, however, that Max Ehrenstein had destroyed this myth a decade earlier and that it was at least conceivable that progesterone could be changed into an oral form without necessarily changing its potency.

Progesterone ($C_{21}H_{30}O_2$) contains four rings of carbon atoms. Following some hints in the literature Djerassi thought that the removal of the methyl group at position 19, thus forming 19-norprogesterone, would increase its potency. His hunch proved to be sound. He was also aware that an acetylene bond introduced into position 17 of the male hormone testosterone increased its oral activity; although known as "ethisterone," it had found no use.

Djerassi's crucial step was to propose that ethisterone's potency could be enhanced, as with progesterone, by removing a methyl group. By October 1951 he had produced testosterone minus a methyl group, but with an added acetylene group. The precise result was 19-nor-17a-ethinyltestosterone, which proved to be a highly active oral progestational hormone. A patent was filed in November 1951. After the appropriate testing it received Federal approval in 1962 under the name Ortho-Novum. Djerassi received one dollar for the patent, a standard payment by a pharmaceutical company to its staff.

In 1951 Djerassi left Syntex for Wayne State University, Detroit, where he remained until 1959 when he was appointed professor of chemistry at Stanford. He continued to work for Syntex, as vice-president in charge of research (1957–69) and as president of research from (1969–72).

He has also served since 1968 with Zoecon, a company partly owned by Syntex and specializing in pest control by using natural juvenile hormones that prevent insects maturing and breeding. In 1977 Zoecon was taken over by Occidental Petroleum and was then sold in 1982 to Sandoz, a Swiss pharmaceutical company. Djerassi has remained as chairman of the board.

Djerassi's business interests have had little impact on his productivity with over 600 papers to his credit. He has also published a novel (*Cantor's Dilemma*), a collection of verse, and his autobiography, *The Pill, Pigmy Chimps, and Degas' Horse* (1992).

Döbereiner, Johann Wolfgang

(1780–1849)

GERMAN CHEMIST

> I love science more than money.
> —Explaining his failure to patent his
>   invention of the Döbereiner lamp

Born the son of a coachman in Hof an der Saale, Germany, Döbereiner (**du(r)**-be-rIn-er) had little formal education and worked as an assistant to apothecaries in several places from the age of 14. He was largely self-taught in chemistry and was encouraged by Leopold Gmelin whom he met at Strasbourg. After several failures in business, he was appointed assistant professor of chemistry at Jena (1810).

In 1823 he discovered that hydrogen would ignite spontaneously in air over platinum sponge, and subsequently developed the *Döbereiner lamp* to exploit this phenomenon. Döbereiner was interested in catalysis in general and discovered the catalytic action of manganese dioxide in the decomposition of potassium chlorate. His law of triads (1829), based on his observation of regular increments of atomic weight in elements with similar properties, was an important step on the way to Dmitri Mendeleev's periodic table. Thus in triads such as calcium, strontium, and barium or chlorine, bromine, and iodine, the middle element has an atomic weight that is approximately the average of the other two. It is also intermediate in chemical properties between the other two elements. Döbereiner also worked in organic chemistry.

Dobzhansky, Theodosius

(1900–1975)

RUSSIAN–AMERICAN GENETICIST

> Nothing in biology makes sense except in the light of evolution.
> —Title of article in the *American Biology Teacher* (1973)

Dobzhansky (dob-**zhan**-ski), who was born in Nemirov, in Ukraine, graduated in zoology from Kiev University in 1921; he remained there to teach zoology before moving to Leningrad, where he taught genetics. In 1927 he took up a fellowship at Columbia University, New York, where he worked with T. H. Morgan. Morgan was impressed by Dobzhansky's ability and, when the fellowship was completed, offered him a teaching post at the California Institute of Technology. Dobzhansky accepted and became an American citizen in 1937.

Dobzhansky studied the fruit fly (*Drosophila*) and demonstrated that the genetic variability within populations was far greater than had been imagined. The high frequency of potentially deleterious genes had previously been overlooked because their effects are masked by corresponding dominant genes. Dobzhansky found that such debilitating genes actually conferred an advantage to the organism when present with the normal type of gene, and therefore they tended to be maintained at a high level in the population. Populations with a high genetic load – i.e., many concealed lethal genes – proved to be more versatile in changing environments. This work profoundly influenced the theories on the mathematics of evolution and natural selection with regard to Mendelism.

In addition, Dobzhansky wrote many influential books, including *Genetics and the Origin of Species* (1937), a milestone in evolutionary genetics.

Doisy, Edward Adelbert

(1893–1986)

AMERICAN BIOCHEMIST

Doisy was born in Hume, Illinois, and educated at the University of Illinois and at Harvard, where he obtained his PhD in 1920. From 1919 to 1923 he worked at the Washington University School of Medicine. In 1923 he was appointed to the chair of biochemistry at the St. Louis University Medical School, a position he retained until his retirement in 1965.

Doisy worked initially on ovarian biochemistry. In 1929 he succeeded in isolating the hormone estrone ($C_{18}H_{12}O_2$), and soon after the more potent estradiol ($C_{18}H_{24}O_2$). In 1938 he isolated, and in the following year synthesized, vitamin K, recently discovered by Carl Dam. He discovered that the vitamin existed in two forms, the physiologically active form K_1, extracted from alfalfa, and K_2, differing in a side chain and derivable from rotten fish. For his discovery of the chemical nature of vitamin K, technically a naphthoquinone, Doisy shared the 1943 Nobel Prize for physiology or medicine with Dam.

Dokuchaev, Vasily Vasilievich

(1846–1903)

RUSSIAN SOIL SCIENTIST

> Climate, vegetation, and animal life are distributed on the earth's surface, from north to south, in a strictly determined order.
> —*Collected Works,* Vol. VI

Dokuchaev (dok-uu-**cha**-ef) was born in Milyukovo near Smolensk, Russia, the son of the village priest. He too was originally trained for the priesthood but later turned to the study of science at St. Petersburg University where he graduated in 1871. He was immediately appointed to the faculty, initially as curator of the geological collection but he also served as professor of geology until poor health forced him to retire in 1897.

Dokuchaev made the first comprehensive scientific study of the soils of Russia, details of which are to be found in his *Collected Works* (9 vols., 1949–61). He also, in the 1890s, set up at the Kharkov Institute of Agriculture and Forestry, the first department of soil science in Russia.

In the West he is mainly known for his work on the classification of soils, his insistence that soil is a geobiological formation, and his use of soil to define the different geographical zones. It is also owing to Dokuchaev that the Russian term "chernozem," used to describe a black soil rich in humus and carbonates, has entered most languages.

Dollfus, Audouin Charles

(1924–   )

FRENCH ASTRONOMER

Dollfus (**dol**-foos), the son of an aeronaut, studied at the university in his native city of Paris. In 1946 he joined the staff of the astrophysical division of the Paris Observatory at Meudon and is now head of the Laboratory for Physics of the Solar System.

Dollfus has established a reputation as an authority on the solar system and a leading planetary observer. He began a study of Saturn's rings in 1948 and soon noted the presence of occasional brightness ripples. Work in the 1950s showed that they could not be explained by the effects of the known satellites and Dollfus concluded that other forces seemed to be acting, possibly attributable to an unknown satellite very close to the rings. A favorable viewing time, with the rings appearing edge-on to an Earth-bound observer, came in 1966. Although early visual attempts to detect the satellite failed, Dollfus was more successful when he examined photographic plates taken with the 43-inch (1.1-m) reflecting telescope of the Pic du Midi Observatory in December 1966, virtually the last opportunity for favorable viewing before 1980. On these he found the image of an unknown satellite.

Following independent confirmation, the satellite was named Janus and was widely accepted as Saturn's tenth satellite, its period having been calculated by Dollfus as 18 hours. When no such satellite was found by the Pioneer II and Voyager I spacecraft in 1979 and 1980, Dollfus rechecked his measurements. It now appears that he photographed one of the "twin" satellites that appeared in the spacecraft pictures and that recent calculations have shown to move in nearly identical orbits with periods of about 16.7 hours.

Döllinger, Ignaz Christoph von

(1770–1841)

GERMAN BIOLOGIST

After studying medicine in his native city of Bamberg, then at Würzburg, Vienna, and Pavia (Italy), Döllinger (**du(r)l**-ing-er) gained his doctorate at Bamberg in 1794. In 1796 he was appointed professor of medicine at the University of Bamberg, and in 1803 became professor of physiology and normal and pathological anatomy at Würzburg. From 1823 Döllinger was curator of academic sciences at Munich and then became (1826) professor of anatomy and physiology and director of the anatomical museum of the University of Munich. He was one of the pioneers of the use of the microscope in medical studies and made investigations of blood circulation, the spleen and liver, glandular secretions, and the eye, as well as comparative anatomy studies. His embryological work exercised a considerable influence on Louis Agassiz.

Dollond, John

(1706–1761)

BRITISH OPTICIAN

Dollond was born in London, the son of Huguenot refugees. He started life as a silk weaver but later joined his eldest son, Peter, in making optical instruments, and devoted years of experiment to developing an achromatic lens. The problem confronting lens makers at the time was chromatic aberration – the fringe of colors that surrounds and disturbs images formed by a lens. This put a limit on the power of lenses (and of refracting telescopes), for the stronger the lens, the more chromatically disturbed the images became. Chromatic aberration is caused by the different wavelengths that make up white light being refracted to different extents by the glass, each being focused at a different point.

In 1758 Dollond succeeded in making lenses without this defect by using two different lenses, one of crown glass and one of flint glass (one convex and one concave), so made that the chromatic aberration of one was neutralized by the aberration of the other. In fact he was not the first to make such a lens, since Chester Hall had already done so in 1753, but Dollond managed to patent the idea because he was the first to publicize the possibility.

In 1761 he was appointed optician to George III but died of apoplexy later that year.

Domagk, Gerhard

(1895–1964)

GERMAN BIOCHEMIST

If I could start again, I would perhaps become a psychiatrist and search for a causal therapy of mental disease, which is the most terrifying problem of our times.
—On his scientific career

Domagk (**doh**-mahk), who was born in Lagow, now in Poland, graduated in medicine from the University of Kiel in 1921 and began teaching at the University of Greifswald and later at the University of Münster. At this time he carried out important researches into phagocytes – special cells that attack bacteria in the body. He became interested in chemotherapy and in 1927 he was appointed director of research in experimental pathology and pathological anatomy at the giant chemical factory I. G. Farbenindustrie at Wuppertal-Elberfeld. Pursuing the ideas of Paul Ehrlich, Domagk tested new dyes produced by the Elberfeld chemists for their effect against various infections. In 1935 he reported the effectiveness of an orange-red dye called prontosil in combating streptococcal infections. For the first time a chemical had been found to be active *in vivo* (in a living organism) against a common small bacterium. Earlier dyes used as drugs were active only against infections caused by much larger protozoa.

The work was followed up in research laboratories throughout the world – Alexander Fleming neglected penicillin to work on prontosil in the early 1930s – but the most significant ramifications were discovered by Daniele Bovet and his coworkers. Prontosil and the sulfa drugs that followed were effective in saving many lives, including those of Franklin D. Roosevelt Jr., Winston Churchill, and Domagk's own daughter. In 1939 Domagk was offered the Nobel Prize for physiology or medicine. The Nazis forced him to withdraw his acceptance because Hitler was annoyed with the Nobel Committee for awarding the 1935 Peace Prize to a German, Carl von Ossietzky, whom Hitler had imprisoned. In 1947 Domagk was finally able to accept the prize. In his later years he undertook drug research into cancer and tuberculosis.

Donati, Giovanni Battista

(1826–1873)

ITALIAN ASTRONOMER

After graduating from the university in his native city of Pisa, Donati (do-**nah**-tee) joined the staff of the Florence Observatory in 1852, and was appointed director in 1864. He died from bubonic plague in 1873.

Much of his work was concerned with comets. He discovered six new comets, one of which, first appearing in June 1858 has since been known as *Donati's comet*. He went on in 1864 to make the first observations of a comet's chemical composition. Spectroscopic observation of the 1864 comet produced a line spectrum with three lines named alpha, beta, and gamma by Donati. The three lines were also seen in an 1866 comet by Secchi. The lines were shown by Huggins in 1868 to be due to the presence of carbon.

Dondi, Giovanni de

(1318–1389)

ITALIAN ASTRONOMER AND CLOCKMAKER

Dondi (**don**-dee), born the son of a professor of medicine and clock designer in Chiogga, Italy, taught medicine and astronomy at the universities of Padua and Pavia. He became famous throughout the whole of Europe for his construction of a marvelous astronomical clock that he began in 1348 and that took him 16 years to complete. It was built for the duke of Milan and was put in his library in Pavia. Although the clock has long been destroyed, Dondi wrote a treatise on it, which has survived. It was weight driven, had a verge and foliot escapement, and was made of brass and bronze. It was completely unlike a modern clock being so unconcerned with the time of day that it did not even have hands. It was intended to show the movements of the planets and the time of the movable and fixed ecclesiastical festivals. It involved advanced gear work and showed mechanical skill of a high order. Such was his fame that Dondi was known throughout Europe as "John of the Clock."

Donnan, Frederick George

(1879–1956)

BRITISH CHEMIST

Donnan, the son of a Belfast merchant, was born in Colombo, the capital of Ceylon (now Sri Lanka). He was educated at Queen's College, Belfast, and the universities of Leipzig and Berlin where he obtained his PhD in 1896 and some of the German expertise in physical chemistry. On his return to England he worked at University College, London, with Sir William Ramsay from 1898 until 1904, when he accepted the post of professor of physical chemistry at the University of Liverpool. In 1913 Donnan returned to succeed Ramsay at University College, remaining there until his retirement in 1937.

Donnan is mainly remembered for the *Donnan membrane equilibrium* (1911) – a theory describing the equilibrium which arises in the passage of ions through membranes.

Doodson, Arthur Thomas

(1890–1968)

BRITISH MATHEMATICAL PHYSICIST

Doodson, the son of a manager of a cotton mill in Worsley in the north of England, was educated at the University of Liverpool. After working at University College, London, from 1916 to 1918 he joined the

Tidal Institute, Liverpool, in 1919 as its secretary. Doodson remained through its re-formation as the Liverpool Observatory and Tidal Institute as assistant director (1929–45) and as director until his retirement in 1960.

Much of Doodson's early work was on the production of mathematical tables and the calculation of trajectories for artillery. Proving himself an ingenious, powerful, and practical mathematician he found an ideal subject for his talents in the complicated behavior of the tides. He made many innovations in their accurate computation and, with H. Warburg in 1942, produced the *Admiralty Manual of Tides*.

Doppler, Christian Johann

(1803–1853)

AUSTRIAN PHYSICIST

Christian Doppler, the son of a stonemason from the Austrian city of Salzburg, studied mathematics at the Vienna Polytechnic. In 1835 he started teaching at a school in Prague and six years later was appointed professor of mathematics at the Technical Academy there.

Doppler's fame comes from his discovery in 1842 of the *Doppler effect* – the fact that the observed frequency of a wave depends on the velocity of the source relative to the observer. The effect can be observed with sound waves. If the source is moving toward the observer, the pitch is higher; if it moves away, the pitch is lower. A common example is the fall in frequency of a train's whistle or a vehicle siren as it passes. Doppler's principle was tested experimentally in 1843 by Christoph Buys Ballot, who used a train to pull trumpeters at different speeds past musicians who had perfect pitch.

Doppler also tried to apply his principle to light waves, with limited success. It was Armand Fizeau in 1848 who suggested that at high relative velocities the apparent color of the source would be changed by the motion: an object moving toward the observer would appear bluer; one moving away would appear redder. The shift in the spectra of celestial objects (the *Doppler shift*) is used to measure the rate of recession or approach relative to the Earth.

Dorn, Friedrich Ernst

(1848–1916)

GERMAN PHYSICIST

Dorn, who was born in Guttstadt (now Dobre Miasto in Poland), studied at Königsberg and in 1873 was made professor of physics at Breslau. In 1886 he transferred to a professorship at Halle and started working with x-rays. He is noted for his discovery, in 1900, that the radioactive element radium gives off a radioactive gas, which Dorn called "radium emanation." The gas was isolated in 1908 by William Ramsay, who named it "niton." The name radon was adopted in 1923. Dorn's discovery is the first established demonstration of a transmutation of one element into another.

Douglas, Donald Wills

(1892–1981)

AMERICAN AIRCRAFT ENGINEER

Douglas, the son of an assistant bank cashier in New York City, was educated at the U.S. Naval Academy and the Massachusetts Institute of Technology. He gained his first experience of aircraft design working for the Glenn L. Martin Company of California on the development of a heavy bomber.

In 1920 he set up on his own with $600 and the backing of David Davis, a wealthy sportsman willing to invest $40,000 to produce a plane capable of flying nonstop across America. Although the *Cloudster*, the result of their venture, only reached Texas it was in fact the first aircraft in history capable of lifting a useful load exceeding its own weight.

By 1928, on the strength of some profitable navy contracts, Douglas was ready to go public with his new Douglas Aircraft Company. The company had many years of success, with such planes as the DC-3, first flown in 1935, contributing substantially to their profits. In 1967 the company was taken over by the McDonnell Aircraft Company and re-formed as the McDonnell–Douglas Corporation.

Douglass, Andrew Ellicott

(1867–1962)

AMERICAN ASTRONOMER AND DENDROCHRONOLOGIST

Douglass came from a family of academics in Windsor, Vermont, with both his father and grandfather being college presidents. He graduated from Trinity College, Hartford, Connecticut in 1889 and in the same year was appointed to an assistantship at Harvard College Observatory. In 1894 he went with Percival Lowell to the new Lowell Observatory in Flagstaff, Arizona, moving to the University of Arizona in 1906 as professor of astronomy and physics.

Douglass's first interest was the 11-year sunspot cycle. In trying to trace its history he was led to the examination of tree rings in the hope that he would find some identifiable correlation of sunspot activity with terrestrial climate and vegetation. Soon the tree rings became the center of his studies.

The only previously established method of dating the past, except by inscriptions, was the geological varve-counting technique, which was developed from 1878. But this was of no use if there were no varves (thin seasonally deposited layers of sediment in glacial lakes) to be found. Douglass soon found that he could identify local tree rings with confidence and use them in dating past climatic trends. He thus founded the field of dendrochronology. By the late 1920s he had a sequence of over a thousand tree rings with six thin rings, presumably records of a severe drought, correlated with the end of the 13th century. In 1929 he found some timber that contained the six thin rings and a further 500 in addition. This took him to the eighth century and over the years he managed to get as far as the first century. This was extended still further and by careful analysis scholars have now established a sequence going back almost to 5000 BC.

The dated rings of Arizona and New Mexico were found however not to correlate with sequences from other parts of the world: the tree-ring clock was a purely local one. The search for a more universal clock continued, and the method of radiocarbon dating was developed by Willard Libby in 1949.

Drake, Frank Donald

(1930–   )

AMERICAN ASTRONOMER

Drake, who was born in Chicago, Illinois, graduated in 1952 from Cornell University and obtained his PhD in 1958 from Harvard. He worked initially at the National Radio Astronomy Observatory (NRAO), West Virginia (1958–63) and at the Jet Propulsion Laboratory, California (1963–64) before returning to Cornell and serving as professor of astronomy from 1964. He was appointed professor of astronomy at the University of California in 1984.

Although Drake has made significant contributions to radio astronomy, including radio studies of the planets, he is perhaps best known for his pioneering search for extraterrestrial intelligence. In April 1959 he managed to gain approval from the director at NRAO, Otto Struve, to proceed with his search, which was called "Project Ozma." The name was taken from the Oz stories of Frank Baum. Drake began in 1960, using the NRAO 26-meter radio telescope to listen for possible signals from planets of the Sunlike stars Tau Ceti and Epsilon Eridani, both about 11 light-years away. He decided to tune to the frequency of 1,420 megahertz at which radio emission from hydrogen occurs. This would have considerable significance for any civilization capable of building radio transmitters.

No signals were received although at one time excitement was generated when signals from a secret military radar establishment were received while the antenna was pointed at Epsilon Eridani. In July 1960 the project was terminated to allow the telescope to fulfill some of its other obligations. Drake revived the project in 1975, in collaboration with Carl Sagan, when they began using the Arecibo 1,000-foot (305-meter) radio telescope to listen to several nearby galaxies on frequencies of 1,420, 1,653, and 2,380 megahertz. No contact was made nor was it likely, they declared, for "A search of hundreds of thousands of stars in the hope of detecting one message would require remarkable dedication and would probably take several decades." He has published a number of works on this issue including *Is Anyone There? The Search for Extra Terrestrial Intelligence* (1992).

Draper, Henry

(1837–1882)

AMERICAN ASTRONOMER

> I think we are by no means at the end of what can be done. If I can stand 6 hours'
> exposure in midwinter another step forward will result.
> —Remark made in the last months of his life, describing his work
> photographing stars and planets

Draper, the son of the distinguished physician and chemist John W. Draper, was born in Prince Edward County, Virginia. He studied at the City University of New York, completing the course in medicine in 1857 before he was old enough to graduate. He obtained his MD in 1858, spending the preceding months in Europe where his interest in astronomy was aroused by a visit to the observatory of the third earl of Rosse at Parsonstown, Ireland. On his return to New York he joined the Bellevue Hospital and was later appointed professor of natural science at the City University in 1860. Draper later held chairs of physiology (1866–73) and analytical chemistry (1870–82) and in 1882 succeeded his father briefly as professor of chemistry. He retired in 1882 in order to devote himself to astronomical research but died prematurely soon after.

One of the most important events in Draper's life was his marriage in 1867 to Anna Palmer, daughter and heiress to Courtlandt Palmer who had made a fortune in hardware and New York real estate. His wife's money allowed him to purchase a 28-inch (71-cm) reflecting telescope and to begin a 15-year research partnership.

Draper was interested in the application of the new technique of photography to astronomy. He started by making daguerrotypes of the Sun and Moon but in 1872 succeeded for the first time in obtaining a photograph of a stellar spectrum, that of Vega. In 1879 he found that dry photographic plates had been developed and that these were more sensitive and convenient than wet collodion. By 1882 he had obtained photographs of over a hundred stellar spectra plus spectra of the Moon, Mars, Jupiter, and the Orion nebula. He also succeeded in directly photographing the Orion nebula, first with a 50-minute exposure in 1880 and then, using a more accurate clock-driven telescope, with a 140-minute exposure. He thus helped to establish photographic astronomy as an important means of studying the heavens.

At the time of his death his widow hoped to continue his work herself, but with prompting from Edward Pickering at the Harvard College Observatory, she set up the Henry Draper Memorial Fund. It was with the aid of this fund that the famous *Henry Draper Catalogue*, some nine volumes with details of the spectra of 225,000 stars, was published from 1918 to 1924 through the labors of Pickering and Annie Cannon.

Draper, John William

(1811–1882)

BRITISH–AMERICAN CHEMIST

How is it that the Church produced no geometers in her autocratic reign of twelve hundred years?
—*The Conflict Between Science and Religion* (1890)

Draper, who was born in St. Helens, Lancashire, in northwestern England, was educated at University College, London, before he emigrated to America in 1833. He qualified in medicine at the University of Pennsylvania in 1836. After a short period teaching in Virginia he moved to New York University (1838) where he taught chemistry and in 1841 helped to start the medical school of which he became president in 1850.

Most of his chemical work was done in the field of photochemistry. He was one of the first scientists to use Louis Daguerre's new invention (1837) of photography. He took the first photograph of the Moon in 1840 and in the same year took a photograph of his sister, Dorothy, which is the oldest surviving photographic study of the human face. In 1843 he obtained the first photographic plate of the solar spectrum. He was also one of the first to take photographs of specimens under a microscope. On the theoretical level Draper was one of the earliest to grasp that only those rays that are absorbed produce chemical change and that not all rays are equally powerful in their effect. He also, in a series of papers (1841–45), showed that the amount of chemical change is proportional to the intensity of the absorbed radiation multiplied by the time it has to act. Draper's work was continued and largely confirmed by the work of Robert Bunsen and Henry Roscoe in 1857. Draper's work also resulted in the development of actinometers (instruments to measure the intensity of light) which he named "tithonometers." He also wrote on a wide variety of other topics.

Draper's son Henry was an astronomer of note after whom the famous Harvard catalog of stellar spectra was named.

Dreyer, Johann Louis Emil

(1852–1926)

DANISH ASTRONOMER

Dreyer (**drI**-er), the son of a general of the Danish Army, was born in Copenhagen and studied at the university there, obtaining his MA in 1874 and his PhD in 1882. He began his career in 1874 as an assistant at the observatory of William Parsons, third earl of Rosse, in Parsonstown, Ireland, moving in 1878 to another assistantship at the Dunsink Observatory, Dublin. In 1882 Dreyer was appointed director of the Armagh Observatory, in what is now Northern Ireland, a post he occupied until his retirement in 1916 when he settled in Oxford, England.

Dreyer's major contribution to astronomy was his three catalogs. He began by preparing in 1878 a supplement to John Herschel's catalog of 5,000 nebulae. The work naturally led to the production of a totally new work, the *New General Catalogue of Nebulae and Clusters of Stars* (1888) containing details of 7,840 celestial objects and known invariably as the NGC. It listed all the nebulae and clusters that had been discovered up to 1888 and included many galaxies that had not yet been identified as such. This in turn was followed by the two *Index Catalogues* (IC), the first in 1895 containing details of a further 1,529 nebulae and clusters (and galaxies) and the second in 1908 adding a further 3,857. The catalogs with over 13,000 nebulae, galaxies, and clusters were reissued in a single volume in 1953. Many of the objects listed are still referred to by their NGC or IC numbers.

Dreyer is also remembered as a historian of astronomy. In 1890 he published a biography of his countryman, *Tycho Brahe*, and followed this with Brahe's *Omnia opera* (15 vols. 1913–29; Complete Works). He had earlier published his *History of Planetary Systems from Thales to Kepler* (1906), a work, despite its age, still without any competitor in the English language.

Drickamer, Harry George

(1918–)

AMERICAN PHYSICIST

Born in Cleveland, Ohio, Drickamer was educated at the University of Michigan where he obtained his PhD in 1946. He then joined the staff of the University of Illinois, Urbana, serving first as professor of physical chemistry and then as professor of chemical engineering from 1953 until his retirement in 1990. He has specialized in the study of the structure of solids by means of high pressures, producing in the course of his researches pressures of the order of some 500,000 atmospheres.

Driesch, Hans Adolf Eduard

(1867–1941)

GERMAN BIOLOGIST

Born in Bad Kreuznach, in southwest Germany, Driesch (dreesh) held professorships at Heidelberg, Cologne, and Leipzig, and was visiting professor to China and America. A student of zoology at Freiburg, Jena, and Munich, he was for some years on the staff of the Naples Zoological Station.

Driesch carried out pioneering work in experimental embryology. He separated the two cells formed by the first division of a sea-urchin embryo and observed that each developed into a complete larva, thus demonstrating the capacity of the cell to form identical copies on division. He was also the first to demonstrate the phenomenon of embryonic induction, whereby the position of and interaction between cells within the embryo determine their subsequent differentiation.

Driesch is perhaps best known for his concept of entelechy – a vitalistic philosophy that postulates the origin of life to lie in some unknown vital force separate from biochemical and physiological influences. This also led him to investigate psychic research and parapsychology.

Dubois, Eugène

(1858–1940)

DUTCH PHYSICIAN AND PALEONTOLOGIST

Dubois (doo-**bwah**) was born in Eijsden in the Netherlands and studied medicine at the University of Amsterdam. After briefly working there as a lecturer in anatomy, he served as a military surgeon in the Dutch East Indies, now Indonesia, from 1887 to 1895. On his return to Amsterdam he held the chair of geology, paleontology, and mineralogy from 1899 until his retirement in 1928.

The decision to go to the Indies was no accident. Dubois was determined to find the "missing link" and had reasoned that such a creature would have originated in proximity to the apes of Africa or the orang-utang of the Indies. After several years fruitless search in Sumatra, Dubois moved to Java and in 1890 discovered his first humanoid remains (a jaw fragment) at Kedung Brubus. The following year, at Trinil on the Solo river, he found the skullcap, femur, and two teeth of what he was later to name *Pithecanthropus erectus*, more commonly known as Java man. He published these findings in 1894.

Although Dubois's estimate of the cranial capacity of *Pithecanthropus* was, at 850 cubic centimeters (later estimates ranged up to 940 cubic centimeters), on the low side for a hominid, the femur it had been found with indicated to Dubois that it must be a form with a very erect posture. However, many doubted this, stating the usual objections that the remains belonged to different creatures, to apes or (Rudolf Virchow's view) to deformed humans. So irritated did Dubois become by this reception that he withdrew the fossils from view, keeping them locked up for some 30 years.

When they were once more made available to scholars in 1923 and Peking man was discovered in 1926 it at last became widely agreed that *Pithecanthropus* was, as Dubois had earlier claimed, a link connecting apes and man. By this time however Dubois would have no part of such a consensus and began to insist the bones were those of a giant gibbon, a view he maintained until his death.

Du Bois-Reymond, Emil Heinrich

(1818–1896)

GERMAN NEUROPHYSIOLOGIST

The more one advances in the knowledge of physiology, the more one will have reason for ceasing to believe that the phenomena of life are essentially different from physical phenomena.

Of Swiss and Huguenot descent, Du Bois-Reymond (doo bwah-ray-**mon**) was born in Berlin and educated at the university there and in Neuchâtel (Switzerland). He is famous as the first to demonstrate how electrical currents in nerve and muscle fibers are generated. He began his studies under the eminent physiologist Johannes Müller at Berlin with work on fish capable of discharging electric currents as an external shock (e.g., eels). Turning his attention to nerve and muscle activity he then showed (1843) that applying a stimulus to the nerve brings about a drop in the electrical potential at the point of stimulus. This reduction in potential is the impulse, which travels along the nerve as waves of "relative negativity." This variation in negativity is the main cause of muscle contraction. Du Bois-Reymond's pioneering research, for which he devised a specially sensitive galvanometer capable of measuring the small amounts of electricity involved, was published as *Untersuchungen über tierische Elektricität* (2 vols. 1848–84; Researches on Animal Electricity): a landmark in electrophysiology, although subject to later elaboration. Du Bois-Reymond's collaboration with fellow physiologists Hermann von Helmholtz, Carl Ludwig, and Ernst von Brücke was of great significance in linking animal physiology with physical and chemical laws.

Du Bois-Reymond was elected a member of the Berlin Academy of Sciences in 1851 and succeeded Müller as professor of physiology at Berlin in 1858. He was also instrumental in establishing the Berlin Physiological Institute, opened in 1877, then the finest establishment of its kind.

Dubos, René Jules

(1901–1982)

FRENCH–AMERICAN MICROBIOLOGIST

Dubos (doo-**bos**) was born in Saint Brice, France, and graduated in agricultural sciences from the National Agronomy Institute in 1921. After a period with the International Institute of Agriculture in Rome as assistant editor, he emigrated to America in 1924.

Dubos was awarded his PhD in 1927 from Rutgers University for research on soil microorganisms, continuing his work in this field at the Rockefeller Institute for Medical Research. Reports that soil microorganisms produce antibacterial substances particularly interested him and in 1939 he isolated a substance from *Bacillus brevis* that he named tyrothricin. This is effective against many types of bacteria but unfortunately also kills red blood cells and its medical use is therefore limited. However, the discovery stimulated such workers as Selman Waksman and Benjamin Duggar to search for useful antibiotics and led to the discovery of the tetracyclines. He won the 1969 Pulitzer Prize for his book *So Human an Animal*.

Duesberg, Peter

(1936–   )

AMERICAN MOLECULAR BIOLOGIST

Born in Germany, Duesberg (**dooz**-berg) was educated at the University of Frankfurt where he obtained his PhD in chemistry in 1963. He immediately moved to the U.S. to work at the University of California, Berkeley, and was appointed professor of molecular biology in 1974.

Duesberg established his reputation in molecular biology by his discovery of cancer-causing genes (oncogenes) in the retrovirus first described by Peyton Rous in 1910. In 1970 Duesberg and his Berkeley colleagues identified three genes, gag, pol, and env, which encode the proteins of the viral capsid, the enzyme reverse transcriptase, and the proteins of the viral envelope, respectively.

Consequently when Gallo and Montagnier identified the HIV retrovirus in 1983 as the cause of AIDS, Duesberg was well qualified to comment on their judgment. In 1987 he published in *Cancer Research* a paper entitled *Retroviruses as Carcinogens and Pathogens: Expectation and Reality* in which he surveyed the published literature, citing 278 references in the process. The paper turned Duesberg into an international celebrity, winning praise from a few but savage rejection and complaints of irresponsibility from the majority of his colleagues.

Duesberg attacked what he saw as a complacent orthodoxy by denying there was any evidence for the claim that HIV was responsible for AIDS. Being antibody positive would cause him no worry, he insisted, and he would be even prepared to inject himself with pure HIV to establish his point.

In defence of his claim Duesberg offered six main arguments:

1. Many AIDS cases are HIV negative.
2. T-cells, the site of HIV attack, are regenerated more quickly than they are destroyed.
3. Viruses typically cause disease in the absence of antibodies; HIV stimulates the production of antibodies.
4. HIV should cause AIDS on infection, not years later.
5. In general retroviruses sustain rather than destroy cells.
6. No known virus discriminates between men and women.

Duesberg's views have been vigorously defended in a popular book by Jad Adams, *AIDS: the HIV Myth* (London, 1989). They have also been vigorously rejected by Robert Gallo and other virologists, and dismissed by them as more inept than challenging.

Despite a hostile reaction to his work from lay and professional press alike, Duesberg continues to campaign vigorously for his views. So much so that in 1995 he collected his previously published papers on the issue in his *Infectious AIDS: Have We Been Misled?* and went on to produce in 1996 a new comprehensive survey of the whole field in his *Inventing the AIDS Virus*.

Du Fay, Charles François de Cisternay

(1698–1739)

FRENCH CHEMIST

Du Fay (doo fay), a Parisian by birth, started his career in the French army, rising to the rank of captain. He left to become a chemist in the Académie Française and in 1732 became superintendent of the Jardin du Roi. His great achievement was to discover the two kinds of electricity, positive and negative, which he named "vitreous" and "resinous." This was based on his discovery that a piece of gold leaf charged from an electrified glass rod would attract and not repel a piece of electrified amber. This was the "two-fluid theory" of electricity, which was to be opposed by Benjamin Franklin's "one-fluid theory" later in the century.

Duggar, Benjamin Minge

(1872–1956)

AMERICAN PLANT PATHOLOGIST

Duggar was born into the farming community of Gallion, Alabama, and soon developed an interest in agriculture. He graduated with honors from the Mississippi Agricultural and Mechanical College, in 1891. He devoted his career to studying plant diseases, and while professor of plant physiology at Cornell University wrote *Fungus Diseases of Plants* (1909), the first publication to deal purely with plant pathology.

Duggar is known for his work on cotton diseases and mushroom culture, but he made his most important discovery after retiring from academic life. In 1945 he became consultant to the American Cyanamid Company, and soon isolated the fungus *Streptomyces aureofaciens*. Three years' work with this organism resulted in Duggar extracting and purifying the compound chlortetracycline (marketed as Aureomycin), the first of the tetracycline antibiotics. This drug was on the market by December 1948, and has proved useful in combating many infectious diseases.

Duggar was one of the foremost coordinators of plant science research in America and was editor of many important publications.

Duhamel du Monceau, Henri-Louis

(1700–1782)

FRENCH AGRICULTURALIST AND
TECHNOLOGIST

Duhamel (doo-a-**mel**) first took an interest in science following lectures at the Jardin du Roi in his native city of Paris during the 1720s. His study of the parasitic fungus found to attack saffron bulbs earned him admission to the French Academy of Sciences in 1728. In 1739 Duhamel was appointed inspector-general of the navy, his duties including supervision of the timber used by the French fleet.

During the 1730s he undertook a series of chemical investigations in collaboration with the chemist Jean Grosse. His most important work during this period was *Sur la base du sel marin* (1736; On the Composition of Sea Salt) in which he distinguished between potassium and sodium salts.

His major work was his contribution to agriculture with studies of French and English methods of practice. He published a series of writings entitled *Traité de la culture des terres* (1775; Treatise on Land Cultivation) in which he adapted Jethro Tull's system to France taking into account his own readings, experiments, and case histories.

Duhem, Pierre Maurice Marie

(1861–1916)

FRENCH PHYSICIST, PHILOSOPHER, AND HISTORIAN

> A physical theory...is a system of mathematical propositions, deduced from a small number of principles, which has the object of representing a set of experimental laws as simply, as completely, and as exactly as possible.
> —*The Aim and Structure of Physical Theory* (1906)

The son of a commercial traveler, Duhem (doo-**em**) was born in Paris and educated at the Ecole Normale. In his doctoral thesis he had managed to annoy Berthelot, an influential figure in French science and politics, and consequently found himself permanently exiled to the provinces. After teaching at the universities of Lille and Rennes (1887–94), he settled finally at the University of Bordeaux where he remained until his death from a heart attack in 1916. There had been a move shortly before his death to create a chair in the history of science for Duhem in Paris at the Collège de France. Duhem would have none of it, insisting that he was a physicist and that "he would not enter Paris by a side door."

As a historian, his reputation is immense. His most important work, *Le système du monde* (vols. 1–5, 1913–17; vols. 6–10, 1954–59; The Global System), was one of the first attempts to argue for a deep continuity in the history of science. He saw and documented an unbroken tradition linking medieval and modern science, and was able to trace the influence of such medieval writers as Buridan and Jordanus upon such moderns as Leonardo and Galileo.

Duhem's influence on the philosophy of science has also been influential in the form of the *Duhem-Quine thesis*. Scientific theories, he argued, are seldom falsified by experience; more commonly they are modified by such techniques as redefining terms and introducing new hypotheses. His views were presented in his *The Aim and Structure of Physical Theory* (Paris, 1906; New York, 1954).

As a scientist Duhem published books on thermodynamics (1886), hydrodynamics (1891), chemical mechanics (1897–99), electricity (1902), and elasticity (1906). He took the general position that it was impossible to reduce physics and chemistry to mechanics. For, he argued, mechanics had become "a branch of a more general science. This science embraces not only movement which displaces bodies in space but also every change of qualities, properties, physical state, and chemical constitution. This science is contemporary thermodynamics or, according to the word created by Rankine, Energetics." Duhem's final attempted synthesis, *Traité d'énergétique* (1911; Treatise on Energetics), shunned atomism and failed to extend the new science to electricity and magnetism.

Dujardin, Félix

(1801–1860)

FRENCH BIOLOGIST AND CYTOLOGIST

Largely self-educated, Dujardin (doo-zhar-**dan**), who was born in Tours, France, studied geology, botany, optics, and crystallography while working variously as a hydraulics engineer, librarian, and teacher of geometry and chemistry at Tours. In 1839 he was elected to the chair of geology and mineralogy at Toulouse, and in the following year was appointed professor of botany and zoology and dean of the Faculty of Sciences at Rennes. As a skilled microscopist, Dujardin carried out extensive studies of the microorganisms (infusoria) occurring in decaying matter. These led him, in 1834, to suggest the separation of a new group of protozoan animals, which he called the rhizopods (i.e., rootfeet). He was the first to recognize and appreciate the contractile nature of the protoplasm (which he termed the *sarcode*) and also demonstrated the role of the vacuole for evacuating waste matter. Such studies enabled Dujardin to refute the supposition, reintroduced by Christian Ehrenberg, that microorganisms have organs similar to those of the higher animals. Dujardin also investigated the cnidarians (jellyfish, sea anemones, corals, etc.), echinoderms (sea-urchins, starfish, etc.), as well as the platyhelminths, or flatworms, the last mentioned providing the basis for subsequent parasitological investigations.

Dulbecco, Renato

(1914–)

ITALIAN–AMERICAN PHYSICIAN
AND MOLECULAR BIOLOGIST

Born in Catanzaro, Italy, Dulbecco (dul-**bek**-oh) obtained his MD from the University of Turin in 1936 and taught there until 1947 when he moved to America. He taught briefly at Indiana before moving to California in 1949, where he served as professor of biology (1952–63) at the California Institute of Technology. Dulbecco then joined the staff of the Salk Institute where, apart from the period 1971–74 at the Imperial Cancer Research Fund in London, he has remained.

Beginning in 1959 Dulbecco introduced the idea of cell transformation into biology. In this process special cells are mixed *in vitro* (Latin, meaning literally "in glass," i.e., in a test tube) with such tumor-producing viruses as the polyoma and SV40 virus. With some cells a "productive infection" results, where the virus multiplies unchecked in the cell and finally kills its host. However, in other cells this unlimited multiplication does not occur and the virus instead induces changes similar to those in cancer cells; that is, the virus alters the cell so that it reproduces without restraint and does not respond to the presence of neighboring cells. A normal cell had in fact been transformed into a "cancer cell" *in vitro*.

The significance of this work was to provide an experimental setup where the processes by which a normal cell becomes cancerous can be studied in a relatively simplified form. It was for this work that Dulbecco was awarded the Nobel Prize for physiology or medicine in 1975, sharing it with Howard Temin and David Baltimore.

In March 1986 Dulbecco published a widely read paper in *Science*, entitled *A Turning Point in Science*, in which he argued that "if we wish to learn more about cancer, we must now concentrate on the cellular genome." The paper appeared shortly after various groups of scientists had held a meeting at Sante Fe to discuss sequencing the entire human genome. Dulbecco's timely paper publicized the project, gave it some authority, and linked it with a practical purpose.

Dulong, Pierre-Louis

(1785–1838)

FRENCH CHEMIST AND PHYSICIST

Born in Rouen, France, Dulong (doo-**long**) studied chemistry at the Ecole Polytechnique (1801–03) and later studied medicine. He was an assistant to Claude-Louis Berthollet before becoming professor of physics at the Ecole Polytechnique (1820), and later its director (1830).

In 1813 Dulong accidentally discovered the highly explosive nitrogen trichloride, losing an eye and nearly a hand in the process. He is best known for the law of atomic heats (1819), discovered in collaboration with Alexis-Thérèse Petit.

Dumas, Jean Baptiste André

(1800–1884)

FRENCH CHEMIST

> I do not claim to have discovered it, for it does no more than reproduce more precisely and in a more generalized form opinions that could be found in the writings of a large number of chemists.
>
> —Concerning his substitution theory of chemistry

Dumas (doo-**mah**) was educated in classics at the college in his native city of Alais and intended to serve in the navy. However, after Napoleon's final defeat he changed his mind and became apprenticed to an apothecary. In 1816 he went to Geneva, again to work for an apothecary. His first research was in physiological chemistry, investigating the use of iodine in goiter (1818). He also studied chemistry in Geneva and was encouraged by Friedrich von Humboldt to go to Paris, where he became assistant lecturer to Louis Thenard at the Ecole Polytechnique (1823). He subsequently worked in many of the Parisian institutes, becoming professor at the Ecole Polytechnique (1835) and at the Sorbonne (1841).

Dumas's early work included a method for measuring vapor density (1826), the synthesis of oxamide (1830), and the discoveries of the terpene cymene (1832), anthracene in coal tar (1832), and urethane (1833). In 1834 Dumas and Eugène Peligot discovered methyl alcohol (methanol) and Dumas recognized that it differed from ethyl alcohol by one $-CH_2$ group. The subsequent discovery that Chevreul's "ethal" was cetyl alcohol (1836) led Dumas to conceive the idea of a series of compounds of the same type (this was formalized into the concept of homologous series by Charles Gerhardt).

Dumas was both a prolific experimentalist and a leading theorist and he took a vigorous part in the many controversies that bedeviled organic chemistry at the time. He was originally an exponent of the "etherin" theory (in which ethyl alcohol (ethanol) and diethyl ether were considered to be compounds of etherin (ethene) with one and two molecules of water, respectively). However, he was converted to the radical theory (an attempt to formulate organic chemistry along the dualistic lines familiar in inorganic chemistry) by Justus von Liebig in 1837. He then introduced his own theory – the substitution theory – which was his greatest work. It had been noticed that candles bleached with chlorine gave off fumes of hydrogen chloride when they burned. Dumas discovered that during bleaching the hydrogen in the hydrocarbon oil of turpentine became replaced by chlorine. This seemed to contradict Jöns Berzelius's electrochemical theory and the latter was bitterly opposed to the substitution theory. Liebig, too, was hostile at first. Dumas then prepared trichloroacetic acid (1838) and showed that its properties were similar to those of the parent acetic acid. This convinced Liebig but not Berzelius. Further work on this series of acids, combined with the substitution theory, led him to a theory of types (1840), essentially similar to the modern concept of functional groups, although the credit for this theory was disputed between Dumas and Auguste Laurent.

Dumas also carried out important work on atomic weights. He had been an early supporter of Amedeo Avogadro but he never properly distinguished between atoms and molecules and the problems this raised caused him to abandon the theory. He also supported William Prout's hypothesis that atomic weights were whole-number multiples of that of hydrogen. In 1840, working with Jean Stas, he obtained the figure 12.000 for carbon instead of the figure 12.24 in use at that time.

Following the revolution of 1848 Dumas became involved in administration, becoming minister of agriculture and commerce (1849–51), minister of education, and permanent secretary of the Academy of Sciences (1868).

Dunning, John Ray

(1907–1975)

AMERICAN PHYSICIST

Born in Shelby, Nebraska, Dunning was educated at the Wesleyan University, Nebraska, and at Columbia University, New York, where he obtained his PhD in 1934. He took up an appointment at Columbia in 1933, being made professor of physics in 1950.

Dunning was one of the key figures in the Manhattan project to build the first atomic bomb. It had been shown by Niels Bohr that the isotope uranium–235 would be more likely to sustain a neutron chain reaction than normal uranium. Only 7 out of every 1,000 uranium atoms occurring naturally are uranium–235, which presents difficulties in extraction. Various techniques were tried and Dunning was placed in charge of the process of separation known as gaseous diffusion. This involved turning the uranium into a volatile compound (uranium hexafluoride, UF_6) and passing the vapor through a diffusion "filter." As ^{235}U atoms are slightly less massive than the normal ^{238}U they pass through the filter a little faster and can thus be concentrated. The difference in mass is so small, however, that simply to produce a gas enriched with ^{235}U atoms required its passage through thousands of filters.

As early as 1939 Dunning had shown that the process would work but to produce ^{235}U in the quantities required by the Manhattan project was a daunting prospect and the engineering problems were immense. The gas is extraordinarily corrosive and a single leak in one of the hundreds of thousands of filters would lose the precious ^{235}U. But as the other projects ran into even more formidable difficulties it was largely through gaseous diffusion that sufficient enriched uranium was made available for the bomb to be built.

Durand, William Frederick

(1859–1958)

AMERICAN ENGINEER

Born in Beacon Falls, Connecticut, Durand graduated from the U.S. Naval Academy in 1880 and entered the Engineering Corps of the U.S. Navy (1880–87). He then took a post as professor of mechanical engineering at Michigan State College in 1887. He moved to Cornell in 1891 to the chair of marine engineering and, in 1904, he accepted the professorship of mechanical engineering at Stanford, a position he held until his retirement in 1924.

Durand worked mainly on problems connected with the propeller, both marine and, after 1914, aeronautical. He was general editor of an important standard work, *Aerodynamic Theory*, produced in six volumes (1929–36). He also served on the National Advisory Committee for Civil Aeronautics (NACA) (1915–33) and, in 1941, was recalled to advise the government on the construction of an American jet-propelled airplane.

Du Toit, Alexander Logie

(1878–1949)

SOUTH AFRICAN GEOLOGIST

Du Toit (doo toit), who was born at Rondebosch, near Cape Town in South Africa, studied at the South Africa College (now the University of Cape Town), the Royal Technical College, Glasgow, and the Royal College of Science, London.

After a short period teaching at Glasgow University (1901–03) he returned to South Africa and worked with the Geological Commission of the Cape of Good Hope (1903–20), during which he explored the geology of South Africa. For the next seven years he worked for the Irrigation Department and produced six detailed monographs on South African geology. He served as a consulting geologist to De Beers Consolidated Mines during the period 1927–41.

Following a visit to South America in 1923, du Toit became one of the earliest supporters of Alfred Wegener's theory of continental drift, publishing his observations in *A Geological Comparison of South America with South Africa* (1927). He noted the similarity between the continents and developed his ideas in *Our Wandering Continents* (1937), in which he argued for the separation of Wegener's Pangaea into the two supercontinents, Laurasia and Gondwanaland.

Dutrochet, René Joachim Henri

(1776–1847)

FRENCH PHYSIOLOGIST

Born in Néon, France, Dutrochet (doo-tro-**shay**) began medical studies while serving in the army in Paris in 1802. After graduating in 1806 he served as an army surgeon in Spain. However, through illness he resigned his post in 1809 and thereafter devoted his time to natural science.

In 1814 he published his investigations into animal development, suggesting a unity of the main features during the early stages. Later research into plant and animal physiology led to his assertion that respiration is similar in both plants and animals. In 1832, Dutrochet showed that gas exchange in plants was via minute openings (stomata) on the surface of leaves and the deep cavities with which they communicate. He further demonstrated that only cells containing chlorophyll can fix carbon and thus transform light energy into chemical energy. Dutrochet studied osmosis and suggested it may be the cause of ascent and descent of sap in plants. Although sometimes lacking in accuracy, the importance of his work lies mainly in his endeavor to demonstrate that the vital phenomena of life can be explained on the basis of physics and chemistry.

Dutton, Clarence Edward

(1841–1912)

AMERICAN GEOLOGIST

Born in Wallingford, Connecticut, Dutton graduated from Yale in 1860 and then entered the Yale Theological Seminary. He joined the army in 1862 during the Civil War and remained in the army although not always on active service. He became interested in geology and joined the Geographical and Geological Survey of the Rocky Mountains and the West in 1875.

The term "isostasy" was introduced into geology by Dutton in 1889. This described a theory propounded by George Airy in which it is supposed that mountain ranges and continents rest on a much denser base. As mountains are eroded the land rises while the settling sediment will compensate by depressing some other part of the Earth.

After his return to the army in 1890 Dutton turned to the study of earthquakes and volcanoes. His research was published in 1904 in his *Earthquakes in the Light of the New Seismology*.

Du Vigneaud, Vincent

(1901–1978)

AMERICAN BIOCHEMIST

Born in Chicago, Illinois, Du Vigneaud (doo **veen**-yoh) graduated from the University of Illinois in 1923; he remained there to take his master's degree before going to the University of Rochester. There he studied the hormone insulin, gaining his PhD in 1927. The research on insulin marked the beginning of his interest in sulfur compounds, particularly the sulfur-containing amino acids – methionine, cystine, and cysteine.

In 1938 Du Vigneaud became head of the biochemistry department of Cornell University Medical College. Two years later he had isolated vitamin H (biotin) and by 1942 had determined its structure. He then went on to examine the hormones secreted by the posterior pituitary gland, especially oxytocin and vasopressin. He found oxytocin to be composed of eight amino acids, worked out the order of these, and in 1954 synthesized artificial oxytocin, which was shown to be as effective as the natural hormone in inducing labor and milk flow. This was the first protein to be synthesized and for this achievement Du Vigneaud received the Nobel Prize for chemistry in 1955.

Du Vigneaud's other work included research on penicillin and on methyl groups. He was professor of chemistry at Cornell University from 1967 to 1975 and subsequently professor of biochemistry there.

Dyson, Sir Frank Watson

(1868–1939)

BRITISH ASTRONOMER

Dyson, the son of a Baptist minister from Ashby-de-la-Zouche in Leicestershire, England, graduated in mathematics from Cambridge University in 1889; in 1891 he was elected to a fellowship. After first working as chief assistant at the Royal Observatory at Greenwich from 1894 to 1905, he was Astronomer Royal for Scotland from 1905 to 1910 and then returned to Greenwich as Astronomer Royal, serving from 1910 to 1933. He was knighted in 1915.

Dyson's early observational work was done in collaboration with William G. Thackeray: they measured the positions of over 4,000 circumpolar stars that had first been observed by Stephen Groombridge at the beginning of the 19th century. They were thus able to determine the proper motions of the stars. Dyson could then extend the work of Jacobus Kapteyn on star streaming to fainter stars.

Dyson observed the total solar eclipses of 1900, 1901, and 1905, obtaining spectra of the atmospheric layers of the Sun. He also organized the detailed observations of the total solar eclipse in 1919, sending expeditions to Principe in the Gulf of Guinea and Sobral in Brazil. The measured positions of stars near the Sun's rim during the eclipse provided evidence for the bending of light in a gravitational field, as predicted by Einstein in his theory of general relativity; this was the first experimental support for the theory.

Dyson, Freeman John

(1923–)

BRITISH–AMERICAN THEORETICAL PHYSICIST

The son of Sir George Dyson, director of the Royal College of Music, Dyson was born at Crowthorne in England and educated at Cambridge University. During World War II he worked at the headquarters of Bomber Command. In 1947 he went on a Commonwealth Fellowship to Cornell University and in 1953 joined the Institute of Advanced Studies, Princeton, where he served as professor of physics until his retirement in 1994.

Dyson has worked on a number of topics but is best known for his contribution to quantum electrodynamics, i.e., the application of quantum theory to interactions between particles and electromagnetic radiation. The observation in 1946 by Willis Lamb of a small difference between the lowest energy levels of the hydrogen atom was an experimental result against which such theories could be tested. In the period 1946–48 independent formulations of quantum electrodynamics were put forward by Julian Schwinger, Sin-Itiro Tomonaga, and Richard Feynman. Dyson showed that the three methods were all consistent and brought them together into a single general theory.

Dyson later became known to a wider public through his work on the nuclear test ban treaty and for his quite serious considerations of space travel and the "greening of the galaxy." He also reached a wider audience with the publication of his autobiography *Disturbing the Universe* (1980) and his 1985 Gifford Lectures, *Infinite in All Directions* (1988).

Eastman, George

(1854–1932)

AMERICAN INVENTOR

Eastman, who was born in Waterville, New York, began his career in banking and insurance but turned from this to photography. In 1880 he perfected the dry-plate photographic film and began manufacturing this. He produced a transparent roll film in 1884 and in the same year founded the Eastman Dry Plate and Film Company. In 1888 he introduced the simple hand-held box camera that made popular photography possible. The Kodak camera with a roll of transparent film was cheap enough for all pockets and could be used by a child. It was followed by the Brownie camera, which cost just one dollar.

Eastman gave away a considerable part of his fortune to educational institutions, including the Massachusetts Institute of Technology. He committed suicide in 1932.

Ebashi, Setsuro

(1922–   )

JAPANESE BIOCHEMIST

Ebashi (e-**bash**-ee), who was born in the Japanese capital of Tokyo, received his MD from the university there in 1944 and his PhD in 1954. He became professor of pharmacology there in 1959 and, since 1963, has held the chair of biochemistry.

Ebashi has, for many years, been one of the leading workers in the field of muscle contraction. His work has thrown considerable light on the identity and workings of the so-called "relaxing factor." As early as 1952, B. Marsh had isolated a substance from muscle that produces relaxation in muscle fibers, and he noted that its effect could be neutralized by the presence of calcium ions.

While the process of muscle contraction appeared to be initiated by the release of calcium ions from the sarcoplasmic reticulum, Ebashi and his colleagues were able to show in the 1960s that such ions were not enough. The presence of two globular proteins, troponin and tropomyosin, is also necessary. Neither protein alone is sufficient as only the complex of both sensitizes muscle to calcium ions.

The globular proteins appear to prevent the interaction of myosin and actin as first described by Hugh Huxley. However, once a certain level of calcium is reached such inhibition is prevented and contraction occurs. Later x-ray analysis by many workers seems to have confirmed Ebashi's model.

Eccles, Sir John Carew

(1903–   )

AUSTRALIAN PHYSIOLOGIST

Born in Melbourne, Australia, Eccles was educated at the university there and at Oxford University. In Oxford he worked with Charles Sherrington on muscular reflexes and nervous transmission across the synapses (nerve junctions) from 1927 to 1937. He then worked in Australia at the Institute of Pathology from 1937 to 1943. After a period in New Zealand, as professor of physiology at the University of Otago from 1944 to 1951, Eccles returned to Australia to the Australian National University, Canberra, where he served as professor of physiology from 1951 to 1966. In 1966 Eccles moved to the U.S., working first in Chicago and finally, from 1968 until his retirement in 1975, at the State University of New York, Buffalo.

While at Canberra Eccles carried out work on the chemical changes that take place at synapses, pursuing the findings of Alan Hodgkin and Andrew Huxley, with whom he subsequently shared the 1963 Nobel Prize for physiology or medicine. Eccles showed that excitation of different nerve cells causes the synapses to release a substance (probably acetylcholine) that promotes the passage of sodium and potassium ions and effects an alternation in the polarity of the electric charge. It is in this way that nervous impulses are communicated or inhibited by nerve cells. Eccles is the author of *Reflex Activity of the Spinal Cord* (1932) and *The Physiology of Nerve Cells* (1957).

After his retirement Eccles began to publish a number of works on the mind-body problem. Notable among them are *The Self and the Brain* (1977), written in collaboration with Karl Popper, *The Human Mystery* (1979), and *The Creation of the Self* (1989).

Eckert, John Presper Jr.

(1919–1995)

AMERICAN COMPUTER SCIENTIST

Born in Philadelphia, Pennsylvania, Eckert was educated at the Moore School of Electrical Engineering at the University of Pennsylvania in his native city. After graduating in 1941 he immediately joined the faculty. Soon after he began his long and profitable career with his colleague, J. W. Mauchly. Together they built the historically important computers, ENIAC, EDSAC, and UNIVAC.

In 1946 Eckert resigned from the Moore School to set up the Electronic Control Co. with his colleague, Mauchly. As they failed to raise any money on Wall Street they began with a $25,000 loan from Eckert's father. Initially things went well but the constraints of a fixed-price contract with the U.S. Census led them into virtual bankruptcy. Consequently, they were forced to sell out to Remington Rand in 1950. They received $200,000 plus a guaranteed executive position for eight years in a separate UNIVAC Division.

While some of the initial ideas emerged from Mauchly, Eckert has been described as "the mainspring of the whole operation." Thus it was Eckert who solved the problem of the vacuum tubes. How does one ensure that sufficient numbers of the 17,000 tubes of ENIAC work at any one time to keep the computer running? The answer was stringent testing and, less obviously, to run the tubes well below their rated voltage and so extend their working lives.

It was also Eckert who devised the mercury delay lines, used as memory stores in early computers, and successfully deployed by M. V. Wilkes in EDSAC.

Eddington, Sir Arthur Stanley

(1882–1944)

BRITISH ASTROPHYSICIST AND
MATHEMATICIAN

We used to think that if we knew one, we knew two, because one and one are two. We are
finding that we must learn a great deal more about "and".
—Quoted by A. L. Mackay in *The Harvest of a Quiet Eye* (1977)

Born at Kendal in northwestern England, Eddington moved with his
mother and sister to the southwestern county of Somerset after the
death of his father in 1884. He was a brilliant scholar, graduating from
Owens College (now the University of Manchester) in 1902 and from
Cambridge University in 1905. From 1906 to 1913 he was chief assistant
to the Astronomer Royal at Greenwich after which he returned to Cambridge as Plumian Professor of Astronomy. He was knighted in 1930.
Eddington was a Quaker throughout his life.

Eddington was the major British astronomer of the interwar period.
His early work on the motions of stars was followed, from 1916 onward,
by his work on the interior of stars, which was published in his first
major book, *The Internal Constitution of the Stars* (1926). He introduced
"a phenomenon ignored in early investigations, which may have considerable effect on the equilibrium of a star, viz. the pressure of radiation."
He showed that for equilibrium to be maintained in a star, the inwardly
directed force of gravitation must be balanced by the outwardly directed
forces of both gas pressure and radiation pressure. He also proposed
that heat energy was transported from the center to the outer regions of
a star not by convection, as thought hitherto, but by radiation.

It was in this work that Eddington gave a full account of his mass-
luminosity relationship, which was discovered in 1924 and shows that the
more massive a star the more luminous it will be. The value of the relation is that it allows the mass of a star to be determined if its intrinsic
brightness is known. This is of considerable significance since only the

masses of binary stars can be directly calculated. Eddington realized that there was a limit to the size of stars: relatively few would have masses exceeding 10 times the mass of the Sun while any exceeding 50 solar masses would be unstable owing to excessive radiation pressure.

Eddington wrote a number of books for both scientists and laymen. His more popular books, including *The Expanding Universe* (1933), were widely read, went through many editions, and opened new worlds to many enquiring minds of the interwar years. It was through Eddington that Einstein's general theory of relativity reached the English-speaking world. He was greatly impressed by the theory and was able to provide experimental evidence for it. He observed the total solar eclipse of 1919 and submitted a report that captured the intellectual imagination of his generation. He reported that a very precise and unexpected prediction made by Einstein in his general theory had been successfully observed; this was the very slight bending of light by the gravitational field of a star – the Sun. Further support came in 1924 when Einstein's prediction of the reddening of starlight by the gravitational field of the star was tested: at Eddington's request Walter Adams detected and measured the shift in wavelength of the spectral lines of Sirius B, the dense white-dwarf companion of the star Sirius. Eddington thus did much to establish Einstein's theory on a sound and rigorous foundation and gave a very fine presentation of the subject in his *Mathematical Theory of Relativity* (1923).

Eddington also worked for many years on an obscure but challenging theory, which was only published in his posthumous work, *Fundamental Theory* (1946). Basically, he claimed that the fundamental constants of science, such as the mass of the proton and the mass and charge of the electron were a "natural and complete specification for constructing a universe" and that their values were not accidental. He then set out to develop a theory from which such values would follow as a consequence, but never completed it.

Edelman, Gerald Maurice

(1929–   )

AMERICAN BIOCHEMIST

Born in New York City, Edelman was educated at Ursinus College, the University of Pennsylvania, and Rockefeller University, where he obtained his PhD on human immunoglobulins in 1960. He remained at Rockefeller where he was appointed professor of biochemistry in 1966 and Vincent Astor Distinguished Professor in 1974. Edelman left Rockefeller in 1992 to set up and direct the Neuroscience Institute at the Scripps Research Institute, La Jolla, California.

Edelman was interested in determining the structure of human immunoglobulin. The molecule is very large and it was first necessary to break it into smaller portions, which was achieved by reducing and splitting the disulfide bonds. Following this, Edelman proposed that the molecule contained more than one polypeptide chain and, moreover, that two kinds of chain exist, light and heavy. Such studies helped Rodney Porter propose a structure for the antibody immunoglobulin G (IgG) in 1962.

Edelman was more interested in attempting to work out the complete amino-acid sequence of IgG. As it contained 1,330 amino acids it was by far the largest protein then attempted. By 1969 he was ready to announce the results of his impressive work, the complete sequence, and was able to show that while much of the molecule was unchanging the tips of the Y-like structure were highly variable in their amino-acid sequence. It thus seemed obvious that such an area would be identical with the active antigen binding region in Porter's structure and that such variability represented the ability of IgG to bind many different antigens. It was for this work that Edelman and Porter shared the 1972 Nobel Prize for physiology or medicine.

Edelman has also speculated on antibody formation and the mechanism behind the spurt in production after contact with an antigen. In the former area he argued in 1966 for a major modification of the clonal theory of Macfarlane Burnet. In the latter case he suggested, in 1970, that the signal to the immune system to increase production is set off by the change in shape of the antibody molecule as it combines with its antigen.

Following his biochemical successes Edelman turned to the neurosciences. In such works as *Neural Darwinism* (1987) and *Bright Air, Brilliant Mind* (1993), he produced a distinctive theory of the development and nature of the mind. We are, he claims, at the beginning of a neuroscientific revolution from which we will learn "how the mind works, what governs our nature, and how we know the world."

Edelman was struck by a number of similarities between the immune system and the nervous system. Just as a lymphocyte can recognize and respond to a new antigen, the nervous system can respond similarly to novel stimuli. Neural mechanisms are selected, he argued, in the same manner as antibodies. Although the 10^9 cells of the nervous system do not replicate, there is considerable scope for development and variation in the connections that form between the cells. Frequently used connections will be selected, others will decay or be diverted to other uses. There are two kinds of selection: developmental, which takes place before birth, and experiential. There are also innate "values," built in preferences that is, for such features as light and warmth over the dark and the cold.

In Edelman's model, higher consciousness, including self-awareness and the ability to create scenes in the mind, have required the emergence during evolution of a new neuronal circuit. To remember a chair or one's grandmother is not to recall a bit of coded data from a specific location; it is rather to create a unity out of scattered mappings, a process called by Edelman a "reentry." Edelman's views have been dismissed by many as obscure; some neurologists, however, consider Edelman to have begun what will eventually turn out to be a major revolution in the neurosciences.

Edison, Thomas Alva

(1847–1931)

AMERICAN PHYSICIST AND
INVENTOR

In 1879 the performance of the Edison telephone was illustrated in the theatre of the Royal Institution....Perhaps the most striking illustration of the pliant power of the instrument was its capability to reproduce a whistled tune. Mr. Edison's whistling at the Circus was heard in Albemarle Street almost as distinctly as if it had been produced upon the spot.
—John Tyndall, *On Sound* (1883)

My personal desire would be to prohibit entirely the use of alternating currents. They are unnecessary as they are dangerous...I can therefore see no justification for the introduction of a system which has no element of permanency and every element of danger to life and property.
—Quoted by R. L. Weber in *A Random Walk in Science*

Genius is one percent inspiration and ninety-nine percent perspiration.
—Quoted in *Life* (1932)

Edison was born in Milan, Ohio, and was taught at home by his mother – he had been expelled from school as "retarded," perhaps because of his deafness. From the age of seven he lived in Port Huron, Michigan, and when he was twelve years old began to spend much of his time on the railroad between Port Huron and Detroit, selling candy and newspapers to make money. However, he was also fascinated by the telegraph system, designing his own experiments and training himself in telegraphy. He became a casual worker on telegraphy (1862–68), reading and experimenting as he traveled. At the age of 21 he bought a copy of Faraday's *Experimental Researches in Electricity* and was inspired to undertake serious systematic experimental work.

While Edison was living in a Wall Street basement (1869) he was called in to carry out an emergency repair on a new telegraphic gold-price indicator in the Gold Exchange. He was so successful that he was taken on as a supervisor. Later he remodeled the equipment and, soon after being commissioned to improve other equipment, his skill became legendary.

For a while Edison had a well-paid job with the Western Union Telegraph Company, but he gave it up to set up a laboratory of his own at Menlo Park, New Jersey. This he furbished with a wide range of scientific equipment, costing $40,000, and an extensive library. He employed 20 technicians and later a mathematical physicist. The laboratory was the first organized research center outside a university and produced many inventions. In 1877 Edison became known internationally after the phonograph was invented. His original instrument used a cylinder coated with tinfoil to record sounds, and was not commercially practical. In 1878, after seeing an exhibition of glaring electric arc lights, he declared that he would invent a milder cheap alternative that could replace the gas lamp. Because of his past successes, he managed to raise the capital to do this and the Edison Electric Light Company was set up. It took 14 months to find a filament material but by October 1879, Edison was able to demonstrate 30 incandescent electric lamps connected in parallel with separate switches. Three years later a power station was opened in New York and this was the start of modern large-scale electricity generation. Edison later merged his electric-light company with that of Joseph Swan who developed the carbon-filament light independently. Also in his work on incandescent filaments, Edison discovered that a current flows in one direction only between the filament and a nearby electrode. The use of this *Edison effect* in the thermionic valve was independently achieved by J. A. Fleming. In 1887 Edison's laboratory moved to larger premises in West Orange, now a national monument. In his lifetime he took out over 1,000 patents covering a variety of applications, including telephone transmission, cinematography, office machinery, cement manufacture, and storage batteries. No other inventor has been so productive.

Edlén, Bengt

(1906–   )

SWEDISH PHYSICIST

Born at Gusum in Sweden, Edlén (ed-**lyen**) studied at the University of Uppsala where he gained his PhD in 1934 and also served on the faculty from 1928 until 1944. He was then appointed professor of physics at the University of Lund, a post he retained until his retirement in 1973.

Edlén is recognized for his research on atomic spectra and its applications to astrophysics. In the early 1940s he carried out important work on the emission lines, first described in 1870, in the Sun's corona, i.e., the outermost layer of the solar atmosphere. The problem with the 20 "well-measured lines" was that none had ever been observed in a laboratory light source. At one time they were thought to indicate the presence of an unknown element, conveniently described as "coronium," but it had become apparent when Edlén began his work that the periodic table no longer contained any suitable gaps.

Edlén succeeded in showing in 1941 that the coronal lines were mainly caused by iron, nickel, calcium, and argon atoms deprived of 10–15 electrons; i.e., by highly charged positive ions. The implications of such extreme ionization were not lost on Edlén who was quick to point out that it must indicate temperatures of over a quarter of a million degrees in the solar corona.

Edsall, John Tileston

(1902–)

AMERICAN BIOCHEMIST

Edsall was born in Philadelphia, Pennsylvania, and educated at Harvard and at Cambridge University, England. He joined the Harvard faculty in 1928 and from 1951 to 1973 served there as professor of biochemistry.

Edsall is basically a protein chemist. He spent much time establishing basic data on the constitution and properties of numerous proteins – information that has since been reproduced in innumerable textbooks. With Edwin Cohn he was the author of the authoritative work *Proteins, Amino Acids and Peptides* (1943).

In later years Edsall turned his attention to the history of biochemistry, his books in this field including *Blood and Hemoglobin* (1952).

Egas Moniz, Antonio

(1874–1955)

PORTUGUESE NEUROLOGIST

> Frontal leukotomy...one of the most important discoveries ever made in psychiatric therapy...a great number of suffering people and total invalids have recovered and have been socially rehabilitated.
> —Herbert Olivecrona, presentation speech at award of the 1949 Nobel Prize

Egas Moniz (eg-**ash** mon-**ish**) was born at Avanca in Portugal and educated at the University of Coimbra, where he gained his MD in 1899. After postgraduate work in Paris and Bordeaux he returned to Coimbra, becoming a professor in the medical faculty in 1902. He moved to Lisbon in 1911 to a newly created chair of neurology, a post he retained until his retirement in 1944. At the same time he was pursuing a successful political career, being elected to the National Assembly in 1900. He served as ambassador to Spain in 1917 and in the following year became foreign minister, leading his country's delegation to the Paris Peace Conference.

Egas Moniz achieved his first major success in the 1920s in the field of angiography (the study of the cardiovascular system using dyes that are opaque to x-rays). In collaboration with Almeida Lima, he injected such radiopaque dyes into the arteries, enabling the blood vessels of the brain to be photographed. In 1927 he was able to show that displacements in the cerebral circulation could be used to infer the presence and location of brain tumors, publishing a detailed account of his technique in 1931.

Egas Moniz is better known for his introduction in 1935 of the operation of prefrontal leukotomy. It was for this work, described by the Nobel authorities as "one of the most important discoveries ever made in psychiatric therapy," that they awarded him the 1949 Nobel Prize for physiology or medicine.

The operation consisted of inserting a sharp knife into the prefrontal lobe of the brain, roughly the area above and between the eyes; it required the minimum of equipment and lasted less than five minutes. The technique was suggested to Egas Moniz on hearing an account (by John Fulton and Carlyle Jacobsen in 1935) of a refractory chimpanzee that became less aggressive after its frontal lobes had been excised. Egas Moniz believed that a similar surgical operation would relieve severe emotional tension in psychiatric patients. He claimed that 14 of the first 20 patients operated upon were either cured or improved. The operation generated much controversy, since the extent of the improvement in the patients' symptoms was not easy to judge and the procedure often produced severe side-effects. Today a more refined version of the operation, in which selective incisions are made in smaller areas of the brain, is still quite widely practiced.

Ehrenberg, Christian Gottfried

(1795–1876)

GERMAN BIOLOGIST AND MICROSCOPIST

> Until now my favorite pursuit has been neither naked systematizing nor unsystematic observation, and whenever time and circumstances, together with my ability, allow it, I prefer getting down to the grass-roots level.
>
> —Letter to Nees von Esenbeck (1821)

Ehrenberg (**air**-en-berg) was born in Delitzsch, which is now in Germany, and took an MD degree at the University of Berlin in 1818. In the same year he was elected a member of the Leopoldine German Academy of Researchers in Natural Sciences. Two years later he took part in a scientific expedition to Egypt, Libya, the Sudan, and the Red Sea, sponsored by the Prussian Academy of Sciences and the University of Berlin. During these travels (1820–25) Ehrenberg collected and classified some 75,000 plant and animal specimens, both terrestrial and marine, including microorganisms. On a further expedition in 1829 to Central Asia and Siberia, sponsored by Czar Nicholas I, he was accompanied by Alexander von Humboldt. In 1827 Ehrenberg was appointed assistant professor of zoology at Berlin and was elected a member of the Berlin Academy of Sciences. He became professor of natural science at Berlin in 1839.

Ehrenberg's studies in natural science were primarily concerned with microorganisms, especially the protozoans. His paleontological investigations led him to demonstrate the presence of single-celled fossils in certain rock layers of various geological formations, and he was also able to show that marine phosphorescence (strictly, bioluminescence) was due to the activity of species of animal plankton. He described fungal development from spores, as well as their sexual reproduction, and also carried out detailed studies of corals. His most important thesis lay in the belief that microorganisms were complete in the sense of sharing the same organs as higher animals, and that social behavior provided the basis for a new approach to animal classification. Ehrenberg's theory was demolished, with the help of experimental evidence, by Félix Dujardin. Ehrenberg's publications include *Travels in Egypt, Libya, Nubia and Dongola* (1828) and *The Infusoria as Complete Animals* (1838). His descriptions and classification of fossil protozoans were published as *Microgeology* (1854).

Ehrlich, Paul

(1854–1915)

GERMAN PHYSICIAN, BACTERIOLOGIST, AND CHEMIST

> Success in research needs four Gs: *Glück, Geduld, Geschick* und *Geld* [luck, patience, skill, and money].
> —Quoted by M. Peruz in *Nature* (1988)

Born in Strehlen (now Strzelin in Poland), Ehrlich (**air**-lik) studied medicine at the universities of Breslau, Strasbourg, and Freiburg, gaining a physician's degree at Breslau in 1878. For the next nine years he worked at the Charité Hospital, Berlin, on many topics including typhoid fever, tuberculosis, and pernicious anemia. He was awarded the title of professor by the Prussian Ministry of Education in 1884 for his impressive work in these fields. In 1887 he became a teacher at the University of Berlin but was not paid because of the antisemitic feeling at the time – Ehrlich would not renounce his Jewish upbringing. As a result of his laboratory work he contracted tuberculosis and was not restored to health until 1890, when he set up his own small research laboratory at Steglitz on the outskirts of Berlin.

In 1890 Robert Koch announced the discovery of tuberculin and suggested its use in preventing and curing tuberculosis. He asked Ehrlich to work on it with him at the Moabit Hospital in Berlin. Ehrlich accepted and for six years studied TB and cholera. In 1896 he accepted the post of director of the new Institute for Serum Research and Serum Investigation at Steglitz and in 1899 moved to the Institute of Experimental Therapy in Frankfurt. Here he investigated African sleeping sickness and syphilis along with his other studies. In 1908 he was awarded the Nobel Prize for physiology or medicine for his work on immunity and serum therapy.

Two years later he announced his most famous discovery, Salvarsan – a synthetic chemical that was effective against syphilis – and until the end of his life he worked on the problems associated with the treatment of patients using this compound of arsenic.

Ehrlich is considered to be the founder of modern chemotherapy because he developed systematic scientific techniques to search for new synthetic chemicals that could specifically attack disease-causing microorganisms. Ehrlich sought for these "magic bullets" by carefully altering the chemical structure of dye molecules that selectively stained the microorganisms observable in his microscope but did not stain cells in the host. He was persevering and optimistic – Salvarsan (compound number 606) was not "rediscovered" until almost 1,000 compounds had been synthesized and tried. He made and tested about 3,000 compounds based on the structure of Salvarsan in an attempt to make a drug that was bacteriocidal to streptococci.

Eichler, August Wilhelm

(1839–1887)

GERMAN BOTANIST

Eichler (**Ik**-ler) was born in Neukirchen (which is now in Germany) and studied natural science and mathematics at the University of Marburg, gaining his PhD in 1861. Eichler then became assistant to Karl von Martius at Munich. With Martius he began editing the 15-volume *Flora of Brazil*, continuing this work single-handed after Martius's death in 1868. In 1878 he succeeded Alexander Braun as professor of systematic and morphologic botany at Berlin and also became director of the university's herbarium. The same year he published the second volume of his two-volume *Diagrams of Flowers*, describing the comparative structure of flowers.

In 1886, the year before his death, Eichler developed a plant classification system in which the plant kingdom is split into four divisions: Thallophyta (algae, fungi), Bryophyta (mosses, liverworts), Pteridophyta (ferns, horsetails), and Spermatophyta (seed plants). He further subdivided the Spermatophyta into the Gymnospermae (conifers, cycads, ginkgos) and Angiospermae (flowering plants). This system was later adopted by nearly all botanists, but because of his early death from leukemia Eichler did not live to see the general acceptance of his work.

Eigen, Manfred

(1927–   )

GERMAN PHYSICAL CHEMIST

> A theory has only the alternative of being right or wrong. A model has a third possibility: it may be right, but irrelevant.
> —*The Physicist's Conception of Nature*
> (1973)

Eigen (I-gen), the son of a musician, was born at Bochum in Germany and educated at the University of Göttingen where he obtained his PhD in 1951. He joined the staff of the Max Planck Institute for Physical Chemistry at Göttingen in 1953 and has served as its director since 1964.

In 1954 Eigen introduced the so-called relaxation techniques for the study of extremely fast chemical reactions (those taking less than a millisecond). Eigen's general method was to take a solution in equilibrium for a given temperature and pressure. If a short disturbance was applied to the solution the equilibrium would be very briefly destroyed and a new equilibrium quickly reached. Eigen studied exactly what happened in this very short time by means of absorption spectroscopy. He applied disturbances to the equilibrium by a variety of methods, such as pulses of electric current, sudden changes in temperature or pressure, or changes in electric field.

The first reaction he investigated was the apparently simple formation of a water molecule from the hydrogen ion, H^+, and the hydroxide ion, OH^-. Calculations of reaction rates made it clear that they could not be produced by the collision of the simple ions H^+ and OH^-. Eigen went on to show that the reacting ions are the unexpectedly large $H_9O_4^+$ and $H_7O_4^-$, a proton hydrated with four water molecules and a hydroxyl ion with three water molecules. For this work Eigen shared the 1967 Nobel Prize for chemistry with George Porter and Ronald Norrish.

Eigen later applied his relaxation techniques to complex biochemical reactions. He has also become interested in the origin of nucleic acids and proteins; with his colleague R. Winkler he has proposed a possible mechanism to explain their formation. Much of this and subsequent work was described by Eigen in his *Laws of the Game: How Principles of Nature Govern Chance* (1982).

Eijkman, Christiaan

(1858–1930)

DUTCH PHYSICIAN

Eijkman (**Ik**-man) was born at Nijkerk in the Netherlands and qualified as a physician from the University of Amsterdam in 1883. He served
as an army medical officer in the Dutch East Indies from 1883 to 1885,
when he was forced to return to the Netherlands to recuperate from a severe attack of malaria. In 1886 he returned to the East Indies as a member of an official government committee to investigate beriberi. After the
completion of the committee's work, Eijkman remained in Batavia (now
Djakarta) as director of a newly established bacteriological laboratory.
In 1896 he took up the post of professor of public health at the University of Utrecht.

Eijkman was responsible for the first real understanding of the nature
and possible cure of beriberi. For this work he shared the 1929 Nobel
Prize for physiology or medicine with Frederick Gowland Hopkins.
Beriberi is a disorder caused by dietary deficiency, producing fatal lesions
in the nervous and cardiovascular systems. Physicians of the late 19th century, however, were not trained to recognize its cause: with the clear success of the germ theory recently demonstrated by Robert Koch it was
difficult to realize that symptoms could be produced by the absence of
something rather than by the more obvious presence of a visible pathogen.

Eijkman's discovery was prompted by the outbreak of a disease very
similar to human beriberi among the laboratory chickens. Despite the
most thorough search no causative microorganisms could be identified,
and then, for no obvious reason, the disease disappeared.

On investigation, Eijkman discovered that the symptoms of the disease had developed during a period of five months in which the chickens' diet was changed to hulled and polished rice. With a return to their
normal diet of commercial chicken feed the symptoms disappeared.
Eijkman subsequently found that he could induce the disease with a
diet of hulled and polished rice and cure it with one of whole rice. How-

ever, he failed to conclude that beriberi was a deficiency disease. He argued that the endosperm of the rice produced a toxin that was neutralized by the outer hull: by eating polished rice the toxin would be released in its unneutralized form.

Thus although Eijkman had clearly demonstrated how to cure and prevent beriberi it was left to Hopkins to identify its cause as a vitamin deficiency. It was not until the early 1930s that Robert Williams identified the vitamin as vitamin B_1 (thiamine).

Einstein, Albert

(1879–1955)

GERMAN–SWISS–AMERICAN THEORETICAL PHYSICIST

Everything should be made as simple as possible, but not simpler.
—Quoted in *Reader's Digest*, October 1977

Imagination is more important than knowledge.

—*On Science*

Einstein was born at Ulm in Germany where his father was a manufacturer of electrical equipment. Business failure led his father to move the family first to Munich, where Einstein entered the local gymnasium in 1889, and later to Milan. There were no early indications of Einstein's later achievements for he did not begin to talk until the age of three, nor was he fluent at the age of nine, causing his parents to fear that he might even be backward. It appears that in 1894 he was expelled from his Munich gymnasium on the official grounds that his presence was "disruptive." At this point he did something rather remarkable for a fifteen-year-old boy. He had developed such a hatred for things German that he could no longer bear to be a German citizen. He persuaded his father to apply for a revocation of his son's citizenship, a request the authorities granted in 1896. Until 1901, when he obtained Swiss citizenship, he was in fact stateless.

After completing his secondary education at Aarao in Switzerland he passed the entrance examination, at the second attempt, to the Swiss Federal Institute of Technology, Zurich, in 1896. He did not appear to be a particularly exceptional student, finding the process of working for examinations repellent. Disappointed not to be offered an academic post, he survived as a private tutor until 1902, when he obtained the post of technical expert, third class, in the Swiss Patent Office in Bern. Here he continued to think about and work on physical problems. In 1905 he published four papers in the journal *Annalen der Physik* (Annals of Physics) – works that were to direct the progress of physics during the 20th century.

The first, and most straightforward, was on Brownian motion – first described by Robert Brown in 1828. Einstein derived a formula for the average displacement of particles in suspension, based on the idea that the motion is caused by bombardment of the particles by molecules of the liquid. The formula was confirmed by Jean Perrin in 1908 – it represented the first direct evidence for the existence of atoms and molecules of a definite size. The paper was entitled *Über der von molekularkinetischen Theorie der Wärme geförderte Bewegung von in ruhenden Flüssigkeiten suspendierten Teilchen* (On the Motion of Small Particles Suspended in a Stationary Liquid According to the Molecular Kinetic Theory of Heat).

His second paper of 1905 was *Über einen die Erzeugung und Verwandlung des Lichtes betreffenden heuristischen Gesichtspunkt* (On a Heuristic Point of View about the Creation and Conversion of Light). In this Einstein was concerned with the nature of electromagnetic radiation, which at the time was regarded as a wave propagated throughout space according to Clerk Maxwell's equations. Einstein was concerned with the difference between this wave picture and the theoretical picture physicists had of matter. His particular concern in this paper was the difficulty in explaining the photoelectric effect, investigated in 1902 by Philipp Lenard. It was found that ultraviolet radiation of low frequency could eject electrons from a solid surface. The number of electrons depended on the intensity of the radiation and the energy of the electrons depended on the frequency. This dependence on frequency was difficult to explain using classical theory.

Einstein resolved this by suggesting that electromagnetic radiation is a flow of discrete particles – quanta (or photons as they are now known). The intensity of the radiation is the flux of these quanta. The energy per quantum, he proposed, was $h\nu$, where ν is the frequency of the radiation and h is the constant introduced in 1900 by Max Planck. In this way Einstein was able to account for the observed photoelectric behavior. The work was one of the early results introducing the quantum theory into physics and it won for Einstein the 1921 Nobel Prize for physics.

The third of his 1905 papers is the one that is the most famous: *Zur Elektrodynamik bewegter Körper* (On the Electrodynamics of Moving Bodies). It is this paper that first introduced the special theory of relativity to science. The term "special" denotes that the theory is restricted to certain special circumstances – namely for bodies at rest or moving with uniform relative velocities.

The theory was developed to account for a major problem in physics at the time. Traditionally in mechanics, there was a simple procedure for treating relative velocities. A simple example is of a car moving along a road at 40 mph with a second car moving toward it at 60 mph. A stationary observer would say that the second car was moving at 60 mph relative to him. The driver of the first car would say that, relative to him, the second car was approaching at 100 mph. This common-sense method of dealing with relative motion was well established. The mathematical equations involved are called the Galilean transformations – they are simple equations for changing velocities in one frame of reference to another frame of reference. The problem was that the method did not appear to work for electromagnetic radiation, which was thought of as a wave motion through the ether, described by the equations derived by Maxwell. In these, the speed of light is independent of the motion of the source or the observer. At the time, Albert Michelson and Edward Morley had performed a series of experiments to attempt to detect the Earth's motion through the ether, with negative results. Hendrik Lorentz proposed that this result could be explained by a change of size of moving bodies (the Lorentz–Fitzgerald contraction).

Although Einstein was unaware of the Michelson–Morley experiment, he did appreciate the incompatibility of classical mechanics and classical electrodynamics. His solution was a quite radical one. He proposed that the speed of light *is* a constant for all frames of reference that are moving uniformly relative to each other. He also put forward his "relativity principle" that the laws of nature are the same in all frames of reference moving uniformly relative to each other. To reconcile the two principles he abandoned the Galilean transformations – the simple method of adding and subtracting velocities for bodies in relative motion. He arrived at this rejection by arguments about the idea of simultaneity – showing that the time between two events depends on the motions of the bodies involved. In his special theory of relativity, Einstein rejected the ideas of absolute space and absolute time. Later it was developed in terms of events specified by three spatial coordinates and one coordinate of time – a space–time continuum.

The theory had a number of unusual consequences. Thus the length of a body along its direction of motion decreases with increasing velocity. The mass increases as the velocity increases, becoming infinitely large in theory at the speed of light. Time slows down for a moving body – a phenomenon known as time dilation. These effects apply to all bodies but only become significant at velocities close to the speed of light – under normal conditions the effects are so small that classical laws appear to be obeyed. However, the predictions of the special theory – unusual as they may seem – have been verified experimentally. Thus increase in mass is observed for particles accelerated in a synchrocyclotron. Similarly, the lifetimes of unstable particles are increased at high velocities.

In that same year of 1905 Einstein had one more fundamental paper to contribute: *Ist die Trägheit eines Körpers von seinem Energieinhalt abhängig?* (Does the Inertia of a Body Depend on Its Energy Content?). It was in this two-page paper that he concluded that if a body gives off energy E in the form of radiation, its mass diminishes by E/c^2 (where c is the velocity of light) obtaining the celebrated equation $E = mc^2$ relating mass and energy.

Within a short time Einstein's work on relativity was widely recognized to be original and profound. In 1908 he obtained an academic post at the University of Bern. Over the next three years he held major posts at Zurich (1909), Prague (1911), and the Zurich Federal Institute of Technology (1912) before taking a post in Berlin in 1914. This was probably due in part to the respect in which he held the Berlin physicists, Max Planck and Walther Nernst.

By 1907 Einstein was ready to remove the restrictions imposed on the special theory showing that, on certain assumptions, accelerated motion could be incorporated into his new, general theory of relativity. The theory begins with the fact that the mass of a body can be defined in two ways. The inertial mass depends on the way it resists change in motion, as in Newton's second law. The gravitational mass depends on forces of gravitational attraction between masses. The two concepts – inertia and gravity – seem dissimilar yet the inertial and gravitational masses of a body are always the same. Einstein considered that this was unlikely to be a coincidence and it became the basis of his principle of equivalence.

The principle states that it is impossible to distinguish between an inertial force (that is, an accelerating force) and a gravitational one; the two are, in fact, equivalent. The point can be demonstrated with a thought experiment. Consider an observer in an enclosed box somewhere in space far removed from gravitational forces. Suppose that the box is suddenly accelerated upward, followed by the observer releasing two balls of different weights. Subject to an inertial force they will both fall to the floor at the same rate. But this is exactly how they would behave if the box was in a gravitational field and the observer could conclude that the balls fall under the influence of gravity. It was on the basis of this equivalence that Einstein made his dramatic prediction that rays of light in a gravitational field move in a curved path. For if a ray of light enters the box at one side and exits at the other then, with the upward acceleration of the box, it will appear to exit at a point lower down than its entrance. But if we take the equivalence principle seriously we must expect to find the same effect in a gravitational field.

In 1911 he predicted that starlight just grazing the Sun should be deflected by 0.83 seconds of arc, later increased to 1".7, which, though small, should be detectable in a total eclipse by the apparent displacement of the star from its usual position. In 1919 such an eclipse took place; it was observed by Arthur Eddington at Principe in West Africa, who reported a displacement of 1".61, well within the limits of experimental error. It was from this moment that Einstein became known to a wider public, for this dramatic confirmation of an unexpected phenomenon seemed to capture the popular imagination. Even the London *Times* was moved to comment in an editorial, as if to a recalcitrant government, that "the scientific conception of the fabric of the universe must be changed."

In 1916 Einstein was ready to publish the final and authoritative form of his general theory: *Die Grundlage der allgemeinen Relativitätstheorie* (The Foundation of the General Theory of Relativity). It is this work that gained for Einstein the reputation for producing theories that were comprehensible to the very few. Eddington on being informed that there were only three people capable of understanding the theory is reported to have replied, "Who's the third?" It is true that Einstein introduced into gravitational theory a type of mathematics that was then unfamiliar to most physicists, thus presenting an initial impression of incomprehension. In his theory Einstein used the space–time continuum introduced by Hermann Minkowski in 1907, the non-Euclidean geometry developed by Bernhard Riemann in 1854, and the tensor calculus published by Gregorio Ricci in 1887. He was assisted in the mathematics by his friend Grossmann. The theory of gravitation produced is one that depends on the geometry of space–time. In simple terms, the idea is that a body "warps" the space around it so that another body moves in a curved path (hence the notion that space is curved). Einstein and Grossmann in 1915 succeeded in deriving a good theoretical value for the small (and hitherto anomalous) advance in the perihelion of Mercury. The theory was put to an early test. Because of perturbations in the orbit of Mercury produced by the gravitational attractions of other planets, its perihelion (point in the orbit closest to the Sun) actually precesses by a small amount (9′ 34″ per century). When these perturbation effects were calculated on the basis of Newtonian mechanics, they could only account for a precession rate of 8′ 51″ per century, a figure 43″ too small. In 1915 Einstein, while completing his 1916 paper on General Relativity, calculated Mercury's perihelion precession on the basis of his own theory and found that, without making any extra assumptions, the missing 43″ were accounted for. The discovery, Einstein later reported, gave him palpitations and "for a few days I was beside myself with joyous excitement."

The theory also predicted (1907) that electromagnetic radiation in a strong gravitation field would be shifted to longer wavelengths – the *Einstein shift*. This was used by Walter Adams in 1925 to explain the spectrum of Sirius B. In 1959 Robert Pound and Glen Rebka demonstrated it on Earth using the Mossbauer effect. They found that at a height of 75 feet (23 m) above the ground gamma rays from a radioactive source had a longer wavelength than at ground level. Physicists have been less successful, however, with the prediction in 1916 of the existence of gravitational waves. Despite an intensive search from 1964 onward by Joseph Weber and others, they have yet to be detected.

Einstein was less successful in applying his theory to the construction of a cosmological model of the universe, which he assumed to be uniform in density, static, and lacking infinite distances. He found himself forced to complicate his equations with a cosmological constant, λ. It was left to Aleksandr Friedmann in 1922 to show that the term could be dropped and a solution found that yielded an expanding universe, a solution that Einstein eventually adopted. He later described the cosmological constant as "my greatest mistake."

By the early 1920s Einstein's great work was virtually complete. He wrote in 1921 that: "Discovery in the grand manner is for young people … and hence for me a thing of the past." From the early 1920s he rejected quantum theory – the theory he had done much to establish himself. His basic objection was to the later formulation that included the probability interpretation. "God does not play dice," he said, and, "He may be subtle, but he is not malicious." He felt, like Louis de Broglie, that although the new quantum mechanics was clearly a powerful and successful theory it was an imperfect one, with an underlying undiscovered deterministic basis. For the last 30 years of his life he also pursued a quest for a unified field theory – a single theory to explain both electromagnetic and gravitational fields. He published several attempts at such a theory but all were inadequate. This work was carried out right up to his death.

Also, from about 1925 onward, Einstein engaged in a debate with Niels Bohr on the soundness of quantum theory. He would present Bohr with a series of thought experiments, which seemed undeniable even though they were clearly incompatible with quantum mechanics. The best known of these was presented in a paper written with Boris Podolsky and Nathan Rosen and entitled: *Can Quantum Mechanical Description of Physical Reality Be Considered Complete?* (1935). The *EPR experiment*, as it soon became known, assumed that, after interacting, two particles become widely separated. Quantum theory allows the total momentum of the pair (A, B) to be measured accurately. Thus if the momentum of B is also measured accurately, it is a simple matter, as momentum is conserved, to calculate the momentum of particle A. We can then measure the position of A with as much precision as is practically possible. It would therefore seem to follow that, without violating any laws of physics, both the position and momentum of particle A have been accurately determined. But, according to the uncertainty principle of Heisenberg, we are prevented from ever knowing accurately a particle's position and momentum simultaneously.

The paper troubled Bohr. He spent six weeks going through the text word by word and analyzing every possibility. Eventually he saw that the measurements of A's position and momentum are separate and distinct. The uncertainty principle insisted that no *single* measurement could determine a particle's precise position and momentum, and this central claim remained unchallenged by the EPR experiment. Einstein's correspondence with Bohr about quantum mechanics is published as the *Bohr–Einstein letters*.

Einstein was also involved in a considerable amount of political activity. When Hitler came to power in 1933 Einstein made his permanent home in America where he worked at Princeton. In 1939 he was persuaded to write to President Roosevelt warning him about the possibility of an atomic bomb and urging American research. He was, in later years, a convinced campaigning pacifist. He was also a strong supporter of Zionist causes and, on the death of Chaim Weizmann in 1952 was asked to become president of Israel, but declined.

Einthoven, Willem

(1860–1927)

DUTCH PHYSIOLOGIST

Einthoven (**Int**-hoh-ven), the son of a physician, was born at Semarang on the Indonesian island of Java and educated at the University of Utrecht in the Netherlands, where he gained his MD in 1885. In the following year he moved to Leiden as professor of physiology.

As early as 1887 the English physiologist Augustus Waller had recorded electric currents generated by the heart. He had used the capillary electrometer invented by Gabriel Lippmann in 1873, which – although sensitive to changes of a millivolt – turned out to be too complicated and inaccurate for general use. In 1901 Einthoven first described a recording system using a string galvanometer, which he claimed would overcome the inadequacies of Waller's device.

A string galvanometer consists of a fine wire thread stretched between the poles of a magnet. When carrying a current it is displaced at right angles to the directions of the magnetic lines of force to an extent proportional to the strength of the current. By linking this up to an optical system the movement of the wire can be magnified and photographically recorded. As the differences in potential developed in the heart are conducted to different parts of the body it was possible to lead the current from the hands and feet to the recording instrument to obtain a curve that was later called an *electrocardiogram* (ECG).

Having demonstrated the potentiality of such a machine, two further problems needed solution. Einthoven first had to standardize his ECG so that different machines or two recordings of the same machine would produce comparable readings. It was therefore later established that a 1 millivolt potential would deflect a recording stylus 1 centimeter on standardized paper. The second problem was how to interpret such a curve in order to distinguish normal readings from recordings of diseased hearts. By 1913 Einthoven had worked out the interpretation of the normal tracing and, by correlating abnormal readings with specific cardiac defects identified at post mortem, was able to use the ECG as a diagnostic tool.

For his development of the electrocardiogram Einthoven was awarded the 1924 Nobel Prize for physiology or medicine.

Ekeberg, Anders Gustaf

(1767–1813)

SWEDISH CHEMIST

Ekeberg (**ay**-ke-berg), who was born in the Swedish capital of Stockholm, graduated from the University of Uppsala in 1788 and, after traveling in Europe, began teaching chemistry at Uppsala in 1794. He was an early convert to the system of Antoine Lavoisier and introduced this new chemistry to Sweden. He was partially deaf from a childhood illness but the further loss of an eye (1801) caused by an exploding flask did not impede his work.

Ekeberg is remembered chiefly for his discovery of the element tantalum. In 1802, while analyzing minerals from Ytterby quarry, Sweden, he isolated the new metal. The name supposedly comes from its failure to dissolve in acid, looking like Tantalus in the waters of Hell. It was a long time before it was recognized as a separate element as it was difficult to distinguish from niobium, isolated by Charles Hatchett in 1801. Wollaston failed to distinguish between them and it was as late as 1865 that Jean Marignac conclusively demonstrated the distinctness of the two new metals.

Ekman, Vagn Walfrid

(1874–1954)

SWEDISH OCEANOGRAPHER

Ekman (**ayk**-man), the son of an oceanographer, was born in the Swedish capital of Stockholm and educated at the University of Uppsala, graduating in 1902. He worked at the International Laboratory for Oceanographic Research in Oslo (1902–08) before he moved to Lund, Sweden, as a lecturer in mathematical physics, being made a professor in 1910.

In 1905 Ekman published a fundamental paper, *On the Influence of the Earth's Rotation on Ocean Currents*. This work originated from an observation made by the explorer Fridtjof Nansen that in the Arctic drift ice did not follow wind direction but deviated to the right. He showed that the motion, since known as the *Ekman spiral*, is produced as a complex interaction between the force of the wind on the water surface, the deflecting force due to the Earth's rotation (Coriolis force), and the frictional forces within the water layers.

Ekman also studied the phenomenon of dead water, a thin layer of fresh water from melting ice spreading over the sea, which could halt slow-moving ships. This, he established, resulted from the waves formed between water layers of different densities. The *Ekman current meter*, invented by him, is still in use.

Ellet, Charles

(1810–1862)

AMERICAN CIVIL ENGINEER

Born at Penns Manor in Pennsylvania, Ellet began work as a surveyor and assistant engineer, and then traveled to Europe to study engineering, returning to America in 1832. He concentrated on designing suspension bridges and built his first in 1842 over the Schuylkill River in Pennsylvania, with a span of 358 feet (109 m). He went on to build the world's first long-span wire-cable suspension bridge, with a central span of 1,010 feet (308 m), over the Ohio River (1846–49). The bridge failed in 1854 because of aerodynamic instability.

Ellet also devised a steam-powered ram that helped to win the Mississippi River for the Union in the Battle of Memphis on 6 June 1862. Ellet was mortally wounded in this battle.

Elliott, Thomas Renton

(1877–1961)

BRITISH PHYSICIAN

Elliott was the son of a retailer from the northeastern English city of Durham. He was educated at Cambridge University and University College Hospital, London, where he later served as professor of clinical medicine from the end of World War I until his retirement in 1939.

It was as a research student under John Langley at Cambridge that Elliott made his greatest discovery. In 1901 Langley had injected animals with a crude extract from the adrenal gland and noted that the extract stimulated the action of the sympathetic nerves. Adrenaline (epinephrine) had earlier (1898) been isolated by John Abel at Johns Hopkins University. Elliott therefore decided to inject adrenaline into animals to see if he got the same response as Langley had with the adrenal gland extract. He did indeed achieve increases in heart beat, blood pressure, etc., characteristic of stimulation of the sympathetic nervous system. Elliott is remembered for his subsequent suggestion that adrenaline may be released from sympathetic nerve endings – the first hint of neurotransmitters. Langley discouraged such speculation but later work by Henry Dale and Otto Loewi on acetylcholine supported Elliott's early work.

Elsasser, Walter Maurice

(1904–1991)

GERMAN–AMERICAN
GEOPHYSICIST

Elsasser was born in the German city of Mannheim and educated at the University of Göttingen, where he obtained his doctorate in 1927. He worked at the University of Frankfurt before leaving Germany in 1933 following Hitler's rise to power. He taught at the Sorbonne, Paris, before emigrating to America (1936) where he joined the staff of the California Institute of Technology. He became professor of physics at the University of Pennsylvania (1947–50) and at the University of Utah (1950–58). In 1962 he became professor of geophysics at Princeton and he was appointed research professor at the University of Maryland from 1968 until his retirement in 1974.

Elsasser made fundamental proposals on the question of the origin of the Earth's magnetic field. It had been known for some time that this could not be due to the Earth's iron core for its temperature is too high for it to serve as a simple magnet. Instead he proposed that the molten liquid core contains eddies set up by the Earth's rotation. These eddies produce an electric current that causes the familiar terrestrial magnetic field.

Elsasser also made predictions of electron diffraction (1925) and neutron diffraction (1936). His works include *The Physical Foundation of Biology* (1958) and *Atom and Organism* (1966).

Elton, Charles Sutherland

(1900–1991)

BRITISH ECOLOGIST

Born in the English city of Liverpool, Elton graduated in zoology from Oxford University in 1922. He was assistant to Julian Huxley on the Oxford University expedition to Spitzbergen (1921), where Elton carried out ecological studies of the region's animal life. Further Arctic expeditions were made in 1923, 1924, and 1930. Such experience prompted his appointment as biological consultant to the Hudson's Bay Company, for which he carried out investigations into variations in the numbers of fur-bearing animals, using trapper's records dating back to 1736. In 1932 Elton helped establish the Bureau of Animal Population at Oxford – an institution that subsequently became an international center for information on and research into animal numbers and their ecology. In the same year he became editor of the new *Journal of Animal Ecology*, launched by the British Ecological Society, and in 1936 was appointed reader in animal ecology as well as a senior research fellow by Oxford University.

Elton was one of the first biologists to study animals in relation to their environment and other animals and plants. His demonstration of the nature of food chains and cycles, as well as such topics as the reasons for differences in animal numbers, were discussed in *Animal Ecology* (1927). In 1930 *Animal Ecology and Evolution* was published in which he advanced the notion that animals were not invariably at the mercy of their environment but commonly, perhaps through migration, practiced environmental selection by changing their habitats. Work on the rodent population of Britain, and how it is affected by a changing environment, was turned to eminently practical account at the outbreak of World War II when Elton conducted intensive research into methods of controlling rats and mice and thus conserving food for the war effort. *Voles, Mice and Lemmings: Problems in Population Dynamics* was published in 1942, and *The Control of Rats and Mice* in 1954, the latter becoming accepted as the standard work on the subject.

Elvehjem, Conrad Arnold

(1901–1962)

AMERICAN BIOCHEMIST

Elvehjem (el-ve-yem), the son of a farmer from McFarland, Wisconsin, graduated from and spent his whole career at the University of Wisconsin. He obtained his PhD in 1927, and served as professor of biochemistry from 1936 until 1958, when he became president of the university, a position held until his retirement in 1962.

In 1937, following discoveries by Casimir Funk and Joseph Goldberger, Elvehjem succeeded in producing a new treatment for pellagra. In the 1920s Goldberger had postulated that this disease was caused by a deficiency of "P-P" (pellagra preventive) factor present in milk. In 1913 Funk, while searching for a cure for beriberi, came across nicotinic acid in rice husks. Although it was of little use against beriberi, Elvehjem found that even in minute doses it would dramatically remove the symptoms of blacktongue, the canine equivalent of pellagra. Tests on humans revealed the same remarkable effects on pellagra.

Elvehjem, a prolific author with over 800 papers to his credit, also worked on the role of trace elements in nutrition, showing the essential role played by such minerals as copper, zinc, and cobalt.

Embden, Gustav George

(1874–1933)

GERMAN PHYSIOLOGIST

Embden, the son of a lawyer from Hamburg in Germany, was educated at the universities of Freiburg, Munich, Berlin, and Strasbourg. From 1904 he was director of the chemical laboratory in the medical clinic of the Frankfurt hospital, becoming in 1907 director of the Physiological Institute (which evolved from the medical clinic) and in 1914 director of the Institute for Vegetative Physiology (which in its turn evolved from the Physiological Institute).

In 1918 Otto Meyerhof threw considerable light on the process of cellular metabolism by showing that it involved the breakdown of glucose to lactic acid. Embden spent much time in working out the precise steps involved in such a breakdown, as did many other chemists and physiologists. By the time of his death the details of the metabolic sequence from glycogen to lactic acid, later known as the *Embden–Meyerhof pathway*, had been worked out.

Embden's earlier work concentrated on the metabolic processes carried out by the liver. In his experiments he used a new perfusion technique to maintain the condition of the dissected livers. In this way he discovered the breakdown of amino acids by oxidative deamination, realized that abnormal sugar metabolism can lead to the formation of acetone and acetoacetic acid, and showed that sugar is synthesized from lactic acid.

Emeleus, Harry Julius

(1903–1993)

BRITISH INORGANIC CHEMIST

Emeleus was educated at Imperial College, in his native city of London, and at Karlsruhe and Princeton. He returned to Imperial College in 1931 and taught there until 1945 when he moved to Cambridge University, where he served as professor of inorganic chemistry until his retirement in 1970.

In 1938, in collaboration with John Anderson, he published the well-known work, *Modern Aspects of Inorganic Chemistry*. He also worked on fluorine, publishing a monograph on the subject in 1969: *The Chemistry of Fluorine and its Compounds*.

Emiliani, Cesare

(1922–)

ITALIAN–AMERICAN GEOLOGIST

Emiliani (e-meel-**yah**-ni) was born in the Italian city of Bologna and educated at the university there. He moved to America in 1948, obtaining his PhD from the University of Chicago in 1950. After teaching at Chicago (1950–56) he moved to the University of Miami, where he served as professor of geology at the Institute of Marine Science from 1963 until his retirement in 1993.

Emiliani has specialized in using oxygen isotopic analysis of pelagic microfossils from ocean sediments. Albrecht Penck and Eduard Brückner had, in 1909, established the long-held orthodox view that four ice ages had occurred during the Pleistocene. In his fundamental paper *Pleistocene Temperatures* (1955) Emiliani produced evidence that there had been more. Using the principle established by Harold Urey that the climate of past ages can be estimated by the ratio of oxygen–16 to oxygen–18 present in water (i.e., the less oxygen–18 present the colder the climate must have been), he examined the oxygen–18 content of fossils brought up from the mud of the Caribbean. By choosing fossils that he knew had lived near the surface he could reconstruct the climatic history, and consequently identified seven complete glacial cycles.

Empedocles of Acragas

(*c.* 490 BC–*c.* 430 BC)

GREEK PHILOSOPHER

Empedocles (em-**ped**-oh-kleez) was a poet and a physician as well as a philosopher. Born at Acragas in Greece, he was probably a pupil of Parmenides. Much legend surrounds what is known of his life. Styling himself as a god, he reputedly brought about his own death in an attempt to persuade his followers of his divinity by throwing himself into the volcanic crater of Mount Etna. Fragments of two poems by Empedocles survive: *On Nature* and *Purifications*. There is some difficulty in reconciling the two because the first is purely physical while the second deals with the progress of the soul from fall to redemption.

Empedocles is best known as the originator of the four-element theory of matter (earth, fire, air, and water), which had a persuasive influence until the beginning of modern chemistry in the 18th century. He was noted for his keen observation and was the first to demonstrate that air has weight.

Encke, Johann Franz

(1791–1865)

GERMAN ASTRONOMER

The son of a Lutheran pastor from Hamburg in Germany, Encke (**eng**-ke) was educated at Göttingen where he impressed Karl Gauss. In 1816 he was appointed to the staff of the Seeberg Observatory, Gotha, where he remained until 1825 when he moved to the Berlin Observatory as its director.

A faint comet had first been observed by P. Mechain in 1786. Over the years other reports were made in 1795, 1805, and 1818 of a series of faint comets. Although several astronomers suspected there was only one comet involved, it was Encke who provided in 1819 the necessary computations. He showed that *Encke's comet*, as it became known, had a period of 3.3 years and predicted that it would be at perihelion again on 24 May 1822. His prediction was accurate to within a few hours and Encke thus became, after Halley, only the second man to predict the return of a periodic comet successfully.

Enders, John Franklin

(1897–1985)

AMERICAN MICROBIOLOGIST

Enders, the son of a wealthy banker from West Hartford in Connecticut, was educated at Yale and Harvard where he obtained his PhD in 1930. His career was somewhat delayed by the war, in which he served as a flying instructor, and also by his initial intention to study Germanic and Celtic languages. This was upset by the influence of the bacteriologist Hans Zinsser who "seduced" Enders into science in the late 1920s.

In 1946 Enders set up an Infectious Diseases Laboratory at the Boston Children's Hospital; it was here that he did the work to be later described as opening up a "new epoch in the history of virus research." This referred to his success, in collaboration with Thomas Weller and Frederick Robbins, in 1949 in cultivating polio virus in test tube cultures of human tissue for the first time. They further demonstrated that the virus could be grown on a wide variety of tissue and not just nerve cells.

This at last allowed the polio virus to be studied, typed, and produced in quantity. Without such an advance the triumphs of Albert Sabin and Jonas Salk in developing a vaccine against polio in the 1950s would have been impossible. In 1954 Enders, Weller, and Robbins were awarded the Nobel Prize for physiology or medicine.

By this time Enders had already begun to work on the cultivation of the measles virus. This time, working with T. Peebles, they followed up their success in cultivating the virus with, in 1957, the production of the first measles vaccine.

Engelmann, George

(1809–1884)

AMERICAN BOTANIST

Born the son of a schoolmaster at Frankfurt in Germany, Engelmann was educated at the universities of Heidelberg, Berlin, and Würzburg where he obtained his MD in 1831. In the following year he visited America to invest in some land for a wealthy uncle and decided in 1835 to settle and practice medicine in St. Louis.

Engelmann was not only a plant collector of some importance; he also did much to initiate and organize major collecting expeditions of the flora of the West. It was thus through Engelmann that many of the newly collected specimens passed on their way to eastern scholars as Asa Gray at Harvard. Engelmann's role became more official with the setting up of the Missouri Botanical Garden in 1859 with the backing of the St. Louis businessman Henry Shaw.

He is also remembered for his demonstration that some stocks of American vine were resistant to the pest *Phylloxera*, which had begun to devastate the vineyards of Europe from 1863 onward.

Engelmann, Theodor Wilhelm

(1843–1909)

GERMAN PHYSIOLOGIST

Engelmann, the son of a publisher, was educated at Jena, Heidelberg, and Göttingen, before obtaining his PhD from the university in his native city of Leipzig in 1867. He immediately joined the faculty of the University of Utrecht, serving there as professor of physiology from 1888 until 1897 when he returned to Germany to a similar chair at the University of Berlin, where he remained until his retirement in 1908.

Between 1873 and 1895 Engelmann published a number of papers on muscle contraction. By this time, following the work of such physiologists as William Bowman, the main anatomical details of striated muscle had been established. However an explanation was needed as to why the anisotropic or A bands refract polarized light quite differently to the isotropic or I bands. Engelmann had noted that in contraction the A bands increased in volume while the I bands decreased. He consequently proposed his "imbibition" theory in which the contraction of striped muscle is attributed to a flow of fluid from the I to the A bands.

Engelmann also worked on the nature and mechanism of the heartbeat and in 1875 devised an experiment that proved the heartbeat is myogenic; that is, the contraction originates in the heart muscle and not from an external nerve stimulus. In 1881 he discovered the chemotactic response of certain bacteria to oxygen, and he also demonstrated that red and blue light are far more effective in stimulating plant chloroplasts during photosynthesis than other parts of the spectrum.

Engler, Heinrich Gustav Adolf

(1844–1930)

GERMAN BOTANIST

Engler was born in Sagan (which is now in Poland) and studied botany at Breslau University, gaining his PhD in 1866 for his thesis on the genus *Saxifraga*. After teaching natural history he became custodian of the Munich botanical collection and then professor of botany at Kiel University; in 1884 he returned to Breslau to succeed his former teacher in the chair of botany. At Breslau Engler replanned the botanic garden, ordering the plants according to their geographical distribution. In 1887 he took up the important chair of botany at Berlin and successfully reestablished the garden in Dahlem.

Between 1878 and his retirement from Berlin in 1921, Engler contributed greatly to the development of plant taxonomy with his classifications, presented in such books as *The Natural Plant Families* (1887–1911) and *The Plant Kingdom* (1900–37). Much of his work was drawn from first-hand observation gained during travels through Africa, Europe, India, China, Japan, and America.

Eötvös, Baron Roland von

(1848–1919)

HUNGARIAN PHYSICIST

Born in Budapest, Eötvös (**u(r)t**-vu(r)sh) studied at the University of Königsberg and at Heidelberg where he obtained his PhD in 1870 for a thesis concerning a method of detecting motion through the ether by measuring light intensity. At Königsberg in 1886 he introduced the *Eötvös law* – an equation approximately relating surface tension, temperature, density, and relative molecular mass of a liquid.

He then started teaching at Budapest University, where he was appointed professor in 1872. His work from then on centered on gravitation. In 1888 he developed the *Eötvös torsion balance*, consisting of a bar with two attached weights, the bar being suspended by a torsion fiber. He argued that if the two weights were made from different materials, and if the inertial and gravitational forces were not equivalent, there would be a discernible twisting force, which would cause a slight rotation of the bar about a vertical axis. Observations were made with copper, aluminum, asbestos, platinum, and other materials. No torque was found and Eötvös concluded that the masses of different materials were equivalent to a few parts per billion. His experiments were repeated in the 1960s by Dicke and in 1970 by Braginsky, with results affirming the equivalence to 1 part per 100 billion and 1 part per trillion respectively. The experiment became one of the foundation stones of general relativity since, by failing to distinguish between inertial and gravitational mass experimentally, it supported Einstein's principle of equivalence.

Eötvös spent much of his time trying to improve the Hungarian education system and for a short time was minister of instruction. He was also an excellent mountain climber and a peak in the Dolomites is named for him.

Epicurus

(*c.* 341 BC–270 BC)

GREEK PHILOSOPHER

The atoms come together in different order
and position, like the letters, which, though
they are few, yet, by being placed together in
different ways, produce innumerable words.
—Quoted by Max Muller in *Science of
Language* (1871)

Epicurus, who was born on the Greek island of Samos, traveled to
Athens when he was about 18 years old, and received military training.
He then taught at Mytilene and Lampsacus before returning to Athens
(305 BC) where he founded a school of philosophy and attracted a substantial following.

Epicurus revived Democritean atomism and was little influenced by
his predecessors, Plato and Aristotle. His work is known through substantial fragments in the writings of Diogenes Laërtius and especially
through the long poem, *De rerum natura* (On the Nature of Things), by
his Roman disciple Lucretius. The Epicurean philosophy aimed at the at-
tainment of a happy, though simple, life and used the atomic theory to
sanction the banishment of the old fears and superstitions. Epicurus
also made important additions to the atomic theory, asserting the primacy of sense-perception where Democritus had distrusted the senses,
and he introduced the concept of random atomic "swerve" to preserve
free will in an otherwise deterministic system.

Epstein, Sir Michael Anthony

(1921–   )

BRITISH VIROLOGIST

Epstein, a Londoner, was educated at Cambridge University and at the Middlesex Hospital Medical School in his native city. After serving in the Royal Army Medical Corps (1945–47), he returned to the Middlesex Hospital as an assistant pathologist. He left the Middlesex in 1965 and in 1968 he was appointed professor of pathology at Bristol University, a position he held until his retirement in 1985. He has continued to work in the Department of Clinical Medicine at Oxford.

In 1961 Epstein heard Denis Burkitt describe the distribution of a particularly savage lymphoma throughout Africa. Epstein saw that "anything which has geographical factors such as climate affecting distribution must have some kind of biological cause." That biological cause, Epstein suspected, for no very good reason, was a virus.

Although Epstein received tumor samples from Burkitt, he found them impossible to culture and saw no trace of any virus. After struggling unsuccessfully for two years, Epstein and his assistant Yvonne Barr developed a new approach. Instead of working with small tumor lumps they divided the pieces into single cells. The technique proved successful and for the first time ever human lymphocytes were being grown in a continuous culture.

Yet Epstein initially found no virus until he examined some cells under an electron microscope. The virus was named the *Epstein–Barr virus* and proved to be a member of the herpes family.

The virus turned out to have a worldwide distribution and was identified as the cause of mononeucleosis. Clearly, its presence alone is insufficient to cause lymphoma. For if most of us have the virus, why is lymphoma not distributed more widely? Epstein and Burkitt argued that only in cases in which malaria or some other chronic condition has suppressed a child's immature immune system could the virus provoke lymphoid cells into malignant growth.

Erasistratus of Chios

(*c.* 304 BC–*c.* 250 BC)

GREEK ANATOMIST AND PHYSICIAN

Erasistratus (er-a-**sis**-stra-tus), who was born on the Greek island of Chios, came from a distinctly medical background and studied in Athens, Cos, and Alexandria. Following Herophilus he became the leading figure in the Alexandrian School of Anatomy.

It is possible with Erasistratus, unlike his contemporaries, to make out at least the outline of his physiological system. Every organ and part of the body was served by a "threefold network" of vein, artery, and nerve. Indeed, he believed the body tissues were a plaiting of such vessels, which at their extremities became so fine as to be invisible. The veins carried blood and the nerves and arteries transported nervous and animal spirits respectively.

As an atomist he rejected all attractive and occult forces seeking instead to explain everything in terms of atoms and the void. He thus accounted for the bleeding of severed arteries by assuming the escaped pneuma left a vacuum that was filled by blood from adjoining veins.

One of the most interesting aspects of his thought was his unusual rejection of the humoral theory of disease which, formulated by the Hippocratics and authorized by Galen, became the sterile orthodoxy of Western medicine for 2,000 years. Instead he seems to have argued for a more mechanical concept of disease, attributing it to a "plethora" of blood, vital spirit, or food, which produces a blocking and inflammation of the various vessels.

His objection to the humoral theory found little support and with the passing of Erasistratus the great innovative period of Alexandrian medicine came to an end.

Eratosthenes of Cyrene

(*c.* 276 BC–*c.* 194 BC)

GREEK ASTRONOMER

Eratosthenes (er-a-**tos**-the-neez) was born in Cyrene, now in Libya, and educated at Athens. He then taught in Alexandria where he became tutor to the son of Ptolemy III and librarian. He was prominent in history, poetry, mathematics, and astronomy and was known by the nickname "beta" because, some say, he was the second Plato.

In number theory he introduced the procedure named for him to collect the prime numbers by filtering out all the composites. The method, called the *sieve of Eratosthenes*, was to write down a list of ordered numbers and to strike out every second number after 2, every third number after 3, every fourth number after 4, and so on. The numbers remaining are primes.

Eratosthenes achieved his greatest fame by using a most ingenious and simple method to measure the circumference of the Earth. He was aware that on a certain day the Sun at Syene (now Aswan) was exactly at its zenith (it was known to shine directly down a deep well on that day). He found that on the same day at Alexandria it was south of its zenith by an angle corresponding to 1/50 of a circle (7° 12′). He also knew that the distance between Syene and Alexandria was 5,000 stadia – a distance that he estimated from the time it took a camel train to make the journey. Therefore, 5,000 stadia must be 1/50 of the circumference of the Earth; that is, 250,000 stadia. (Since the exact length of a stade is not known it is impossible to work out exactly how accurate his measurement was but it has been thought to be within 50 miles of the presently accepted value.) Eratosthenes also established an improved figure for the obliquity of the ecliptic (the tilt of the Earth's axis) of 23°51′20″. Finally, he produced the first map of the world, as he knew it, based on meridians of longitude and parallels of latitude.

Ercker, Lazarus

(*c.* 1530–1594)

BOHEMIAN METALLURGIST

Ercker was born in Annaberg, now in Germany, and studied at the University of Wittenberg (1547–48). In 1554 he was made assayer in Dresden, Saxony, and later he became control tester of coins in a town near Prague.

Ercker's main contribution to metallurgy was to write the first systematic account of analytical and metallurgical chemistry. This manual, *Beschreibung allerfürnemisten mineralischen Ertzt und Berckwercksarten* (1574; Description of Leading Ore Processing and Mining Methods), described the testing of alloys, minerals, and compounds containing silver, gold, copper, antimony, mercury, bismuth, and lead.

Erdös, Paul

(1913–1996)

HUNGARIAN MATHEMATICIAN

Paul Erdös has the theory that God has a book containing all the theorems of mathematics with their absolutely most beautiful proofs, and when he wants to express particular appreciation of a proof he exclaims, "This is one from the book!"
—Ross Honsberger, *Mathematical Morsels*

The son of two mathematics teachers from the Hungarian capital of Budapest, Erdös (**er**-du(r)sh) devoted his life to mathematics to an unequalled degree. He was educated at the University of Budapest where he obtained his PhD in 1934. Sensing difficult political times ahead, Erdös moved to Manchester, England, on a four-year fellowship. Shortly before the outbreak of war he left for America. At the height of the McCarthy era he was denied a reentry permit after attending a conference in Amsterdam. Erdös then settled in Israel for several years until, in the 1960s, he was allowed a U.S. visa once more.

With no official job and no family, Erdös lived out of a suitcase and traveled from one mathematical center to another. His life was spent working up to 20 hours a day on mathematical problems, usually with colleagues. In the process he produced over 1,000 papers. He lived on lecture fees, prizes, grants and the hospitality of his wide circle of collaborators. He wrote up to 1,500 letters a year and had more than 250 published collaborators.

Erlanger, Joseph

(1874–1965)

AMERICAN NEUROPHYSIOLOGIST

Erlanger, the son of a German immigrant drawn to California in the gold rush, was born in San Francisco. He was educated at the University of California and at Johns Hopkins University in Baltimore, where in 1899 he obtained his MD. After working on the staff for a few years Erlanger moved to the University of Wisconsin (1906) to accept the chair of physiology. In 1910 he moved to Washington University, St. Louis, where he held the chair of physiology in the Medical School until his retirement in 1944.

Between 1921 and 1931 Erlanger carried out some fundamental research on the functions of nerve fibers with his former pupil and colleague, Herbert Gasser. They investigated the transmission of a nerve impulse along a frog nerve kept in a moist chamber at constant temperature. Their innovation was to study the transmission with the cathode-ray oscillograph, invented by Ferdinand Braun in 1897, which enabled them to picture the changes the impulse underwent as it traveled along the nerve.

Erlanger and Gasser found that on stimulating a nerve, the resulting electrical activity indicating the passage of an impulse was composed of three waves, as observed on the oscillograph. They explained this by proposing that the one stimulus activated three different groups of nerve fibers, each of which had its own conduction rate. They went on to measure these rates, concluding that the fastest fibers (the A-fibers) conduct with a speed of up to 100 meters per second (mps) while the slowest (the C-fibers) could manage speeds of no more than 2 mps. The intermediate B-fibers conducted in the range 2–14 mps. Erlanger and Gasser were able to relate this variation to the thickness of the different nerve fibers, A-fibers being the largest.

It was a short step from this to the theory of differentiated function, in which it was proposed that the slender C-fibers carry pain impulses whereas the thicker A-fibers transmit motor impulses. But it was soon demonstrated that while such propositions may be broadly true the detailed picture is more complex.

Erlanger and Gasser produced an account of their collaboration in *Electrical Signs of Nervous Activity* (1937); they were awarded the 1944 Nobel Prize for physiology or medicine for their work.

Erlenmeyer, Richard August Carl Emil

(1825–1909)

GERMAN CHEMIST

Born near Wiesbaden in Germany, Erlenmeyer (**er**-len-mI-er) studied at Giessen and practiced at first as a pharmacist. In 1855 he became a private pupil of August Kekulé at Heidelberg and later was appointed professor at the Munich Polytechnic (1868–83). He synthesized guanidine and was the first to give its correct formula (1868). He also synthesized tyrosine and formulated the *Erlenmeyer rule*, which states the impossibility of two hydroxy groups occurring on the same carbon atom or of a hydroxy group occurring adjacent to a carbon–carbon double bond (chloral hydrate is an exception to this rule). His son F. G. C. E. Erlenmeyer introduced the Erlenmeyer synthesis of amino acids and synthesized cystine, serine, and phenylalanine.

Ernst, Richard Robert

(1933–   )

SWISS CHEMIST

Born at Winterthur in Switzerland, Ernst (ernst) was educated at the Federal Institute of Technology, Zurich, where he obtained his PhD in 1962. He spent the period from 1963 until 1968 working as a research chemist for Varian Associates, Palo Alto, California, before returning to the Federal Institute where he was appointed professor of physical chemistry in 1976.

The technique of nuclear magnetic resonance (NMR) described by I. I. Rabi in 1944, and developed by Felix Bloch and Edward Purcell in the late 1940s, quickly became a recognized tool for the exploration of atomic nuclei. As nuclei possess a magnetic moment they will tend to align themselves with any strong magnetic field. If, however, nuclei are subjected to radiowaves of the appropriate frequency, they will be raised to a higher energy level, and align themselves in a different direction with respect to the field. With the removal of the radio signal, the nuclei will revert to their original energy state by emitting radiation of a characteristic frequency. The frequency of the radiation emitted allows nuclei to be identified, and the structure of certain molecules determined.

But, the process was time-consuming because, in order to find which radiofrequency a sample responded to, it was necessary to sweep the applied frequency through a range of frequencies. Ernst developed a technique in which the sample was subjected to a single high-energy radio pulse. In this way numerous nuclei would respond and emit an apparently jumbled signal. But Ernst showed that, with the aid of Fourier analysis and a computer, the signal could be unraveled into its separate components. Ernst's procedure considerably increased the sensitivity of NMR.

In 1970 Ernst made a further advance. He found that if he subjected his samples to a sequence of high-energy pulses instead of to a single pulse, it enabled him to use NMR techniques to study much larger molecules. Ernst's "two-dimensional analysis," as it became known, opened the way to investigate complex biological molecules such as proteins. His work also laid the foundation for the development by Peter Mansfield and others of MRI (magnetic resonance imaging).

For his work on NMR Ernst was awarded the 1991 Nobel Prize for chemistry.

Esaki, Leo

(1925–   )

JAPANESE PHYSICIST

Born in the Japanese city of Osaka, Esaki (e-**sah**-ki) graduated in physics at the University of Tokyo in 1947, gaining his doctorate there in 1959. His doctoral work was on the physics of semiconductors, and in 1958 he reported an effect known as "tunneling," which he had observed in narrow p–n junctions of germanium that were heavily doped with impurities. The phenomenon of tunneling is a quantum-mechanical effect in which an electron can penetrate a potential barrier through a narrow region of solid, where classical theory predicts it could not pass.

Esaki was quick to see the possibility of applying the tunnel effect, and in 1960 reported the construction of a device with diodelike properties – the tunnel (or *Esaki*) diode. With negative bias potential, the diode acts as a short circuit, while under certain conditions of forward bias it can have effectively negative resistance (the current decreasing with increasing voltage). Important characteristics of the tunnel diode are its very fast speed of operation, its small physical size, and its low power consumption. It has found application in many fields of electronics, principally in computers, microwave devices, and where low electronic noise is required. Esaki shared the Nobel Prize for physics in 1973 with Brian Josephson and Ivar Giaever.

Esaki worked for the computer firm International Business Machines at the Thomas J. Watson Research Center, Yorktown Heights, New York, until 1992, when he returned to Japan to become president of Tsukuba University, Ibaraki.

Eschenmoser, Albert

(1925–)

SWISS CHEMIST

Born at Erstfeld in Switzerland, Eschenmoser (**esh**-en-moh-ser) was educated at the Federal Institute of Technology, Zurich, where he has taught since 1956 and where, in 1960, he was appointed professor of organic chemistry.

He is best known for his work in synthesizing a number of complex organic compounds. His first success came with colchicine – an alkaloid found in the autumn crocus – which has important applications in genetical research. He also collaborated with Robert Woodward on the synthesis of vitamin B_{12} (cyanocobalamin), which had first been isolated and crystallized by Karl Folkers in 1948. Its empirical formula was soon established and in 1956 Dorothy Hodgkin established its structure. It took many years with samples passing between Zurich and Harvard before Eschenmoser and Woodward were finally able to announce its synthesis in 1965.

Eskola, Pentti Elias

(1883–1964)

FINNISH GEOLOGIST

The son of a farmer from Lellainen in Finland, Eskola (**es**-ko-la) was educated at the universities of Helsinki and Freiburg, Germany, where he obtained his PhD in 1915. He joined the faculty of Helsinki University in 1916, and became professor of geology in 1924, a position he held until his retirement in 1953.

Early in his career Eskola introduced the important notion of metamorphic facies. He pointed out (1915) that in any rock of metamorphic formation that has arrived at chemical equilibrium under conditions of constant temperature and pressure, the mineral composition is controlled only by its chemical composition. Initially he recognized five types of facies, namely, sanidine, hornfels, greenschist, amphibolite, and eclogite. By 1939 he had raised the number to eight while later workers have continued to add further types.

Espy, James Pollard

(1785–1860)

AMERICAN METEOROLOGIST

Espy was born in Washington County, Pennsylvania, and graduated from Transylvania University in Lexington, Kentucky, in 1808. He became principal of the Academy in Cumberland, Maryland (1812–17), and, after teaching mathematics and physics in Philadelphia, he became a full-time meteorologist in 1835. He was made state meteorologist in 1839 and from 1842 took up a national appointment, being attached at various times to the War Department, the Navy, and, after 1852, the Smithsonian, which eventually took over his network of observers and out of which the Weather Bureau was later to grow.

In addition to collecting and issuing basic data, Espy also wrote on questions of theoretical meteorology. He was the first to argue for the convectional theory of precipitation in which the ascent and cooling of moist air with the release of latent heat leads to condensation and the formation of clouds. Much of the evidence for this came from his "nephelescope," a device whereby he could simulate cloud behavior and measure cooling rates. Espy published, in 1841, his *Philosophy of Storms* and then became involved in a prolonged and bitter controversy with William Redfield on the cause and nature of storms. Here he argued that storms consisted of radially convergent winds with the air escaping up the middle. Although his views on storms were influential in Europe, Redfield and Elias Loomis were able to produce convincing contrary evidence.

Euclid

(*c.* 330 BC–*c.* 260 BC)

GREEK MATHEMATICIAN

A line is length without breadth.
—*Elements*

Euclid (**yoo**-klid) is one of the best known and most influential of classical Greek mathematicians but almost nothing is known about his life. He was a founder and member of the academy in Alexandria, and may have been a pupil of Plato in Athens. Despite his great fame Euclid was not one of the greatest of Greek mathematicians and not of the same caliber as Archimedes.

Euclid's most celebrated work is the *Elements*, which is primarily a treatise on geometry contained in 13 books. The influence of this work not only on the future development of geometry, mathematics, and science, but on the whole of Western thought is hard to exaggerate. Some idea of the importance that has been attached to the *Elements* is gained from the fact that there have probably been more commentaries written on it than on the Bible. The *Elements* systematized and organized the work of many previous Greek geometers, such as Theaetetus and Eudoxus, as well as containing many new discoveries that Euclid had made himself. Although mainly concerned with geometry it also deals with such topics as number theory and the theory of irrational quantities. One of the most celebrated number theoretic results is Euclid's proof that there are an infinite number of primes. The *Elements* is in many ways a synthesis and culmination of Greek mathematics. Euclid and Apollonius of Perga were the last Greek mathematicians of any distinction, and after their time Greek civilization as a whole soon became decadent and sterile.

Euclid's *Elements* owed its enormously high status to a number of reasons. The most influential single feature was Euclid's use of the axiomatic method whereby all the theorems were laid out as deductions from certain self-evident basic propositions or axioms in such a way that in each successive proof only propositions already proved or axioms were used. This became accepted as the paradigmatically rigorous way of setting out any body of knowledge, and attempts were made to apply it not just to mathematics, but to natural science, theology, and even philosophy and ethics.

However, despite being revered as an almost perfect example of rigorous thinking for almost 2,000 years there are considerable defects in Euclid's reasoning. A number of his proofs were found to contain mistakes, the status of the initial axioms themselves was increasingly considered to be problematic, and the definitions of such basic terms as "line" and "point" were found to be unsatisfactory. The most celebrated case is that of the parallel axiom, which states that there is only one straight line passing through a given point and parallel to a given straight line. The status of this axiom was long recognized as problematic, and many unsuccessful attempts were made to deduce it from the remaining axioms. The question was only settled in the 19th century when Janos Bolyai and Nicolai Lobachevski showed that it was perfectly possible to construct a consistent geometry in which Euclid's other axioms were true but in which the parallel axiom was false. This epoch-making discovery displaced Euclidean geometry from the privileged position it had occupied. The question of the relation of Euclid's geometry to the properties of physical space had to wait until the early 20th century for a full answer. Until then it was believed that Euclid's geometry gave a fully accurate description of physical space. No less a thinker than Immanuel Kant had thought that it was logically impossible for space to obey any other geometry. However when Albert Einstein developed his theory of relativity he found that the appropriate geometry for space was not Euclid's but that developed by Georg Riemann. It was subsequently experimentally verified that the geometry of space is indeed non-Euclidean.

In mathematical terms too, the discovery of non-Euclidean geometries was of great importance, since it led to a broadening of the conception of geometry and the development by such mathematicians as Felix Klein of many new geometries very different from Euclid's. It also made mathematicians scrutinize the logical structure of Euclid's geometry far more closely and in 1899 David Hilbert at last gave a definitively rigorous axiomatic treatment of geometry and made an exhaustive investigation of the relations of dependence and independence between the axioms, and of the consistency of the various possible geometries so produced.

Euclid wrote a number of other works besides the *Elements*, although many of them are now lost and known only through references to them by other classical authors. Those that do survive include *Data*, containing 94 propositions, *On Divisions*, and the *Optics*. One of his sayings has come down to us. When asked by Ptolemy I Soter, the reigning king of Egypt, if there was any quicker way to master geometry than by studying the *Elements* Euclid replied, "There is no royal road to geometry."

Eudoxus of Cnidus

(*c.* 400 BC–*c.* 350 BC)

GREEK ASTRONOMER AND MATHEMATICIAN

Born in Cnidus, which is now in Turkey, Eudoxus (yoo-**dok**-sus) is reported as having studied mathematics under Archytas, a Pythagorean. He also studied under Plato and in Egypt. Although none of his works have survived they are quoted extensively by Hipparchus. Eudoxus was the first astronomer who had a complete understanding of the celestial sphere. It is only this understanding that reveals the irregularities of the movements of the planets that must be taken into account in giving an accurate description of the heavens. For Eudoxus the Earth was at rest and around this center 27 concentric spheres rotated. The outermost sphere carried the fixed stars, each of the planets required four spheres, and the Sun and the Moon three each. All these spheres were necessary to account for the daily and annual relative motions of the heavenly bodies. He also described the constellations and the changes in the rising and setting of the fixed stars in the course of a year.

In mathematics, Eudoxus is thought to have contributed the theory of proportion to be found in Book V of Euclid – the importance of this being its applicability to irrational as well as rational numbers. The method of exhaustion in Book XII is also attributed to Eudoxus. This tackled in a mathematical way for the first time the difficult problem of calculating an area bounded by a curve.

Euler, Leonhard

(1707–1783)

SWISS MATHEMATICIAN

> Mathematicians have tried in vain to this day
> to discover some order in the sequence of
> prime numbers, and we have reason to be-
> lieve that it is a mystery into which the human
> mind will never penetrate.
> —Quoted by G. Simmons in *Calculus Gems*

Euler (**oi**-ler) was one of the outstanding figures of 18th-century mathematics, and also the most prolific. He was born at Basel in Switzerland
and studied at the university there, where he came to the notice of the
Bernoulli family; he became, in particular, a friend of Daniel Bernoulli.
Having completed his studies Euler applied unsuccessfuly for a post at
Basel University. He was encouraged by his friend Bernoulli to join him
at the St. Petersburg Academy of Science. Bernoulli obtained for Euler
a post in the medical section of the academy and in 1727 Euler left for
Russia to find on arriving that the empress had just died and that the future of the academy was doubtful. Fortunately it survived intact and he
managed to find his way into the mathematical section. In 1733 Bernoulli
left Russia to return to Switzerland and Euler was appointed to replace
him as head of the mathematical section of the academy. Euler was not
particularly happy in the highly repressive political climate and devoted
himself almost exclusively to his mathematics. In 1740 he eventually
left Russia to join Frederick the Great's Berlin Academy. He returned
to Russia in 1766 at the invitation of Catherine the Great, remaining
there for the rest of his life. He had lost the sight of his right eye through
observing the Sun during his first stay in Russia and shortly after returning there his blindness became total. However, such was his facility
for mental calculation and the power of his memory that this did not af-
fect his mathematical creativity.

Euler contributed to almost all areas of mathematics, and did equally
important work in both pure and applied mathematics. One of his most
significant contributions was to the development of analysis. Although
he was working before the development of modern standards of rigor by
such mathematicians as Karl Friedrich Gauss and Augustin Cauchy

and thus lacked a rigorous treatment of such key topics as convergence, nonetheless his work in analysis constitutes a major advance over previous work in the area. He wrote three treatises on different aspects of analysis, which together collect, systematize, and develop what the mathematicians of the 17th century had achieved. These treatises became important and influential textbooks. It is worth noting that unlike some great mathematicians, such as Gauss, Euler was a highly successful and effective teacher. It is a measure of his intuitive insight into mathematics that even though he did lack truly rigorous analytical techniques he was still able to arrive at so many novel and important results. His phenomenal ability for calculation came to his aid here, for he frequently arrived at results, for example about infinite series, by induction from a great many calculations and gave only a highly dubious proof, leaving future mathematicians to give properly rigorous proofs of results that were indeed quite correct.

Outside analysis Euler made extremely important contributions both to the calculus of variations and mechanics. Mechanics was transformed by his treatment of it in his treatise of 1736. In essence he transformed the subject into one to which the full resources of analytical techniques could be applied. In doing so he paved the way for the work of mathematicians such as Joseph Lagrange.

Euler put his expertise in mechanics to practical use in his work on the three-body problem. He was interested in this problem because he wished to investigate the motion of the Moon. He published his first lunar-motion theory in 1753 and then a second theory in 1772. Euler was able to invent methods of approximating solutions that were accurate enough to be of practical use in navigation. Here his prodigious ability as a sheer calculator came into its own.

In addition to these pieces of work Euler made notable contributions to number theory and geometry. Numerous theorems and methods are named for him.

Euler-Chelpin, Hans Karl August Simon von

(1873–1964)

GERMAN–SWEDISH BIOCHEMIST

Euler-Chelpin (oi-ler-**kel**-pin) was born at Augsburg in Germany and educated at the universities of Berlin, Strasbourg, and Göttingen and at the Pasteur Institute. In 1898 he moved to Sweden, being appointed to the staff of the University of Stockholm, where in 1906 he became professor of general and inorganic chemistry. In 1929 he also became director of the Institute of Biochemistry where he remained until his retirement in 1941. Although he became a Swedish citizen in 1902 he served Germany in both world wars.

In 1904 important work by Arthur Harden had shown that enzymes contain an easily removable nonprotein part, a coenzyme. In 1923 Euler-Chelpin worked out the structure of the yeast coenzyme. He showed that the molecule is made up from a nucleotide similar to that found in nucleic acid. It was named diphosphopyridine nucleotide (now known as NAD).

Euler-Chelpin shared the 1929 Nobel Prize for chemistry with Harden for this work. His son, Ulf von Euler, was also a Nobel prizewinner.

Eustachio, Bartolommeo

(c. 1524–1574)

ITALIAN ANATOMIST

The son of a physician from San Severino in Italy, Eustachio (ay-oo-stah-kyoh) received a sound humanist education acquiring a good knowledge of Latin, Greek, and Arabic. In the early 1540s he was appointed physician to the duke of Urbino and, from 1547, served the duke's brother, Cardinal Rovere, with whom he moved to Rome in 1549. While there he also served from 1562 as professor of anatomy at the Sapienza or Papal College.

In 1564 he collected some of his earlier work in his *Opuscula anatomica* (Anatomical Works). It contains his *De auditus organis* (On the Auditory Organs), which describes the eustachian tubes connecting the middle ear to the pharynx and named in his honor (although these were first described by Alcmaeon). It also contained the *De renum structura* (On the Structure of the Kidney), in which he published the first description of the adrenal glands.

Eustachio was not in fact as influential an anatomist as he might have been for his anatomical plates, prepared for a text never completed, were lost and only rediscovered in the early 18th century. They were finally published as the *Tabulae anatomica* in 1714 and republished with full notes by Bernhard Albinus in 1744. It has been claimed that the plates manifest an originality equaled only by Andreas Vesalius and Leonardo da Vinci and that Eustachio's plates of the sympathetic nervous system are the best yet produced.

Evans, Robley Dunglison

(1907–)

AMERICAN PHYSICIST

Born in University Place, Nebraska, Evans was educated at the California Institute of Technology where he obtained his PhD in 1932. He went to the Massachusetts Institute of Technology in 1934 and was appointed professor of physics there in 1945.

In 1940 Evans suggested that radioactive potassium–40 could be of use in geologic dating. It is widespread in the Earth's crust and has an exceptionally long halflife of over a thousand million years. It decays to the stable isotope argon–40 and determination of the ratio of ^{40}K to ^{40}Ar allows estimations of the age of potassium-bearing rocks ranging from 100,000 to about 10 million years. The technique proved to be particularly valuable as it permitted accurate dating beyond the limits of Willard Libby's carbon–14 technique.

Everett III, Hugh

(1930–82)

AMERICAN PHYSICIST

Everett was a doctoral pupil of John Wheeler in the 1950s at Princeton. In 1957 he published a famous paper on the foundations of quantum mechanics describing what has become known as the "many worlds" interpretation. The paper was entitled *Relative State Formulation of Quantum Mechanics*.

The traditional Copenhagen interpretation of quantum mechanics applied only to the submicroscopic world. Everett broke away from this tradition and attempted to apply quantum mechanics to the universe. He established a universal wave function that could be applied to both microscopic entities and macroscopic observers. As a consequence, there is no collapse of the wave function and quantum paradoxes, such as Schrödinger's cat, are avoided.

This approach, however, is not without paradoxical conclusions of its own. In Everett's formulation, the result of a measurement is to split the universe into as many ways as to allow all possible outcomes of the measurement. Thus if an observer were to check the outcome of a die throw, the universe would split into six copies with each one containing one of the six possible outcomes of the throw. Everett proposed that each outcome is realized in a number of parallel universes between which there is no communication.

While Everett's work has inevitably been taken up by many science fiction writers, it has also been taken seriously by other scientists. Gell-Mann, for example, has tried to develop a version of quantum theory that eliminates the role of the observer, in the manner of Everett, but reduces the idea of "many worlds" to one of possible histories of the universe to which a probability value can be assigned.

Ewing, Sir James Alfred

(1855–1935)

BRITISH PHYSICIST

The son of a minister of the Free Church of Scotland, Ewing was educated at the University of Edinburgh where he studied engineering. He served as professor of engineering at the Imperial University, Tokyo, from 1878 until 1883 when he returned to Scotland to a similar post at the University of Dundee. In 1890 he was appointed professor of applied mechanics at Cambridge University, but in 1903 moved into higher levels of administration, first as director of naval education and from 1916 until his retirement in 1929 as principal and vice-chancellor of Edinburgh University.

In Japan he worked on problems in seismology and in 1883 published *Treatise on Earthquake Measurement*. However, his most notable achievement as a physicist was his work on hysteresis, first described by him in 1881. Hysteresis is an effect in which there are two properties, M and N, such that cyclic changes of N cause cyclic variations of M. If the changes of M lag behind those of N, there is hysteresis in the relation of M to N. Ewing came across the phenomena when working on the effects of stress on the thermoelectric properties of a wire. Hysteresis effects were later shown to apply to many aspects of the behavior of materials, in particular in magnetization.

Ewing was put in charge of the cryptologists at the Admiralty from 1914 to 1916. He described his work there in his book *The Man in Room 40* (1939).

Ewing, William Maurice

(1906–1974)

AMERICAN OCEANOGRAPHER

Ewing was born at Lockney in Texas and educated at the Rice Institute, Houston, obtaining his PhD in 1931. He taught at Lehigh University, Pennsylvania from 1934 until moving in 1944 to Columbia University, New York, where he organized the new Lamont Geological Observatory into one of the most important research institutions in the world.

Ewing pioneered seismic techniques to obtain basic data on the ocean floors. He was able to establish that the Earth's crust below the oceans is only about 3–5 miles (5–8 km) thick while the corresponding continental crust averages 25 miles (40 km).

Although the Mid-Atlantic Ridge had been discovered when cables were laid across the Atlantic, its dimensions were unsuspected. In 1956 Ewing and his colleagues were able to show that the ridge constituted a mountain range extending throughout the oceans of the world and was some 40,000 miles (64,000 km) long. In 1957, working with Marie Tharp and Bruce Heezen, he revealed that the ridge was divided by a central rift, which was in places twice as deep and wide as the Grand Canyon.

His group found that the oceanic sediment, expected to be about 10,000 feet (3,000 m) thick, was nonexistent on or within about 30 miles (50 km) of the ridge. Beyond this it had a thickness of about 130 feet (40 m) – much less than the depth of the corresponding continental sediment. All this seemed to be consistent with the new sea-floor spreading hypothesis of Harry H. Hess. Ewing was however reluctant to support it until Frederick Vine and Drummond H. Matthews showed how the magnetic reversals discovered by B. Brunhes in 1909 could be used to test the theory.

Ewing also proposed, with William Donn, a mechanism to explain the periodic ice ages. If the Arctic waters were icefree and open to warm currents this source of water vapor would produce greater accumulations of snowfall. This would increase the Earth's reflectivity and reduce the amount of solar radiation absorbed. Temperatures would fall and glaciers move south, but with the freezing of the Arctic seas the supply of water vapor would be cut off and the ice sheets would retreat. This would cause an increase in solar radiation absorbed and the cycle would begin again. No hard evidence has yet been found in support of the theory.

Ewins, Arthur James

(1882–1957)

BRITISH PHARMACEUTICAL CHEMIST

Ewins was born in Norwood on the outskirts of London and went straight from school to the brilliant team of researchers at the Wellcome Physiological Research Laboratories at Beckenham in Kent. Here he worked on alkaloids with George Barger and in 1914, with Henry Dale, isolated the important neurotransmitter acetylcholine from ergot. Following wartime experience in manufacturing arsenicals with the Medical Research Council, he became head of research with the pharmaceutical manufacturers May and Baker, where he remained until his retirement in 1952. Under Ewins in 1939, the team produced sulfapyridine, one of the most important of the new sulfonamide drugs. An important later discovery was the antiprotozoal drug pentamidine (1948).

Eyde, Samuel

(1866–1940)

NORWEGIAN ENGINEER AND INDUSTRIALIST

Born in Arendal in Norway, Eyde (Id) trained as a civil engineer in Berlin. Up until 1900 he worked in Germany and also on harbor and railroad-station projects in Scandinavia. Here he became interested in industrial electrochemical processes – a subject of some potential in Scandinavia because of the availability of cheap hydroelectric power.

In 1901 Eyde met Kristian Birkeland with whom he developed a process (1903) for reacting atmospheric nitrogen with oxygen in an electric arc. Processes in which nitrogen in the atmosphere is "fixed" in nitrogen compounds are of immense importance in the production of nitrogenous fertilizers for agriculture. The main method is the catalytic reaction with hydrogen developed by Fritz Haber. The *Birkeland–Eyde process*, which gives nitrogen oxides, needed plentiful and cheap supplies of electricity, leading to a significant growth in the production of hydroelectric power. In 1900 Norway had an output of little more than 100,000 kilowatts; by 1905 production had jumped to 850,000 kilowatts. In the same year Birkeland started the company Norsk Hydro-Elektrisk Kvaelstof, with the help of French capital, to produce fertilizers by the Birkeland–Eyde process. As a result of this, Norway's export of chemicals was to treble before the start of World War I. Eyde retired from the firm in 1917. As well as his industrial interests, he was also a member of the Norwegian parliament.

Eyring, Henry

(1901–1981)

MEXICAN–AMERICAN PHYSICAL
AND THEORETICAL CHEMIST

Eyring, a grandson of American missionaries who had become Mexican citizens, was born at Colonia Juarez in Mexico. He thus first came to America in 1912 as a Mexican citizen and did not take American citizenship until 1935. He was educated at the University of Arizona and the University of California, where he obtained his PhD in 1927. He then held a number of junior appointments before joining the Princeton faculty in 1931, becoming professor of chemistry there in 1938. Eyring moved to a similar chair at the University of Utah, holding the post until his retirement in 1966.

Eyring, the author of 9 books and over 600 papers, was as creative a chemist as he was productive. His main work was probably in the field of chemical kinetics with his transition-state theory. Since the time of Sven Arrhenius it had been appreciated that the rate constant of a chemical reaction depended on temperature according to an equation of the form:

$$k = Ae^{-E/RT}$$

The constant A is the frequency factor of the reaction; E_A is the activation energy. The values of A and E_A can be found experimentally for given reactions. Eyring's contribution to the field was to develop a theory capable of predicting reaction rates.

In a reaction, the atoms move – i.e., molecules break and new molecules form. If the potential energy of a set of atoms is plotted against the distances between atoms for chosen arrangements, the result is a surface. Positions of low energy on the surface correspond to molecules; a reaction can be thought of as a change from a low-energy point, over a higher energy barrier, to another low-energy position.

A. Marcelin, in 1915, had shown that reactions could be represented in this way, and in 1928 Fritz London pointed out that it was possible to calculate potential surfaces using quantum mechanics. Eyring, with

Michael Polyani, first calculated such a surface (1929–30) for three hydrogen atoms and Eyring later went on to calculate the potential surfaces for a number of reactions. The activation energy of the reaction is the energy barrier that the system must surmount.

Eyring later (1935) showed how to calculate the frequency factor (A). He assumed that the configuration of atoms at the top of the energy barrier – the "activated complex" – could be treated as a normal molecule except for a vibrational motion in the direction of the reaction path. Assuming that the activated complex was in equilibrium with the reactants and applying statistical mechanics, Eyring derived a general expression for reaction rate. Eyring's theory, called absolute-rate theory, is described in his book (with Samuel Glasstone and Keith J. Laidler) *The Theory of Rate Processes* (1941). It can also be applied to other processes, such as viscosity and diffusion.

Eyring also worked on the theory of the liquid state and made contributions in molecular biology.

Fabre, Jean Henri

(1823–1915)

FRENCH ENTOMOLOGIST

> History...records the names of royal bastards, but cannot tell us the origin of wheat.
> —*Souvenirs entomologiques* (1879–1907; Entomological Recollections)

> If there is one vegetable which is God-given, it is the haricot bean.
> —As above

Although world famous for his detailed studies of insect habits and life histories, Fabre (**fah**-bre) did not attain stature as a field entomologist until late in his life, his earlier years being spent under great difficulty and comparative poverty. Described by Darwin, with whom he corresponded, as "an inimitable observer," Fabre's best-known entomological observations were largely made in his native Provence and the Rhône valley. His enthusiasm for his subject had been stimulated by reading an essay on the habits of the *Cerceris* wasp, which prompted Fabre to make his own detailed observations of these and other parasitic wasps, as well as many other insect groups. His descriptions of their development and behavior, written in a clear simple style, still stand as models of accurate observation. Fabre's earliest entomological observations appeared in *Annales des sciences naturelles* (Annals of the Natural Sciences), but his major publication is the classic *Souvenirs entomologiques* (10 vols. 1879–1907; Entomological Recollections).

Fabricius, David

(1564–1617)

GERMAN ASTRONOMER

Fabricius (fah-**bree**-tsee-uus), who was born in Essen, now in Germany, was a clergyman and amateur astronomer. He engaged in a prolonged correspondence with Johannes Kepler but remained unconvinced by Kepler's Copernican arguments. In 1596 he noticed the variability of the star Omicron Ceti and called it "Mira" (the marvelous). Fabricius was murdered by one of his parishioners. His son Johannes Fabricius was also an astronomer and was one of the discoverers of sunspots.

Fabricius ab Aquapendente, Hieronymus

(1537–1619)

ITALIAN ANATOMIST AND EMBRYOLOGIST

Fabricius (fa-**brish**-ee-us) was born at Aquapendente in Italy and educated at the University of Padua where he studied under Gabriel Fallopius, succeeding him, in 1565, as professor of anatomy.

As an anatomist his most significant work was his *De venarum ostiolis* (1603; On the Valves of the Veins), which contains a clear and detailed description of the venous system and which exercised a considerable influence on his most famous pupil, William Harvey. Fabricius himself entertained no such idea as the circulation of the blood, explaining the role of the valves as retarding the blood flow, thus allowing the tissues to absorb necessary nutriment.

He spent much time observing the development of the chick embryo and published two works *De formato foetu* (1600; On the Formation of the Fetus) and *De formatione ovi et pulli* (1612; On the Development of the Egg and the Chick). These were hailed as elevating embryology into an independent science but they still contain many incorrect assumptions.

Thus for Fabricius semen did not enter the egg but rather initiated the process of generation from a distance in some mysterious way. He also made a now totally unfamiliar distinction between what nourishes and what produces the embryo. Thus he believed both the yolk and albumen merely nourished the embryo. Having eliminated the sperm, yolk, and albumen, Fabricius claimed that the chalaza – the spiral threads holding the yolk in position – produces the chick.

It was while engaged upon this work that he discovered and described the bursa of Fabricius. This is a small pouch in the oviduct of the hen, which Fabricius thought to be a store for semen. In the 1950s however the young research student B. Glick showed that this obscure organ plays a key role in the immune system of chickens, and by implication of humans who must possess a comparable system.

Fahrenheit, (Gabriel) Daniel

(1686–1736)

GERMAN PHYSICIST

Possibly owing to a business failure, Fahrenheit (**fah**-ren-hIt) emigrated to Amsterdam from his native Danzig (now Gdańsk in Poland) to become a glass blower and instrument maker. He specialized in the making of meteorological instruments, and proceeded to develop a reliable and accurate thermometer. Galileo had invented the thermometer in about 1600, using changes in air volume as an indicator. Since the volume of air also varied considerably with changes in atmospheric pressure liquids of various kinds were quickly substituted. Fahrenheit was the first to use mercury in 1714. He fixed his zero point by using the freezing point of a mixture of ice and salt as this gave him the lowest temperature he could reach. His other fixed point was taken from the temperature of the human body, which he put at 96°. Given these two fixed points the freezing and boiling points of water then work out at the familiar 32° and 212°. One advantage of the system is that, for most ordinary purposes, negative degrees are rarely needed.

Using his thermometer, Fahrenheit measured the boiling point of various liquids and found that each had a characteristic boiling point, which changed with changes in atmospheric pressure.

Fairbank, William

(1917–1989)

AMERICAN PHYSICIST

Fairbank was born at Minneapolis in Minnesota and educated at Whitman College, Walla Walla, Washington, and at the University of Washington. He gained his PhD at Yale in 1948. He spent the war years at the Radiation Laboratory of the Massachusetts Institute of Technology. After working at Amherst, Maryland (1947–52) and Duke University, North Carolina (1952–59), Fairbank was appointed professor of physics at Stanford, a post he held until his death from a heart attack in 1989.

In 1977, Fairbank, in collaboration with George Larue, claimed to have experimental evidence for the existence of a quark. The concept of quarks, with an electric charge –1/3 or +2/3 the electron charge, had been proposed by Murray Gell-Mann in 1963 to explain the behavior of hadrons. It was known that it would be unlikely that quarks could be produced at the energies available in particle accelerators. However, it was possible that some might be created in the atmosphere as a result of high-energy cosmic rays. A number of physicists set up ingenious sensitive experiments to "hunt the quark."

Fairbank's technique was a much more sensitive and sophisticated version of Robert Millikan's oil-drop experiment for measuring the charge of the electron. A small sphere (0.25 millimeter diameter) of niobium was suspended between metal plates at a temperature close to absolute zero. The charge on the sphere could be measured by the electric field between the plates.

When Fairbank examined his results he found that in the case of one ball there was "a nonzero residual change of magnitude –0.37 ± 0.03." At first, Fairbank warned, the results did not necessarily imply the presence of a quark as there could well be spurious charge forces present. Consequently, Fairbank spent a good deal of time eliminating these and numerous other possible distortions from his experimental setup.

Theorists were suspicious of Fairbank's work because free quarks are thought to be impossible to produce – the doctrine of "quark confinement." Despite this, Fairbank announced in 1979 that, using modified apparatus, he had detected a second particle with a fractional charge.

While no one has managed to reproduce Fairbank's experiments, he was sufficiently respected as a careful and skillful experimentalist for his work to be taken seriously. Consequently, for some particle physicists at least, the issue of quark confinement remains an open question.

Fajans, Kasimir

(1887–1975)

POLISH–AMERICAN PHYSICAL CHEMIST

Fajans (**fah**-yahns) was born in the Polish capital of Warsaw and gained his doctorate at Heidelberg (1909). He was professor of physical chemistry at Munich (1925–35) before emigrating to America in 1936. He was a member of the Faculty of the University of Michigan (1936–57) and emeritus professor from 1957.

He is best known for *Fajan's laws* (1913), which state that elements emitting alpha particles decrease in atomic number by two while those undergoing beta emission gain in atomic number by one. These were independently discovered by Frederick Soddy. In 1917 Fajans discovered, with Otto Gohring, uranium X_2 – a form of the element protactinium ^{234}Pr.

Fallopius, Gabriel

(1523–1562)

ITALIAN ANATOMIST

Fallopius (fa-**loh**-pee-us) was born in Modena, Italy. He originally intended to enter the Church and served as a canon in his native city for some time before turning to the study of medicine at Ferrara and Padua where he was a pupil of the great Andreas Vesalius. He held the chair of anatomy at the University of Pisa from 1548 until 1551 when he moved to a similar post at the University of Padua, remaining there until his early death at the age of 39.

On the strength of his masterpiece *Observationes anatomicae* (1561; Anatomical Observations) he has been described as a better and more accurate anatomist than his teacher, Vesalius. His main innovations were in the anatomy of the skull and the generative system. In the former area he introduced the terms cochlea and labyrinth, going on to give a clear account of the auditory system.

In his account of the reproductive system he described the clitoris and introduced the term "vagina" into anatomy. He is mainly remembered today, however, for his description of the eponymous fallopian tubes. The tubes, connecting the uterus and the ovaries, were described by him as resembling at their extremity a "brass trumpet" (tuba). This somehow became mistranslated into English as tube. It was many years before their function was understood.

Faraday, Michael

(1791–1867)

BRITISH PHYSICIST AND CHEMIST

Mr. Faraday is not only a man of profound chemical and physical science (which all Europe knows), but a very respectable lecturer. He speaks with ease and freedom, but not with a gossiping, unequal tone, alternately inaudible and bawling, as some very learned professors do; he delivers himself with clearness, precision, and ability.
—Friedrich Ludwig Georg von Raumer in *Cyclopedia of Literary and Scientific Anecdote* (19th century)

Faraday's father was a blacksmith who suffered from poor health and could only work irregularly. Faraday, who was born in Newington, England, knew real poverty as a child and his education was limited for he left school at the age of 13. He began work for a bookseller and binder in 1804 and was apprenticed the following year. His interest in science seems to have been aroused by his reading the 127-page entry on electricity in an Encyclopaedia Britannica he was binding and this stimulated him to buy the ingredients to make a Leyden jar and to perform some simple experiments. He joined the City Philosophical Society, which he attended regularly, broadening his intellectual background still further. The turning point in his life came when he attended some lectures by Humphry Davy at the Royal Institution in 1812. He took very full notes of these lectures, which he bound himself.

By now he was no longer satisfied with his amateur experiments and evening lectures and wanted desperately to have a full-time career in science. He wrote to the President of the Royal Society, Joseph Banks, asking for his help in obtaining any post but received no reply. Faraday now had a little luck. Davy had had an accident and needed some temporary assistance. Faraday's name was mentioned and proved acceptable. While working with Davy he showed him the lecture notes he had taken and bound. When a little later, in 1813, a vacancy for a laboratory assistant arose, Davy remembered the serious young man and hired him at a salary of a guinea a week (less than Faraday had been earning as a bookbinder).

Faraday was to spend the rest of his working life at the Royal Institution, from which he finally resigned in 1861. In 1815 he was promoted to the post of assistant and superintendent of the apparatus of the laboratory and meteorological collection. In 1825 he was made director of the laboratory and, in 1833, he was elected to the newly endowed Fullerian Professorship of Chemistry at the Royal Institution. He had earlier turned down the offer of the chair of chemistry at University College, London, in 1827.

The paucity of the salary paid him was made up by Faraday with consultancy fees and a part-time lectureship he held at the Royal Military Academy, Woolwich. These extra sources took up his time and in 1831, when he was working as hard as he could on his electrical experiments, he gave up all his consultancies. This left him in some financial difficulties and moves were made to arrange for a government pension. He called on the prime minister of the day, Lord Melbourne, who made some sneering remark about such pensions being, in his view, a "gross humbug." This was enough to make Faraday refuse the pension. In fact, Faraday was one of nature's great refusers. Apart from the pension and the chair at University College, he also refused a knighthood and, what must surely be a record, the presidency of the Royal Society, not once, but twice. Faraday also had strong views on awards – "I have always felt that there is something degrading in offering rewards for intellectual exertion, and that societies or academies, or even kings and emperors, should mingle in the matter does not remove the degradation." He had become a fellow of the Royal Society in 1824 but not without some friction between himself and the president, Davy. He was asked to withdraw his application by Davy. Just why Davy behaved in this way is not clear. Some have seen it as jealousy by Davy of someone whose talents so clearly surpassed his own. There is no evidence of this but it is reasonably clear that when Faraday insisted on going ahead with his application Davy voted against him.

Faraday's financial problems were solved when, in 1835, Melbourne apologized, enabling him to accept the pension. After his labors of the 1830s he suffered some kind of breakdown in 1841 and went into the country to rest. Just what was wrong is not known; he wrote in 1842 that he could see no visitors because of "ill health connected with my head." For two years he did no work at all until in 1844 he seemed to be able to resume his experiments. Faraday continued to work but by the 1850s his creativity was in decline. He gave his last childrens' lectures at the Royal Institution in 1860 and resigned from it the following year, taking up residence in a house at Hampton Court made available to him by Prince Albert in 1858.

Faraday's first real successes were made in chemistry. In 1823 he unwittingly liquefied chlorine. He was simply heating a chlorine compound in a sealed tube and noticed the formation of some droplets at the cold end. He realized that this was the result of both temperature and pressure and on and off over the years applied the method to other gases. In 1825 he discovered benzene (C_6H_6) when asked to examine the residue collecting in cylinders of illuminating gas; he called the new compound "bicarburet of hydrogen" because he took its formula to be C_2H. As a working chemist Faraday was one of the best analysts of his day. All his working life he was working and publishing as a chemist but in 1820 he also turned to a new field that was to dominate his life.

Faraday had begun by accepting the view that electricity is composed of two fluids. It was common in the 18th century to see such phenomena as light, heat, magnetism, and electricity to be the result of weightless fluids. In 1820 Hans Christian Oersted made a most surprising discovery: he had found that a wire carrying a current is capable of deflecting a compass needle; the direction in which the needle turned depended on whether the wire was under or over the needle and the direction in which the current was flowing. André Marie Ampère found that two parallel wires attract each other if the current in each is traveling in the same direction but repel each other if the currents are moving in opposite directions. Finally François Arago discovered that a copper disk rotating freely on its own axis would produce rotation in a compass needle suspended over it.

These phenomena were difficult to fit into fluid theories of electricity and magnetism. They enabled Faraday to make his first important discovery in 1821, that of electromagnetic rotation. A magnet was placed upright in a tube of mercury and secured firmly at the bottom with the pole of the magnet above the surface. A wire dipping into the mercury but free to rotate was suspended over the pole. When a current was passed through the mercury and through the wire, the wire rotated around the magnet. If the wire was secured and the magnet allowed to move, then the current caused the magnet to rotate. The first electric motor had been constructed.

When Faraday published his results they were to cause him much distress. William Wollaston had spoken of the possibility of such rotation and many concluded that Faraday had stolen his ideas. Faraday was only too aware of the stories about him but found there was little he could do about them. It may well have been this that Davy thought disqualified him from membership of the Royal Society.

In any case it was not really electromagnetic rotation that interested Faraday. All the new results involved the production of a magnetic force by an electric current and Faraday, with many others, was sure that it should also be possible to induce an electric current by magnetic action. He tried intermittently for ten years without success until in 1832 he hit upon an apparatus in which an iron ring was wound with two quite separate coils of wire. One was connected to a voltaic cell; the other to a simple galvanometer. He showed that on making and breaking the current in the cell circuit, the galvanometer momentarily registered the presence of a current in its circuit. The following few months were some of the most active of his life. He showed that the same results can be obtained without a battery: a magnet moved in and out of a coil of wire produced a current. A steady current could be produced by rotating a copper disk between the poles of a powerful magnet. His results were published in his *Experimental Researches in Electricity, first series* (1831).

Faraday found this deeply satisfying for it reinforced one of his strongest convictions about nature "that the various forms under which the forces of matter are made manifest have one common origin." That electricity and magnetism could interact made this view more plausible. At the time it was by no means clear that the various types of electricity – static, voltaic, animal, magnetic, and thermoelectric – were the same and Faraday spent the period 1833–34 on this problem, publishing his results in the third series of his *Experimental Researches*.

Faraday had also continued the work of Davy on electrolysis – i.e., on the chemical reaction produced by passing an electric current through a liquid. He applied his ideas on the quantity of electricity to this chemical effect and produced what are now known as *Faraday's laws of electrolysis*. By careful analysis he showed that the chemical action of a current is constant for a constant quantity of electricity. This was his first law, that equal amounts of electricity produce equal amounts of decomposition. In the second law he found that the quantities of different substances deposited on the electrode by the passage of the same quantity of electricity were proportional to their equivalent weights.

In his explanations of magnetic and electrical phenomena Faraday did not use the fluid theories of the time. Instead he introduced the concept of lines of force (or tension) through a body or through space. (A similar earlier idea had been put forward by R. J. Boscovich with his picture of point atoms surrounded by shells of force.) Thus Faraday saw the connection between electrical and magnetic effects as vibrations of electrical lines communicated to magnetic lines. His experiments on induction were described in terms of the cutting of magnetic lines of force, which induces the electrical current. He explained electrical induction in dielectrics by the strain in "tubes of induction" – and electrolysis was complete breakdown under such strain.

Faraday was no mathematician, relying instead on his wonderful experimental skill and his imagination. His lines of force were taken up by others more skillful mathematically. In the latter half of the century Clerk Maxwell developed Faraday's ideas into a rigorous and powerful theory, creating an orthodoxy in physics that lasted until the time of Einstein. Faraday's greatness rests in his courage and insight in rejecting the traditional physics and creating an entirely new one. Few can compete with Faraday at the level of originality.

One further effect discovered by Faraday lay in optics. His discovery of *Faraday rotation* in 1845 was one that gave him pleasure for it seemed to be further evidence for the unity of nature by showing that "magnetic force and light were proved to have a relation to each other." Here, he showed that if polarized light is passed through a transparent medium in a magnetic field its plane of polarization will be rotated.

Not the least of Faraday's achievements was as a lecturer and popularizer of science. In 1826 he started the famous Christmas lectures to children at the Royal Institution in London and gave 19 of these lecture courses. For most only the notes exist but a couple of lectures were taken down in shorthand and later published: *The Chemical History of a Candle* and *Lectures on Various Forces of Matter*. The children's Christmas lectures still continue to be given every year by eminent scientists.

Farman, Joe

(1930–)

BRITISH ATMOSPHERIC CHEMIST

Farman has been engaged in the study of the Antarctic atmosphere since 1957, working in recent years for the British Antarctic Survey based in Cambridge, England. The Survey operates five Antarctic stations.

One of the tasks of Farman's team has been to measure Antarctic ozone levels. This is normally done with a spectrophotometer recording the amount of ultraviolet radiation (UV) reaching the Earth's surface. As ozone absorbs UV, the less ozone in the atmosphere, the greater the amount of UV reaching the Earth. The ozone level was measured in Dobson units (DU) and normally had a value of about 400 DUs (after the designer of the spectrophotometer, G. M. Dobson). In 1982 Farman first noted a very low reading of 130 DUs. Initially he merely assumed that his instruments were breaking down. Further, ozone levels were known to fluctuate widely and shortlived, unusual levels, both high and low, had been known before. And as nothing unusual had been detected by the Nimbus satellite, Farman suspected his readings were, in some unknown way, unreliable.

Nonetheless new equipment was installed and when similar low levels were recorded in the following season Farman began to take the matter seriously. An examination of past records revealed that there had been a decline in ozone levels since 1977. He further checked the readings by organizing measurements at another research station 1,000 miles away.

By the end of the 1984 season Farman was convinced that he had detected a persistent seasonal fall in ozone Antarctic levels of about 40%. Soon after the southern winter's end in October, the polar vortex collapses and ozone levels rise as air is drawn in from elsewhere. A check on the Nimbus satellite revealed that it was programmed to ignore readings that varied from the average by more than a third.

Farman was aware of the work of Rowland and began to suspect that ozone depletion was connected with atmospheric CFCs. He published his results in *Nature* in May 1985. All subsequent work, whether by Farman or others, has confirmed his initial measurements of 1982.

Fechner, Gustav Theodor

(1801–1887)

GERMAN PHYSICIST AND PSYCHOLOGIST

Fechner (**fek**-ner), who was born at Gross-Särchen in Germany, studied medicine at the University of Leipzig; after graduating, however, his interest turned toward physics. He did some research on the galvanic battery and, on the strength of this, was appointed professor of physics at Leipzig in 1834. However, partial blindness, caused by overlong study of the Sun, and mental illness forced him to resign five years later.

It was after his recovery that he started trying to put psychology on a scientific basis. He studied the relationship between the intensities of external stimulae and subjective sensations, and elaborated Ernst Weber's work to develop the *Weber–Fechner law* governing this connection. This work, published in 1860, founded the science of psychophysics.

Fechner also became interested in spiritualism, like many scientists of his day, and wrote much on mystical and philosophical subjects. He also wrote satirical poems under the pseudonym of Dr. Mises.

Fehling, Hermann Christian von

(1812–1885)

GERMAN ORGANIC CHEMIST

Fehling (**fay**-ling), who was born in Lübeck, now in Germany, gained his doctorate at Heidelberg in 1837 and studied with Justus von Liebig at Giessen. He was professor of chemistry at the polytechnic school at Stuttgart from 1839 to 1882.

Fehling did much work in organic chemistry, including the preparation and hydrolysis of benzonitrile and the discovery of succinosuccinic ester. However, he is best known for his invention of *Fehling's solution*, used as a test for aldehydes and reducing sugars (e.g., glucose, fructose, lactose). It consists of a solution of copper(II) sulfate (Fehling's I) and an alkaline solution of a tartaric acid salt (Fehling's II). The solutions are boiled with the test material and a positive result is a brick-red precipitate (insoluble copper(I) oxide), formed by the reduction of copper(II) sulfate.

Feigenbaum, Edward Albert

(1936–   )

AMERICAN COMPUTER SCIENTIST

Born at Weehawken, New Jersey, Feigenbaum (**fI**-gen-bowm) first studied electrical engineering at Carnegie Institute of Technology, Pittsburgh; there, under the influence of Herbert Simon, his interests were diverted into the newly emerging field of artificial intelligence (AI). Consequently after completing his PhD in 1960 at Carnegie in cognitive psychology, Feigenbaum spent the period from 1960 to 1964 at the University of California, Berkeley, before being appointed professor of computer science at Stanford University in 1965.

Feigenbaum was an early pioneer in the expert-systems approach to AI. Workers like Allan Newell had tried to provide computers with a general understanding that would enable them to tackle a wide variety of problems. Their ambitions, however, remained unfulfilled. Feigenbaum opted for a more specialized alternative. "We found," he commented, "it was better to be knowledgeable than smart"; to build computers, that is, capable of playing high-level chess, but unable to understand the rules of tick-tack-toe.

Against this background Feigenbaum set out to program a computer to be able, on the basis of data from mass spectrometers and elsewhere, to identify organic compounds. By 1971 he had developed DENDRAL which was capable of formulating hypotheses about molecular structure, and then testing the hypothesis against further data. It finally offered a list of compounds ranked in terms of decreasing likelihood.

DENDRAL has proved to be remarkably successful and, allowing for later improvements and refinements, is recognized to be almost as proficient as a human chemist.

Fermat, Pierre de

(1601–1665)

FRENCH MATHEMATICIAN AND PHYSICIST

> It cannot be denied that he [Fermat] has had many exceptional ideas, and that he is a highly intelligent man. For my part, however, I have always been taught to take a broad overview of things, in order to be able to deduce from them general rules, which might be applicable elsewhere.
>
> —René Descartes

Fermat (fer-**mah**) was one of the leading mathematicians of the early 17th century although not a professional mathematician. Born at Beaumont-de-Lomagne in France, he studied law and spent his working life as a magistrate in the small provincial town of Castres. Although mathematics was only a spare-time activity, Fermat was an extremely creative and original mathematician who opened up whole new fields of enquiry.

Fermat's work in algebra built on and greatly developed the then new theory of equations, which had been largely founded by François Viète. With Pascal, Fermat stands as one of the founders of the mathematical theory of probability. In his work on methods of finding tangents to curves and their maxima and minima he anticipated some of the central concepts of Isaac Newton's and Gottfried Leibniz's differential calculus.

Another area of mathematics that Fermat played a major role in founding, independently of René Descartes, was analytical geometry. This work led to violent controversies over questions of priority with Descartes. Nor were Fermat's disagreements with Descartes limited to mathematics. Descartes had produced a major treatise on optics – the *Dioptrics* – which Fermat greatly disliked. He particularly objected to Descartes's attempt to reach conclusions about the physical sciences by purely *a priori* rationalistic reasoning without due regard for empirical observation. By contrast Fermat's view of science was grounded in a thoroughly empirical and observational approach, and to demonstrate the errors of Descartes's ways he set about experimental work in optics himself. Among the important contributions that Fermat made to optics are his discovery that light travels more slowly in a denser medium, and his formulation of the principle that light always takes the quickest path.

Fermat is probably best known for his work in number theory, and he made numerous important discoveries in this field. But he also left one of the famous problems of mathematics – *Fermat's last theorem*. This theorem states that the algebraic analog of Pythagoras's theorem has no whole number solution for a power greater than 2, i.e., the equation

$$a^n + b^n = c^n$$

has no solutions for *n* greater than 2, if *a*, *b*, and *c* are all integers. In the margin of a copy of a book *Arithmetica of Diophantos*, an early treatise on equations, he wrote:

"To resolve a cube into the sum of two cubes, a fourth power into two fourth powers, or in general any power higher than the second into two of the same kind, is impossible; of which I have found a remarkable proof. The margin is too small to contain it."

Fermat never wrote down his "remarkable proof" and the equation was the subject of much investigation for over 350 years. In June 1993 the British-born mathematician Andrew Wiles presented a proof to a conference at Cambridge in a lecture entitled "Modular forms, elliptic curves, and Galois representations." His proof ran to 1,000 pages – rather more space than Fermat's margin – and it is generally believed that Fermat, given the mathematical techniques available at the time, must have been mistaken in believing that he had a proof of the conjecture.

Fermi, Enrico

(1901–1954)

ITALIAN–AMERICAN PHYSICIST

> Whatever Nature has in store for mankind, unpleasant as it may be, men must accept, for ignorance is never better than knowledge.
> —Quoted by Laura Fermi in *Atoms in the Family*

Fermi (**fer**-mee) was without doubt the greatest Italian scientist since Galileo and in the period 1925–50 was one of the most creative physicists in the world. Unusually in an age of ever-growing specialization he excelled as both an experimentalist and a theoretician.

He was born in Rome and brought up in the prosperous home of his father who, beginning as a railroad official, progressed to a senior position in government service. Fermi's intelligence and quickness of mind were apparent from an early age and he had little difficulty in gaining admission in 1918 to the Scuola Normale in Pisa, a school for the intellectual élite of Italy. He later completed his education at the University of Pisa where he gained his PhD in 1924. After spending some time abroad in Göttingen and Leiden, Fermi returned to Italy where, after some initial setbacks, he was appointed to a professorship of physics at the University of Rome. This in itself was a considerable achievement for one so young, considering the traditional and bureaucratic nature of Italian universities. It was no doubt due to the reputation he had already established with the publication of some 30 substantial papers, and the support of O. M. Corbino, the most distinguished Italian physicist at the time and also a senator. Corbino was determined to modernize Italian physics and had the good sense to see that Fermi, despite his youth, was the ideal man to advance his cause.

Fermi began by publishing the first Italian text on modern physics, *Introduzione alla Fisica Atomica* (1928; Introduction to Nuclear Physics). Soon his reputation attracted around him the brightest of the younger Italian physicists. But the growth of fascism in Italy led to the dispersal of its scientific talent. By 1938 Fermi, with a Jewish wife, was sufficiently alarmed by the growing anti-Semitism of the government to join the general exodus and move to America.

However, before his departure, his period in Rome turned out to be remarkably productive, with major advances being made in both the theoretical and the experimental field. His experimental work arose out of attempts to advance the efforts of Irène and Frédéric Joliot-Curie who had announced in 1934 the production of artificial radioactive isotopes by the bombardment of boron and aluminum with helium nuclei (alpha particles). Fermi realized that the neutron, discovered by James Chadwick in 1932, was perhaps an even better tool for creating new isotopes. Although less massive than an alpha particle, the neutron's charge neutrality allowed it to overcome the positive charge of a target nucleus without dissipating its energy.

Fermi reported that in 1934 he had impulsively and for no apparent reason interposed paraffin between the neutron source and the target. "It was with no advance warning, no conscious prior reasoning ... I took some odd piece of paraffin" and placed it in front of the incident neutrons. The effect was to increase the activation intensity by a factor that ranged from a few tens to a few hundreds. Fermi had stumbled on the phenomenon of slow neutrons. What was happening was that the neutrons were slowing down as the result of collisions with the light hydrocarbon molecules. This in turn meant that they remained in the vicinity of the target nucleus sufficiently long to increase their chance of absorption.

The production of slow neutrons was later to have a profound impact in the field of nuclear energy, both civil and military. However, Fermi's immediate task was to use them to irradiate as many of the elements as possible and to produce and investigate the properties of a large number of newly created radioactive isotopes. It was for this work, for "the discovery of new radioactive substances ... and for the discovery of the selective power of slow neutrons" that Fermi was awarded the 1938 Nobel Prize for physics.

He did however miss one significant phenomenon. In the course of their systematic irradiation of the elements Fermi and his colleagues naturally bombarded uranium with slow neutrons. This would inevitably lead to nuclear fission, but Fermi thought that transuranic elements were being produced and in his Nobel address actually referred to his production of elements 93 and 94, which he named "ausonium" and "hesperium." In 1938 Otto Frisch and Lise Meitner first realized that nuclear fission was taking place in such reactions.

On the theoretical level Fermi's major achievement while at Rome was his theory of beta decay. This is the process in unstable nuclei whereby a neutron is converted into a proton with the emission of an electron and an antineutrino ($n \rightarrow p + e^- + v$). Fermi gave a detailed analysis which introduced a new force into science, the so-called "weak" force. An account was published in Italian in 1933 as an original English version was rejected by the journal *Nature* as being too speculative.

In America Fermi soon found himself caught up in the attempt to create a controlled nuclear chain reaction. In 1942 he succeeded in building the first atomic pile in the stadium of the University of Chicago at Stagg Field. Using pure graphite as a moderator to slow the neutrons, and enriched uranium as the fissile material, Fermi and his colleagues began the construction of the pile. It consisted of some 40,000 graphite blocks, specially produced to exclude impurities, in which some 22,000 holes were drilled to permit the insertion of several tons of uranium. At 2:20 p.m. on 2 December 1942, the atomic age began as Fermi's pile went critical, supporting a self-supporting chain reaction for 28 minutes. In a historic telephone call afterwards Arthur Compton informed the managing committee that "the Italian navigator has just landed in the new world," and that the natives were friendly.

Fermi continued to work on the project and was in fact present in July 1945 when the first test bomb was exploded in the New Mexico desert. He is reported to have dropped scraps of paper as the blast reached him and, from their displacement, to have calculated the force as corresponding to 10,000 tons of TNT.

After the war Fermi accepted an appointment as professor of physics at the University of Chicago where he remained until his untimely death from cancer. His name has been commemorated in physics in various ways. Element 100, *fermium*, and the unit of length of 10^{-13} centimeter, the *fermi*, were named for him, as was the National Accelerator Laboratory, Fermilab, at Batavia, near Chicago.

Fernel, Jean François

(1497–1558)

FRENCH PHYSICIAN

> From his [Fernel's] school there went forth skilled physicians more numerous than soldiers from the Trojan horse, and spread over all regions and quarters of Europe.
> —Guillaume Plancy, *Life of Fernel* (1577)

Fernel (fer-**nel**), the son of an innkeeper from Clermont in France, was educated at the Collège de Sainte Barbe in Paris where he graduated in 1519. After some years devoted to such subjects as philosophy and cosmology, Fernel took up the study of medicine, qualifying in 1530 and being appointed professor of medicine in 1534 at the University of Paris. He was also appointed as physician to Henri II after successfully treating Henri's mistress Diane de Poitiers, although his failure to cure Henri's father, Francis I, of syphilis appears not to have been held against him.

In 1554 Fernel published his *Medicina*, which went through some 30 editions and was one of the standard texts of the late 16th century. It is here that he introduced the terms "physiology" and "pathology" into medicine. The work was however mainly traditional, describing the physiology of Galen with but a few modifications.

Fernel also wrote an interesting account of the status of medicine in his *On the Hidden Causes of Things* (1548) in which he began to question long accepted magical and astrological accounts of diseases. He fell back on the standard medical objection to therapies offered by competitors, namely that any relief obtained would be only superficial and temporary.

Before turning to medicine Fernel had published his *Cosmotheoria* (1528), a work that contained one of the earliest measurements of a meridian, measured with an odometer between Paris and Amiens.

Ferrel, William

(1817–1891)

AMERICAN METEOROLOGIST

> [Ferrel gave] to the science of meteorology a foundation in mechanics as solid as that which Newton laid for astronomy.
> —Cleveland Abbe, *Biographical Memoirs* (1895)

Born in Fulton County, Pennsylvania, Ferrel moved with his family to farm in West Virginia in 1829. Since he received only the most rudimentary education, his early scientific knowledge was entirely self acquired. Despite this he developed an interest in mathematical physics and, after graduating from Bethany College in West Virginia in 1844, began to study the *Principia* of Isaac Newton and the *Mécanique céleste* (Celestial Mechanics) of Pierre Simon de Laplace. He earned his living as a school teacher from 1844 until 1857 when, having established his scientific reputation, he was appointed to the staff of the American Ephemeris and Nautical Almanac. He worked there until 1867 when he joined the U.S. Coast and Geodetic Survey.

In 1856 he published his most significant work, *Essay on the Winds and Currents of the Oceans*. He showed that all atmospheric motion, as well as ocean currents, are deflected by the Earth's rotation. He went on in 1858 to formulate his law, which states that if a mass of air is moving in any direction there is a force arising from the Earth's rotation that always deflects it to the right in the northern hemisphere and to the left in the southern hemisphere. The air tends to move in a circle whose radius depends on its velocity and distance from the equator. Ferrel went on to show how this law could be used to explain storms and the pattern of winds and currents. He was in some ways anticipated by Gustave-Gaspard Coriolis whose name is much better known.

Ferrel also did fundamental work on the solar system. He was able to correct Laplace and show that the tidal action of the Sun and Moon on the Earth is slowly retarding the Earth's rotation. In 1864 he provided the first mathematical treatment of tidal friction. His other works included his three-volume *Meteorological Researches* (1877–82). In 1880 he invented a machine to predict tidal maxima and minima.

Ferrier, Sir David

(1843–1928)

BRITISH NEUROLOGIST

Born in Aberdeen, Scotland, Ferrier graduated in philosophy from the university there in 1863 and then spent some time at Heidelberg studying psychology. He returned to Scotland to study medicine at Edinburgh University and graduated in 1868. Initially he worked in private practice until his appointment as professor of forensic medicine at King's College Hospital, London (1872–89). The chair of neuropathology was created for him in 1889, a post he retained until his retirement in 1908.

Following the fundamental paper of Gustav Fritsch and Eduard Hitzig on cerebral localization, Ferrier began, in 1873, a series of experiments that both confirmed and extended their work. Whereas they had worked only with dogs, Ferrier used a wide variety of mammals, including primates. He was thus able to identify many more different areas in the cerebral hemispheres capable of eliciting movement. This work was soon shown to have practical implications. The surgeon William Macewen saw that the technique could be reversed and that disturbances of movement in a patient could be used to indicate the site of a possible brain tumor.

Ferrier was an important figure in the newly emerging discipline of neurophysiology. He was one of the first editors of the influential journal *Brain* (founded 1878) and was also a founder member of the Physiological Society.

Fessenden, Reginald Aubrey

(1866–1932)

CANADIAN ELECTRICAL ENGINEER

Fessenden was born at Milton in Quebec, Canada. After an education in Canada, he worked for Edison as an engineer and later as head chemist (1886–90) and as an engineer (1890–91) for Westinghouse, Edison's great rival. He was professor of electrical engineering at Purdue University, Indiana (1882–83), and the Western University of Pennsylvania (now the University of Pittsburgh) from 1893 to 1900. He was then appointed special agent for the U.S. Weather Bureau, adapting the technique of radio telegraphy, newly developed by Guglielmo Marconi, to weather forecasting and storm warning. In 1902 he became general manager of the National Electric Signaling Company, a company formed by two Pittsburgh financiers to exploit his ideas. From 1910 he was consultant engineer at the Submarine Signal Company.

Fessenden's inventions were prolific and varied: at the time of his death he held over 500 patents. In 1900 he developed an electrolytic detector that was sufficiently sensitive to make radio telephony feasible. His most significant invention was the technique of amplitude modulation. This involved the use of "carrier waves" to transmit audio signals; he varied the amplitude of a steady high-frequency radio signal so that it corresponded to variations in the sound waves and thus "carried" the audio information. Using this principle he transmitted, on Christmas Eve 1906, what was probably the first program of music and speech broadcast in America. The program was heard by ships' radio operators up to a distance of several hundred miles.

Fessenden had a choleric temperament and a fear of being outwitted by businessmen. He was involved in various lawsuits, one of which was against his financial backers in the National Electric Signaling Company: Fessenden won a judgment of $406,000 and sent the company into bankruptcy.

Feyerabend, Paul Karl

(1924–1994)

AUSTRIAN PHILOSOPHER OF SCIENCE

> Unanimity of opinion may be fitting for a church, for the frightened or greedy victims of some (ancient or modern) myth, or for the weak and willing followers of some tyrant. Variety of opinion is necessary for objective knowledge.
>
> —*Against Method* (1975)

Feyerabend (**fI**-er-ah-bent), who was born in the Austrian capital of Vienna, enlisted in the German army immediately after leaving school in 1942. He was seriously wounded on the Russian front in 1945 and was subsequently awarded the Iron Cross. His education after the war was varied and unusual. He was a student of the Vienna Music Academy, but he also studied history, physics, and astronomy at the University of Vienna. In 1952 he moved to London and attended the seminars given by Karl Popper at the London School of Economics. Though he had never studied philosophy formally, he was appointed in 1955 to a philosophy lectureship at Bristol University. In 1959 Feyerabend moved to the U.S. and in 1962 was appointed professor of philosophy at the University of California, Berkeley, a position he held, along with a similar appointment from 1979 at the Zurich Federal Institute of Technology, until his retirement in 1990.

Feyerabend had arrived at Berkeley at an exciting time. Political radicalism, the free speech movement, and increasing racial toleration were to be found in Berkeley in an exceptionally intense form. Here he began to reexamine the claims of western science to offer the only valid account of nature. Why, he asked, should modern science be preferred to Hopi cosmology or Aristotelian metaphysics? On examination, he argued, the superiority of western science was no more than an assumption. It assumed the achievements of science were gained through the exercise of a distinctive scientific method. Yet, an examination of the works of Copernicus, Galileo, and others revealed that they had succeeded by adopting extrascientific assumptions. Further, early prescientific societies had made such major advances as metalworking and agriculture without recourse to science. Nor, he pointed out, did science give its rivals a fair hearing. Astrology was dismissed out of hand; its principles were untested, and astrologers were denied access to scientific periodicals.

Science had thus, for Feyerabend, flourished by dubious rhetorical devices and by imposing a general consensus by totalitarian methods. As an alternative, in his *Against Method* (London, 1975), a work translated into 16 languages, he argued for an "anarchistic theory of knowledge," guided only by the principle "Anything goes." In *Science and a Free Society* (1978) Feyerabend argued that the democratic process itself is threatened by the authoritarian nature of modern science. His views have been vigorously contested and he has been described in the pages of *Nature* as "currently the worst enemy of science." Shortly before he died Feyerabend completed his autobiography *Killing Time* (1995), in which he revealed that in 1993 he had been diagnosed as having an inoperable brain tumor.

Feynman, Richard Phillips

(1918–1988)

AMERICAN THEORETICAL PHYSICIST

For a successful technology, reality must take precedence over public relations, for Nature cannot be fooled.
—Final report of the inquiry into the *Challenger* space shuttle disaster of 1986

The father of Feynman (**fIn**-man) had been brought with his immigrant parents from Minsk, Byelorussia, in 1895. Feynman himself was born in New York and educated at the Massachusetts Institute of Technology and at Princeton, where he completed his PhD in 1942 under the supervision of John Wheeler. In 1943 Feynman moved to Los Alamos to work on the Manhattan Project in the theoretical division under Hans Bethe. He was soon recognized to be, in the words of Robert Oppenheimer, "the most brilliant young physicist here." Feynman's own writings about the period deal less with the bomb than with his wife, Arline who was dying of TB. He had married her in 1942 against much family opposition. She moved into a sanatorium in nearby Albuquerque and died in June 1945, a month before the first atomic bomb was tested.

In 1945 Feynman moved to Cornell as professor of physics, a post he held until 1950 when he was appointed to a similar position at the California Institute of Technology, where he remained for the rest of his career. While at Cornell he began to consider anew some of the outstanding problems in quantum electrodynamics (QED) – an area of physics dealing with the interactions between electrons and photons. The electron was seen as a point charge. As the strength of a charged body diminishes with distance in accordance with the inverse square law, it will vary as $1/r^2$. But what about the strength of the charge at the electron itself where r = 0? At this point the charge (and for a point, density) of the electron must be infinite. To handle this and other similar absurdities physicists developed a number of artificial mathematical techniques which would allow them to "renormalize" their equations so as to remove the infinite terms. Yet the charge on the electron is finite and can be measured accurately. Theoretical calculations, it was felt, should reach the same value without requiring artificial manipulation.

Freeman Dyson has described Feynman at this time as claiming that "he couldn't understand the official version of quantum mechanics," and that he had to "reinvent quantum mechanics" in a form he could understand. Feynman first presented his new approach in a paper, turned down by the *Physical Review*, entitled *Space-Time Approach to Non-Relativistic Quantum Mechanics* (1948) in which he introduced the notion of path integrals, also referred to as "sum over histories."

In Feynman's approach, the probability of an event that can happen in a number of different ways, such as finding an electron at a certain place, was the sum of the probabilities of all the possible ways the event could happen. When all the probabilities were added, Feynman noted, the result was Schrödinger's wave function.

In a 1949 paper, *Space-Time Approach to Quantum Electrodynamics*, Feynman showed how to calculate these path integrals using simple sketches which have since become widely known as *Feynman diagrams*. It was for work in this field that Feynman shared the 1965 Nobel Physics prize with Julian Schwinger and Sin-Itiro Tomonaga. His first reaction had been to decline what he terms "Alfred Nobel's other mistake" on the grounds that he would thereafter become a celebrity and not just someone who wanted to talk about physics. Warned that a refusal would mark him in the media as an even bigger celebrity, Feynman agreed to accept the award.

Feynman also worked on problems connected with superconductivity and with particle physics. In 1955 he devized a new model to represent the structure of liquid helium. During a visit to Stanford in 1968 Feynman began to work on the strong nuclear interaction. He attributed to the proton a set of constituents he named "partons," which were point-like and did not interact with each other. Their value lay in their ability to explain the inelastic scattering results emerging from the Stanford Linear Accelerator (SLAC).

With the publication in 1963 of the *Feynman Lectures in Physics*, Feynman began to be known outside the small community of theoretical physicists. However, he gained international celebrity in the 1980s following a number of TV programs and the publication of *Surely You're Joking Mr Feynman* (1985). The picture of a man of rare seriousness and honesty, with little time for honors, institutions, and formality, yet who clearly enjoyed the life of the flesh as well as the mind, had rarely been presented with such clarity. Despite his reluctance to accept the Nobel award, Feynman seems to have enjoyed his fame, and even to accentuate his unconventional character.

When he was asked to serve in 1986 on the presidential commission to investigate the explosion of the *Challenger* space shuttle, he assumed that he was being asked to contribute to a genuine scientific investigation. Pointed in the right direction by sympathetic colleagues, Feynman soon realized that the immediate cause of the explosion had been the O-ring seals used in the booster rocket. On the morning of the shuttle's launch the temperature was below freezing and the seals failed to retain their elasticity at low temperatures. Feynman also found out that the NASA officials had been warned about this potential failure. Feynman demonstrated the point, unannounced, at a televised meeting of the commission. He placed the O-rings in a glass of iced water for a few minutes and showed that, for several seconds after their removal, the seals had lost their resilience.

Feynman wrote up his findings as a separate appendix. He was aware that, while the commission would not actually suppress any evidence, much that was critical of NASA could be scattered throughout the report and consequently picked up by only the most careful of readers.

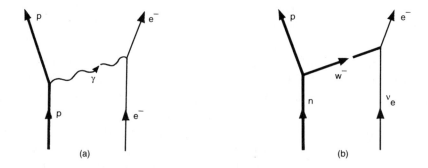

FEYNMAN DIAGRAM   Diagrams for (a) electromagnetic scattering of an electron by a proton; (b) scattering of a neutrino by a neutron.

Before the commission agreed to publish his report in a form acceptable to Feynman, he first found it necessary to threaten to resign and issue the report elsewhere. Feynman found his Washington experiences genuinely distressing. Much of his life had been spent trying to understand various natural phenomena. The work had been hard, demanding many hours of intense intellectual concentration. He went to Washington intending to put the same effort into the service of the commission. Yet he found himself working with people who, though not crooks, liars, or lazy, were only marginally interested in the truth. It was more important for them to find a story acceptable to a community consisting of the Washington establishment, NASA, and "the American people," rather than to set out to establish what happened.

By this time, however, Feynman was a seriously ill man. In 1978 a malignant growth had been removed from his abdomen. A second cancer, involving bone marrow, was diagnosed in 1986. The abdominal cancer returned in late 1987 and soon after Feynman died from kidney failure.

Fibiger, Johannes Andreas Grib

(1867–1928)

DANISH PHYSICIAN

Fibiger (**fee**-bi-ger), born the son of a physician at Silkeborg in Denmark, was educated at the University of Copenhagen, completing his medical studies in 1890. After some hospital work and further study in Berlin under Robert Koch and Emil von Behring, Fibiger joined the Institute of Pathological Anatomy at the University of Copenhagen in 1897, serving there as its director from 1900.

It was realized that cancers could be chemically induced by factors in the environment but all attempts to induce such cancers artificially had failed. Fibiger thought he could change this when, in 1907, he observed extensive papillomatous tumors virtually filling the stomachs of three wild rats. Microscopic examination showed the presence in the stomachs of formations similar to nematode worms, and Fibiger naturally concluded that these parasites were the cause of the tumors. A search of a further 1,200 wild rats, however, produced no additional cases of cancer. This suggested to him that the nematodes were transmitted by an intermediate host, and a report published in 1878 confirmed that such nematodes had been found as parasites of a common kind of cockroach. Before long Fibiger found rats from a sugar refinery that fed regularly on the cockroaches there: examination of 61 of these rats showed that 40 had nematodes in their stomachs and 7 of these 40 had the earlier identified tumor.

By 1913 Fibiger was able to claim that he could induce such malignancies in rats by feeding them with cockroaches infested with nematode larvae, noting a proportional relationship between the number of parasites and the degree of anatomic change in the stomach. It was for this work, described somewhat extravagantly by the Nobel Committee as the "greatest contribution to experimental medicine in our generation," that Fibiger was awarded the 1926 Nobel Prize for physiology or medicine.

Although no one disputed that Fibiger had induced cancer it was never completely accepted that such growths were caused by the nematodes. In any case Fibiger's work had little impact on experimental cancer research: simpler methods of carcinogenesis were almost universally preferred.

Fibonacci, Leonardo

(*c.* 1170– *c.* 1250)

ITALIAN MATHEMATICIAN

Fibonacci (fee-boh-**nah**-chee) lived in Pisa and is often referred to as Leonardo of Pisa. Although he was probably the most outstanding mathematician of the Middle Ages virtually nothing is known of his life. The modern system of numerals, which originated in India and had first been introduced to the West by al-Khwarizmi, first became widely used in Europe owing to Fibonacci's popularization of it. His father served as a consul in North Africa and it is kown that Fibonacci studied with an Arabian mathematician in his youth, from whom he probably learned the decimal system of notation.

Fibonacci's main work was his *Liber abaci* (1202; Book of the Abacus) in which he expounded the virtues of the new system of numerals and showed how they could be used to simplify highly complex calculations. Fibonacci also worked extensively on the theory of proportion and on techniques for determining the roots of equations, and included a treatment of these subjects in the *Liber abaci*. In addition it contains contributions to geometry and Fibonacci later published his *Practica geometriae* (1220; Practice of Geometry), a shorter work that was devoted entirely to the subject.

Fibonacci was fortunate in being able to gain the patronage of the Holy Roman Emperor, Frederick II, and a later work, the *Liber quadratorum* (1225; Book of Square Numbers) was dedicated to his patron. This book, whch is generally considered Fibonacci's greatest achievement, deals with second order Diophantine equations. It contains the most advanced contributions to number theory since the work of Diophantus, which were not to be equaled until the work of Fermat. He discovered the "Fibonacci sequence" of integers in whch each number is equal to the sum of the preceding two (1, 1, 2, 3, 5, 8, ...).

Finch, George Ingle

(1888–1970)

AUSTRALIAN PHYSICAL CHEMIST

Finch was born at Orange in Australia and educated at Wolaroi College in his native country and the Ecole de Médecine in Paris. Finding the study of medicine unappealing, Finch moved to Switzerland where he studied physics and chemistry, first at the Federal Institute of Technology in Zurich and afterward at the University of Geneva. On moving to Britain in 1912 he worked briefly as a research chemist at the Royal Arsenal, Woolwich, joining the staff of Imperial College, London, in 1913. Finch remained there until his retirement in 1952, having been appointed professor of applied physical chemistry in 1936. After his retirement Finch spent the period 1952–57 in India as director of the National Chemical Laboratory.

Finch worked mainly on the properties of solid surfaces. In the 1930s he developed the technique of low-energy electron diffraction, using the wavelike properties of electrons, demonstrated by George Thomson and Clinton J. Davisson in 1927, to investigate the structure of surfaces. X-rays are neutral and too penetrating to provide much information about surfaces or thin films; electrons, however, are charged and are deflected after penetrating no more than a few atoms below the surface. With this new and powerful tool Finch began the study of lubricants and the Beilby layer – a thin surface layer produced by polishing, and differing in its properties from the underlying material. Finch had earlier worked on the mechanism of combustion in gases as initiated by an electric discharge.

Finch was also widely known as a mountaineer. As one of the leading climbers of his generation he was a member of the 1922 Everest expedition, climbing to the then unequaled height of 27,300 feet (8,321 m).

Finlay, Carlos Juan

(1833–1915)

CUBAN PHYSICIAN

Finlay's father was a Scottish physician who had fought with Simon Bolivar. Carlos, who was born at Puerto Principe, now Camagüey, in Cuba, was educated in Paris and at the Jefferson Medical College, Philadelphia, where he graduated in 1855. He then returned to Cuba where he spent his life in general practice.

In 1881 Finlay published a prophetic paper *The Mosquito Hypothetically Considered as the Agent of the Transmission of Yellow Fever*, naming the species *Culex fasciatus* (now *Aëdes aegypti*) as the vector. He had been struck by the presence of *Aëdes* in houses during epidemics and noted that the yellow fever and mosquito seasons seemed to coincide. Although he campaigned vigorously for his theory he only succeeded in turning himself into a figure of mild ridicule.

There were a number of complicating factors that undermined Finlay's work. Firstly yellow fever is caused by a virus, a microorganism only discovered in 1898 and far too small to be detected by the microscopic techniques of the late 19th century. Further, with the newly established germ theory of Robert Koch, scientists were demanding visual evidence for the existence of the supposed pathogen. As Finlay could not isolate the causative organism he attempted to demonstrate its existence by such clinical techniques as transmitting the disease from a sick patient via *Aëdes* to a healthy individual. But here too, although he repeated such experiments many times, he failed to produce any coherent results. As it turned out, it was only the female mosquito, and then only one who had bitten a victim in the first three days of infection who could, two weeks later, transmit the disease. Consequently many of Finlay's failures could be explained by using the wrong type of mosquito or the right type at the wrong time. But to discover such facts required more ambitious resources than Finlay commanded.

He did however live to see such resources come to Cuba with the arrival of the 4th U.S. Yellow Fever Commission in 1900 under the command of Walter Reed. Finlay interested Reed in his views, and Reed, in a classic series of trials, completely vindicated them.

Finsen, Niels Ryberg

(1860–1904)

DANISH PHYSICIAN

Finsen (**fin**-sen), the son of a leading civil servant, was born at Thorshavn on the Faeroe Islands, which are part of Denmark; he was educated in Reykjavik and at the University of Copenhagen, where he qualified as a physician in 1890. After teaching anatomy for some time Finsen founded (1895) the Institute of Phototherapy, which he directed until his early death at the age of 43.

In the 1890s, following up some earlier work suggesting that light had the ability to kill bacteria, Finsen began a systematic appraisal of its therapeutic effects. Arguing that it was light, acting slowly and weakly, rather than heat that was effective, he devised various filters and lenses to separate and concentrate the different components of sunlight. He found that it was the short ultraviolet rays, either natural or artificial, that turned out to have the greatest bactericidal power.

Finsen found phototherapy to be of most use against lupus vulgaris, a skin infection produced by the tubercle bacillus. He claimed that on exposure to ultraviolet rays the skin regained its normal color and the ulcerations began to heal. For this Finsen received the third Nobel Prize for physiology or medicine in 1903.

It was, however, an avenue that few physicians were willing to explore. The use of ultraviolet radiation was mainly restricted to the treatment of lupus vulgaris and even this was superseded by x-rays and, more importantly, by such drugs as cortisone when they became available in the 1950s.

Fischer, Edmond H.

(1920–)

AMERICAN BIOCHEMIST

Born in Shanghai, China, Fischer was educated at the University of Geneva, where, after graduation, he worked as assistant in the organic chemistry laboratories (1946–47). After spending two years as a research fellow with the Swiss National Foundation (1948–50) he moved to the University of Washington, Seattle, as a Rockefeller Foundation research fellow (1950–53). After a brief spell at the California Institute of Technology in 1953, he was appointed assistant professor of biochemistry at the University of Washington, subsequently becoming associate professor (1956–61) and professor (1961–90).

Fischer's most acclaimed work was done at Seattle in the 1950s and 1960s in collaboration with the biochemist Edwin Krebs. In 1955–56 the pair discovered how the enzyme (glycogen phosphorylase) that catalyzes the release of glucose from glycogen in the body is "switched on." The enzyme receives a phosphate group from ATP (adenosine triphosphate – the body's major energy carrier) in a transfer reaction catalyzed by a second enzyme, which Fischer and Krebs termed a "protein kinase." They went on to show that glycogen phosphorylase is then switched off by removal of the phosphate group by a further enzyme (called a protein phosphatase). The addition and removal of the phosphate group reversibly changes the shape of the enzyme molecule, thereby switching it between the inactive and active forms.

These findings opened the way to a major new field of research suggesting how enzymes might function in various physiological processes, such as hormone regulatory mechanisms, gene expression, and fertilization of the egg. Their work also had implications for the understanding of certain diseases; for instance, abnormally phosphorylated proteins have been identified in muscular dystrophy and diabetes, while protein kinases may play a significant role in certain cancers and in airway constriction in asthma.

In recognition of his contributions to our understanding of enzymes Fischer was awarded the 1992 Nobel Prize for physiology or medicine, which he shared with his long-time coworker, Krebs.

Fischer, Emil Hermann

(1852–1919)

GERMAN ORGANIC CHEMIST AND BIOCHEMIST

The son of a successful businessman from Euskirchen, now in Germany, Fischer joined his father's firm on leaving school (1869) but left in 1871 to study chemistry with August Kekulé at Bonn. He was not happy with the chemistry instruction there and came close to abandoning chemistry for physics. In 1872, however, he moved to Strasbourg to study with Adolf von Baeyer. Here, he gained his doctorate in 1874 for work on phthaleins. The same year he made the vital discovery of phenylhydrazine, a compound that was later to prove the vital key for unlocking the structures of the sugars.

Fischer became Baeyer's assistant and together they moved to Munich (1875). At Munich, working with his cousin, Otto Fischer, he proved that the natural rosaniline dyes are derivatives of triphenylmethane. In 1879 Fischer became assistant professor of analytical chemistry and soon after became financially independent. He was then professor at Erlangen (1882), Würzburg (1885), and Berlin (1892).

Fischer has some claim to be called the father of biochemistry. He carried out extremely comprehensive work in three main fields: purines, sugars, and peptides, the last two effectively founding biochemistry on a firm basis of organic chemistry. The work on purines, begun in 1882, resulted in the synthesis of many important compounds, including the alkaloids caffeine and theobromine, and purine itself (1898). Fischer's early structures were incorrect but from 1897 the correct structures were used.

In 1884 Fischer discovered that phenylhydrazine produces well-defined crystalline compounds with sugars, thus affording a reliable means of identification. In 1887 he synthesized first fructose (from acrolein dibromide) and later mannose and glucose. By 1891 he was able to deduce the configurations of the 16 possible aldohexoses, which he represented in the form of the famous *Fischer projection formulae*.

In 1899 Fischer turned to amino acids and peptides and devised a peptide synthesis that eventually produced a polypeptide containing 18 amino acids (1907). Fischer's other work included the first synthesis of a nucleotide (1914), the "lock-and-key" hypothesis of enzyme action, work on tannins, and attempts to prepare very high-molecular-weight compounds. He was awarded the 1902 Nobel Prize for chemistry for his work on purines and sugars.

Fischer, Ernst Otto

(1918–)

GERMAN INORGANIC CHEMIST

Fischer, the son of a physics professor, was educated in his native city at the Munich Institute of Technology, where he obtained his PhD in 1952. He taught at the University of Munich serving as professor of inorganic chemistry from 1957 to 1964, when he became the director of the Institute for Inorganic Chemistry at the Institute of Technology.

Fischer is noted for his work on inorganic complexes. In 1951 two chemists, T. Kealy and P. Pauson, were attempting to join two five-carbon (cyclopentadiene) rings together and discovered a compound $C_5H_5FeC_5H_5$, which they proposed had an iron atom joined to a carbon atom on each ring.

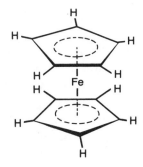

FERROCENE   Originally the structure was thought to be that on the left. E. O. Fischer showed it to be a sandwich compound with the iron atom positioned between the two rings.

Fischer, on reflection, considered such a structure inadequate for he failed to see how it could provide sufficient stability with its carbon–iron–carbon bonds. The British chemist Geoffrey Wilkinson suggested a more novel structure in which the iron atom was sandwiched between two parallel rings and thus formed bonds with the electrons in the rings, rather than with individual carbon atoms. Compounds of this type are called "sandwich compounds."

By careful x-ray analysis Fischer confirmed the proposed structure of ferrocene, as the compound was called, and for this work shared the Nobel Prize for chemistry with Wilkinson in 1973. Fischer went on to do further work on transition-metal complexes with organic compounds and is one of the leading workers in the field of organometallic chemistry.

Fischer, Hans

(1881–1945)

GERMAN ORGANIC CHEMIST

Fischer, the son of a chemicals industrialist from Höchst-am-Main in Germany, gained his doctorate in chemistry at the University of Marburg in 1904. He also studied medicine at the University of Munich, gaining his MD in 1908. He was assistant to Emil Fischer before occupying chairs of medical chemistry at Innsbruck (1916) and Vienna (1918). In 1921 he succeeded Heinrich Wieland as professor at the Technical Institute in Munich.

Fischer's life work was the study of the immensely important biological molecules hemoglobin, chlorophyll, and the bile pigments, especially bilirubin. He showed that hemin – the nonprotein, iron-containing portion of the hemoglobin molecule – consists of a system of four pyrrole rings, linked by bridges, with iron in the center. He synthesized hemin in 1929 and extensively investigated similar molecules – the porphyrins. He was awarded the Nobel Prize for chemistry for this work in 1930. He then turned to the chlorophylls and showed that they are substituted porphins with magnesium rather than iron in the center. The bile acids were shown by Fischer to be degraded porphins, and he synthesized bilirubin in 1944. Fischer took his own life at the end of World War II, after his laboratories had been destroyed in the bombing of Munich.

Fischer, Otto Philipp

(1852–1932)

GERMAN ORGANIC CHEMIST

Otto Fischer was the cousin of Emil Fischer, with whom he collaborated in some of his work. He was born at Euskirchen, now in Germany, gained his doctorate at Strasbourg (1874), and was professor of chemistry at Erlangen from 1885 to 1925. His most notable work was with dyestuffs: he discovered malachite green, a triphenylmethane dye (1877), and determined the structures of pararosaniline (1880; with Emil) and mauveine (1890).

Fisher, Sir Ronald Aylmer

(1890–1962)

BRITISH STATISTICIAN AND GENETICIST

> Natural selection is a mechanism for generating an exceedingly high degree of improbability.
>
> —Quoted by A. L. Mackay in *The Harvest of a Quiet Eye* (1977)

Fisher, a Londoner by birth, studied mathematics and physics at Cambridge University, graduating in 1912. In the years before joining Rothamsted Experimental Station in 1919 he undertook a variety of jobs, including farm work in Canada, employment with an investment company, and teaching in various private schools. In this period he also produced two important papers marking his interest in both statistics and genetics. The first, published in 1915, described a solution for the exact distribution of the correlation coefficient, a problem that had been perplexing other statisticians. The second paper was *The Correlation between Relatives on the Supposition of Mendelian Inheritance* (1918). This demonstrated that the inheritance of continuous variation, which had been thought of as non-Mendelian, is in fact governed by many additive genes, each of small effect and each inherited in a Mendelian manner. Thus continuous variation may be analyzed following Mendelian rules. This work later led to the development of the science of biometric genetics. At Rothamsted, Fisher was appointed to sort out the accumulation of over 60 years' data on field trials. He modified the significance test, enabling more confident conclusions to be drawn from small samples of data, and developed the analysis of variance technique. He emphasized the need for random rather than systematic experimental design so that error due to environmental variation could be analyzed quantitatively. His book *Statistical Methods for Research Workers* (1925) is one of the most influential works in statistics.

Fisher's major researches in genetics at Rothamsted were brought together in *The Genetical Theory of Natural Selection* (1930). In this book he argued that Mendelism, far from contradicting Darwinism as some people believed, actually provides the missing link in the theory of evolution by natural selection by showing that inheritance is by means of particulate entities (genes) rather than by physical blending of parental characteristics. (In 1936 Fisher published a paper arguing that probabilistically Mendel's famous results were "too good to be true.") The book also summarizes his views on eugenics and on genes controlling dominant characteristics. He believed that dominance develops gradually by selection, showing selection rather than mutation to be the driving force in evolution.

The Genetical Theory of Natural Selection led to Fisher's appointment as Galton Professor of Genetics at University College, London, in 1933. Here he did important work clarifying the genetics of the Rhesus blood groups. He accepted the chair of genetics at Cambridge University in 1943, remaining there until 1959 although he retired officially in 1957. He spent the last three years of his life working for the Commonwealth Scientific and Industrial Research Organization (CSIRO) in Adelaide. Fisher was knighted in 1952.

Fitch, Val Logsdon

(1923–   )

AMERICAN PHYSICIST

Born in Merriman, Nebraska, Fitch was educated at McGill and Columbia universities and obtained his PhD from Columbia in 1954. He then joined the Princeton staff, being appointed professor of physics there in 1960.

Working with Leo James Rainwater, Fitch was the first to observe radiation from muonic atoms, i.e., from species in which a muon is orbiting a nucleus rather than an electron. This work indicated that the sizes of atomic nuclei were smaller than had been supposed. He went on to study kaons and in 1964 collaborated with James Cronin, James Christenson, and René Turley in an experiment that disproved charge–parity conservation. In 1980 Fitch and Cronin shared the Nobel Prize for physics for this fundamental work.

Fittig, Rudolph

(1835–1910)

GERMAN ORGANIC CHEMIST

Fittig (**fit**-ik) was born in Hamburg, now in Germany, and gained his doctorate at Göttingen in 1858, becoming a professor at Tübingen (1870) and at Strasbourg (1876–1902). He was a prolific experimentalist with many discoveries and syntheses to his credit, including pinacol, diphenyl, mesitylene, cymene, coumarone, and phenanthrene in coal tar. He also did extensive work on lactones and unsaturated acids. His name is remembered in the *Wurtz–Fittig reaction*, a variation of the Wurtz reaction for synthesizing alkylaryl hydrocarbons. An example is the reaction to form methylbenzene (toluene):

$$CH_3Cl + C_6H_5Cl + 2Na \rightarrow C_2H_5CH_3 + 2NaCl$$

Fitzgerald, George Francis

(1851–1901)

IRISH PHYSICIST

I am not in the very least sensitive to having made mistakes. I rush out with all sorts of crude notions in hope that they may set others thinking and lead to some advance.
—Letter to Oliver Heaviside, 4 February 1889

Fitzgerald graduated from Trinity College in his native Dublin in 1871 and then joined the staff there, rising to the position of professor in 1881. His work was mainly concerned with the development of electromagnetism from James Clerk Maxwell's equations, in which he became interested after Heinrich Hertz had demonstrated the existence of the radio waves predicted by theory. Like Hendrik Lorentz, he constructed an electromagnetic theory of the reflection and refraction of light.

His name is best known for the *Lorentz–Fitzgerald contraction* – an effect suggested to explain the negative result of the Michelson–Morley experiment. The suggestion was that a body moving relative to an observer contracted slightly in the dimension parallel to the direction of motion, the amount of the contraction being dependent on the velocity. Thus, light emitted by a moving body would have a different speed, but would travel over a different path length. The contraction in size was supposed to result from the effect of the ether on the electromagnetic forces holding the atoms together. The Lorentz–Fitzgerald contraction received an alternative explanation in Einstein's theory of relativity.

Fitzroy, Robert

(1805–1865)

BRITISH HYDROGRAPHER AND METEOROLOGIST

Fitzroy, who was born near Bury St. Edmunds in the eastern English county of Suffolk, was educated at the Royal Naval College, Portsmouth, and in 1828 took command of the *Beagle*, on a survey of the South American coast. In 1831 he made a second voyage in the *Beagle* to complete his survey, taking with him as naturalist the then unknown Charles Darwin. After his return in 1836 he devoted himself to the publication, in 1839, of his *Narrative*, a three-volume account of the voyage. The third volume, known as *The Voyage of the Beagle*, was the work of Darwin.

Fitzroy served as a member of Parliament (1841–43) and was then appointed governor of New Zealand until his dismissal in 1845. He retired from active duty in 1850 but later (1854) took up the newly created post of meteorological statist and remained there until his death. He organized a number of observation stations, designed the barometer named for him, and began the publication of storm warnings that evolved into daily weather forecasts. One of the earliest textbooks on meteorology, *The Weather Book* (1863), was published by him.

He had a reputation for having a quick temper and, while suffering from depression, committed suicide.

Fizeau, Armand Hippolyte Louis

(1819–1896)

FRENCH PHYSICIST

Fizeau (fee-**zoh**), a Parisian by birth, started by studying medicine but his interest turned to optics before he finished the course. In collaboration with Léon Foucault he first tried to improve the newly developed process of photography and, in 1845, they took the first clear pictures of the Sun.

In 1849 he obtained a value for the speed of light in air, using an ingenious toothed-wheel apparatus. Light was directed through a gap between two teeth and reflected back between the teeth from a distant mirror. The wheel was rotated, the rate of rotation being changed until the reflected flashes were blocked by the tooth of the wheel. The speed of light could then be calculated from the rate of rotation of the wheel. Fizeau's experiment was performed using a path of 8 kilometers (5 mi) between Suresnes and Montmartre.

The next year both he and Foucault simultaneously proved that light traveled faster in air than in water, thus giving experimental support to the wave theory of light. Fizeau is also known for analyzing the Doppler effect for light waves. The change in wavelength with relative speed is sometimes called the *Doppler–Fizeau shift*.

Fizeau was elected a member of the Paris Academy in 1860 and was awarded the Royal Society's Rumford medal in 1875.

Flammarion, Nicolas Camille

(1842–1925)

FRENCH ASTRONOMER

Owing to his family's poverty, Flammarion (fla-ma-**ryon**), who was born at Montigny-le-Roi, France, was forced to leave school and abandon his intention of going into the priesthood. Instead he got a post in the Paris Observatory in 1858 but eventually was dismissed by Urbain Leverrier who accused him of being a poet rather than a scientist. Flammarion made serious contributions to astronomy, including founding the French Astronomical Society in 1887, and built himself a private observatory at Juvisy. However, he is best known as a popularizer of astronomy. His general attitude to astronomy was made clear when he published at the age of 19 *Plurality of Inhabited Worlds* (1862). This was translated into 12 languages, including Chinese and Arabic, and became a best seller in France, making Flammarion famous. His *Popular Astronomy* (1879) was one of the most popular books of the late 19th century. Giovanni Schiaparelli's discovery of "canals" on Mars in 1877 received enthusiastic support from Flammarion. He went even further, claiming that he could discern changes in the lunar craters that could be cultivated fields.

Flamsteed, John

(1646–1719)

ENGLISH ASTRONOMER

In carrying out views of practical utility, with a scrupulous attention to accuracy in the most minute details, in fortitude of resolution under adverse circumstances, and persevering adherence to continuity and regularity of observation throughout a long career, he had few rivals in any age or country.
— Robert Grant, *History of Physical Astronomy* (1852)

Flamsteed was born in Denby, England. Because of ill health, which was to dog his career, he was forced to leave school early and was therefore largely self-educated. He started his scientific career under the patronage of William Brouncker, the first president of the Royal Society, having impressed him by computing an almanac of celestial events for 1670.

A major problem of the time – one tackled at some time by all major astronomers of the 17th century – was the determination of longitude at sea. A suggestion had been made that the motion of the Moon against the stellar background could be used to determine standard time. Flamsteed, asked by Brouncker to comment on this proposal, pointed out that the scheme was impractical because of the inaccuracy of contemporary tables. Charles II subsequently commanded that accurate tables should be constructed, appointing Flamsteed as first Astronomer Royal with this responsibility in 1675, and building the Royal Greenwich Observatory for him, which was opened in 1676. The limited nature of the royal patronage is indicated by the fact that Flamsteed was paid a salary of £100 a year but was expected to provide his own instruments and staff. He eventually managed to put together two small telescopes and then began his decades of observation, made more difficult by his lack of staff and the crippling headaches from which he suffered. In order to make ends meet he was forced to become a clergyman at Burstow in Surrey from 1684 until his death.

The results of his labors were eventually published posthumously in 1725 as the *Historia coelestis Britannica* (British Celestial Record). It contains the position of over 3,000 stars calculated to an accuracy of ten seconds of arc. It was the first great modern comprehensive telescopic catalog and established Greenwich as one of the leading observatories of the world. The publication of the work was not without its difficulties. It involved Flamsteed in a long and bitter dispute with Newton. Flamsteed was reluctant to rush into print with his catalog, claiming, it seemed to Newton, far too much time for the checking of his numerous observations. The dispute lasted from Newton's assumption of the presidency of the Royal Society in 1703 until Flamsteed's death. It involved the virtual seizure of Flamsteed's papers by Newton, the editing and partial publication by Edmond Halley, and their total rejection by Flamsteed who even went so far as to acquire 300 of the 400 printed copies of his own work and burn them. He managed, however, to revise the first volume to his satisfaction before his death in 1719.

Sources and Further Reading

D'ALEMBERT

Hankins, Thomas L. *Jean D'Alembert – Science and the Enlightenment*. New York: Oxford University Press, 1970.

DALTON

Cardwell, D. S. L., ed. *John Dalton and the Progress of Science*. New York: Barnes and Noble, 1968.

Thackray, Arnold. *John Dalton: Critical Assessments of his Life and Science*. Cambridge, MA: MIT Press, 1972.

DART

Dart, R. *Adventures with the Missing Link*. Philadelphia, PA: The Institutes Press, 1967.

Reader, John. *Missing Links. The Hunt for Earliest Man*. Boston, MA: Little, Brown, and Co., 1988.

DARWIN, Charles

Darwin, Charles. *The Origin of Species*. New York: Mentor Books, 1958.

Desmond, Adrian, and James Moore. *Darwin*. New York: Warner Books, 1992.

DAVY

Harré, Rom. *Great Scientific Experiments*. Oxford: Phaidon Press, 1981.

Knight, David. *Humphry Davy, Science and Power*. New York: Cambridge University Press, 1996.

DAWKINS

Dawkins, Richard. *The Selfish Gene*. New York: Oxford University Press, 1976.

———. *The Blind Watchmaker*. New York: W. W. Norton, 1986.

DE BROGLIE

Broglie, Prince L. de. *The Revolution in Physics: a Non-Mathematical Survey of Quanta*. New York: Noonday Press, 1953.

Hoffmann, Banesh. *The Strange Story of the Quantum*. New York: Dover Publications, 1959.

DEDEKIND

Bell, E. T. *Men of Mathematics*. New York: Simon and Schuster, 1937.

Kneale, W., and M. Kneale. *The Development of Logic*. New York: Oxford University Press, 1962.

DE LA BECHE

Secord, James A. *Controversy in Victorian Geology: The Cambrian-Silurian Dispute*. Princeton, NJ: Princeton University Press, 1990.

DELBRÜCK

Judson, H. F. *The Eighth Day of Creation*. New York: Simon and Schuster, 1979.

DESARGUES

Field, J. V., and J. J. Gray. *The Geometrical Work of Girard Desargues*. Berlin: Springer-Verlag, 1987.

DESCARTES

Cottingham, John, ed. *The Cambridge Companion to Descartes*. New York: Cambridge University Press, 1992.

DIOPHANTUS

Heath, T. L., ed. *Diophantus of Alexandria*. New York: Dover Publications, 1964.

DIRAC

Kragh, Helge. *Dirac: a Scientific Biography*. New York: Cambridge University Press, 1990.

Kursunoglu, B. N., and E. P. Wigner. *Reminiscences about a Great Physicist*. New York: Cambridge University Press, 1987.

DJERASSI

Djerassi, Carl. *The Pill, Pygmy Chimps and Degas' Horse: The Autobiography of Carl Djerassi*. New York: Basic Books, 1992.

DYSON, Freeman

Dyson, Freeman. *Disturbing the Universe*. New York: Harper and Row, 1979.

——. *Infinite in all Directions*. New York: Harper and Row, 1988.

ECCLES

Eccles, J. C. *The Understanding of the Brain*. New York: McGraw Hill, 1977.

Eccles, J. C., and K. R. Popper. *The Self and Its Brain*. Berlin: Springer-Verlag, 1977.

ECKERT

Slater, Robert. *Portraits in Silicon*. Cambridge, MA: MIT Press, 1987.

EDDINGTON

Chandrasekhar, S. *Eddington: the Most Distinguished Astrophysicist of his Time*. New York: Cambridge University Press, 1983.

Eddington, A. *The Nature of the Physical World*. New York: Cambridge University Press, 1929.

——. *The Expanding Universe*. New York: Cambridge University Press, 1933.

EDELMAN

Edelman, Gerald M. *Neural Darwinism*. New York: Basic Books, 1987.

——. *Bright Air, Brilliant Fire*. New York: Basic Books, 1992.

EDISON

Friedel, R. D., and P. Israel. *Edison's Electric Light: Biography of an Invention*. New Brunswick, NJ: Rutger's University Press, 1986.

Josephson, Matthew. *Edison*. London: Macdonald and Jane's, 1959.

EINSTEIN

Bernstein, Jeremy. *Einstein*. New York: HarperCollins, 1973.

Einstein, Albert. *Relativity: the Special and General Theory*. New York: Crown Publishing, Random House, 1961.

EINTHOVEN

Baldry, P. E. *The Battle Against Heart Disease*. New York: Cambridge University Press, 1971.

EUCLID

Heath, T. L. *The Thirteen Books of Euclid's Elements*, 3 vols. New York: Dover Publications, 1956.

Gjertsen, Derek. *The Classics of Science*. New York: Lilian Barber Press, 1984.

EULER

Bell, E. T. *Men of Mathematics*. New York: Simon and Schuster, 1937.

Dunham, William. *The Great Theorems of Mathematics*. New York: John Wiley, 1990.

EWING, William Maurice

Sullivan, Walter. *Continents in Motion*. New York: McGraw-Hill, 1974.

FARADAY

Faraday, Michael. *The Forces of Matter*. Buffalo, NY: Prometheus Books, 1993.

Gooding, David, and Frank James, eds. *Faraday Rediscovered: Essays on the Life and Work of Michael Faraday 1791–1867*. New York: Stockton Press, 1985.

FERMAT

Bell, E. T. *Men of Mathematics*. New York: Simon and Schuster, 1937.

Stewart, Ian. *From Here to Infinity*. New York: Oxford University Press, 1996.

FERMI

Fermi, Laura. *Atoms in the Family – My Life with Enrico Fermi*. New York: American Institute of Physics, 1987.

Segré, Emilio. *Enrico Fermi, Physicist*. Chicago, IL: University of Chicago Press, 1970.

FEYERABEND

Feyerabend, Paul. *Killing Time*. Chicago, IL: University of Chicago Press, 1995.

FEYNMAN

Feynman, Richard. *Surely You're Joking, Mr. Feynman*. New York: W. W. Norton, 1985.

Gleick, James. *Genius*. New York: Pantheon Books, Random House, 1992.

FISHER

Box, Joan Fisher. *R. A. Fisher: the Life of a Scientist*. New York: John Wiley, 1978.

Fisher, R. A. *The Genetical Theory of Natural Selection*. New York: Dover Publications, 1958

Glossary

absolute zero The zero value of thermodynamic temperature, equal to 0 kelvin or −273.15°C.

acceleration of free fall The acceleration of a body falling freely, at a specified point on the Earth's surface, as a result of the gravitational attraction of the Earth. The standard value is 9.80665 m s^{-2} (32.174 ft s^{-2}).

acetylcholine A chemical compound that is secreted at the endings of some nerve cells and transmits a nerve impulse from one nerve cell to the next or to a muscle, gland, etc.

acquired characteristics Characteristics developed during the life of an organism, but not inherited, as a result of use and disuse of organs.

adrenaline (epinephrine) A hormone, secreted by the adrenal gland, that increases metabolic activity in conditions of stress.

aldehyde Any of a class of organic compounds containing the group –CHO.

aliphatic Denoting an organic compound that is not aromatic, including the alkanes, alkenes, alkynes, cycloalkanes, and their derivatives.

alkane Any of the saturated hydrocarbons with the general formula C_nH_{2n+2}.

alkene Any one of a class of hydrocarbons characterized by the presence of double bonds between carbon atoms and having the general formula C_nH_{2n}. The simplest example is ethylene (ethene).

alkyne Any one of a class of hydrocarbons characterized by the presence of triple bonds between carbon atoms. The simplest example is ethyne (acetylene).

allele One of two or more alternative forms of a particular gene.

amino acid Any one of a class of organic compounds that contain both an amino group (–NH$_2$) and a carboxyl group (–COOH) in their molecules. Amino acids are the units present in peptides and proteins.

amount of substance A measure of quantity proportional to the number of particles of substance present.

anabolism The sum of the processes involved in the synthesis of the constituents of living cells.

androgen Any of a group of steroid hormones with masculinizing properties, produced by the testes in all vertebrate animals.

antibody A protein produced by certain white blood cells (lymphocytes) in response to the presence of an antigen. An antibody forms a complex with an antigen, which is thereby inactivated.

antigen A foreign or potentially harmful substance that, when introduced into the body, stimulates the production of a specific antibody.

aromatic Denoting a chemical compound that has the property of aromaticity, as characterized by benzene.

asteroid Any of a large number of small celestial bodies orbiting the Sun, mainly between Mars and Jupiter.

atomic orbital A region around the nucleus of an atom in which an electron moves. According to wave mechanics, the electron's location is described by a probability distribution in space, given by the wave function.

ATP Adenosine triphosphate: a compound, found in all living organisms, that functions as a carrier of chemical energy, which is released when required for metabolic reactions.

bacteriophage A virus that lives and reproduces as a parasite within a bacterium.

bacterium (*pl.* **bacteria**) Any one of a large group of microorganisms that all lack a membrane around the nucleus and have a cell wall of unique composition.

band theory The application of quantum mechanics to the energies of electrons in crystalline solids.

baryon Any of a class of elementary particles that have half-integral spin and take part in strong interactions. They consist of three quarks each.

beta decay A type of radioactive decay in which an unstable nucleus ejects either an electron and an antineutrino or a positron and a neutrino.

black body A hypothetical body that absorbs all the radiation falling on it.

bremsstrahlung Electromagnetic radiation produced by the deceleration of charged particles.

carbohydrate Any of a class of compounds with the formula $C_nH_{2m}O_m$. The carbohydrates include the sugars, starch, and cellulose.

carcinogen Any agent, such as a chemical or type of radiation, that causes cancer.

catabolism The sum of the processes involved in the breakdown of molecules in living cells in order to provide chemical energy for metabolic processes.

catalysis The process by which the rate of a chemical reaction is increased by the presence of another substance (the catalyst) that does not appear in the stoichiometric equation for the reaction.

cathode-ray oscilloscope An instrument for displaying changing electrical signals on a cathode-ray tube.

cellulose A white solid carbohydrate, $(C_6H_{10}O_5)_n$, found in all plants as the main constituent of the cell wall.

chelate An inorganic metal complex in which there is a closed ring of atoms, caused by attachment of a ligand to a metal atom at two points.

chlorophyll Any one of a group of green pigments, found in all plants, that absorb light for photosynthesis.

cholesterol A steroid alcohol occurring widely in animal cell membranes and tissues. Excess amounts in the blood are associated with atherosclerosis (obstruction of the arteries).

chromatography Any of several related techniques for separating and analyzing mixtures by selective adsorption or absorption in a flow system.

chromosome One of a number of threadlike structures, consisting mainly of DNA and protein, found in the nucleus of cells and constituting the genetic material of the cell.

codon The basic coding unit of DNA and RNA, consisting of a sequence of three nucleotides that specifies a particular amino acid in the synthesis of proteins in a cell.

collagen A fibrous protein that is a major constituent of the connective tissue in skin, tendons, and bone.

colligative property A property that depends on the number of particles of substance present in a substance, rather than on the nature of the particles.

continental drift The theory that the Earth's continents once formed a single mass, parts of which have drifted apart to their present positions.

cortisone A steroid hormone, produced by the cortex (outer part) of the adrenal gland, that regulates the metabolism of carbohydrate, fat, and protein and reduces inflammation.

critical mass The minimum mass of fissile material for which a chain reaction is self-sustaining.

cryogenics The branch of physics concerned with the production of very low temperatures and the study of phenomena occurring at these temperatures.

cyclotron A type of particle accelerator in which the particles move in spiral paths under the influence of a uniform vertical magnetic field and are accelerated by an electric field of fixed frequency.

cytoplasm The jellylike material that surrounds the nucleus of a living cell.

dendrochronology A method of dating wooden specimens based on the growth rings of trees. It depends on the assumption that trees grown in the same climatic conditions have a characteristic pattern of rings.

dialysis The separation of mixtures by selective diffusion through a semipermeable membrane.

diffraction The formation of light and dark bands (diffraction patterns) around the boundary of a shadow cast by an object or aperture.

diploid Describing a nucleus, cell, or organism with two sets of chromosomes, one set deriving from the male parent and the other from the female parent.

DNA Deoxyribonucleic acid: a nucleic acid that is a major constituent of the chromosomes and is the hereditary material of most organisms.

dissociation The breakdown of a molecule into radicals, ions, atoms, or simpler molecules.

distillation A process used to purify or separate liquids by evaporating them and recondensing the vapor.

ecology The study of living organisms in relation to their environment.

eigenfunction One of a set of allowed wave functions of a particle in a given system as determined by wave mechanics.

electrolysis Chemical change produced by passing an electric current through a conducting solution or fused ionic substance.

electromagnetic radiation Waves of energy (electromagnetic waves) consisting of electric and magnetic fields vibrating at right angles to the direction of propagation of the waves.

electromotive force The energy supplied by a source of current in driving unit charge around an electrical circuit. It is measured in volts.

electromotive series A series of the metals arranged in decreasing order of their tendency to form positive ions by a reaction of the type $M = M^+ + e$.

electron An elementary particle with a negative charge equal to that of the proton and a rest mass of 9.1095×10^{-31} kilograms (about 1/1836 that of the proton).

electron microscope A device in which a magnified image of a sample is produced by illuminating it with a beam of high-energy electrons rather than light.

electroweak theory A unified theory of the electromagnetic interaction and the weak interaction.

enthalpy A thermodynamic property of a system equal to the sum of its internal energy and the product of its pressure and its volume.

entomology The branch of zoology concerned with the study of insects.

entropy A measure of the disorder of a system. In any system undergoing a reversible change the change of entropy is defined as the energy absorbed divided by the thermodynamic temperature. The entropy of the system is thus a measure of the availability of its energy for performing useful work.

escape velocity The minimum velocity that would have to be given to an object for it to escape from a specified gravitational field. The escape velocity from the Earth is 25,054 mph (7 miles per second).

ester A compound formed by a reaction between an alcohol and a fatty acid.

estrogen Any one of a group of steroid hormones, produced mainly by the ovaries in all vertebrates, that stimulate the growth and maintenance of the female reproductive organs.

ethology The study of the behavior of animals in their natural surroundings.

excitation A change in the energy of an atom, ion, molecule, etc., from one energy level (usually the ground state) to a higher energy level.

fatty acid Any of a class of organic acids with the general formula R.CO.OH, where R is a hydrocarbon group.

fermentation A reaction in which compounds, such as sugar, are broken down by the action of microorganisms that form the enzymes required to catalyze the reaction.

flash photolysis A technique for investigating the spectra and reactions of free radicals.

free energy A thermodynamic function used to measure the ability of a system to perform work. A change in free energy is equal to the work done.

free radical An atom or group of atoms that has an independent existence without all its valences being satisfied.

fuel cell A type of electric cell in which electrical energy is produced directly by electrochemical reactions involving substances that are continuously added to the cell.

fungus Any one of a group of spore-producing organisms formerly classified as plants but now placed in a separate kingdom (Fungi). They include the mushrooms, molds, and yeasts.

galaxy Any of the innumerable aggregations of stars that, together with gas, dust, and other material, make up the universe.

gene The functional unit of heredity. A single gene contains the information required for the manufacture, by a living cell, of one particular polypeptide, protein, or type of RNA and is the vehicle by which such information is transmitted to subsequent generations. Genes correspond to discrete regions of the DNA (or RNA) making up the genome.

genetic code The system by which genetic material carries the information that directs the activities of a living cell. The code is contained in the sequence of nucleotides of DNA and/or RNA (*see* codon).

genome The sum total of an organism's genetic material, including all the genes carried by its chromosomes.

global warming *See* greenhouse effect.

glycolysis The series of reactions in which glucose is broken down with the release of energy in the form of ATP.

greenhouse effect An effect in the Earth's atmosphere resulting from the presence of such gases as CO_2, which absorb the infrared radiation produced by the reradiation of solar ultraviolet radiation at the Earth's surface. This causes a rise in the Earth's average temperature, known as "global warming."

half-life A measure of the stability of a radioactive substance, equal to the time taken for its activity to fall to one half of its original value.

halogens The nonmetallic elements fluorine, chlorine, bromine, iodine, and astatine.

haploid Describing a nucleus or cell that contains only a single set of chromosomes; haploid organisms consist exclusively of haploid cells. During sexual reproduction, two haploid sex cells fuse to form a single diploid cell.

heat death The state of a closed system when its total entropy has increased to its maximum value. Under these conditions there is no available energy.

histamine A substance released by various tissues of the body in response to invasion by microorganisms or other stimuli. It triggers inflammation and is responsible for some of the symptoms (e.g., sneezing) occurring in such allergies as hay fever.

histology The study of the tissues of living organisms.

hormone Any of various substances that are produced in small amounts by certain glands within the body (the endocrine glands) and released into the bloodstream to regulate the growth or activities of organs and tissues elsewhere in the body.

hydrocarbon Any organic compound composed only of carbon and hydrogen.

hydrogen bond A weak attraction between an electronegative atom, such as oxygen, nitrogen, or fluorine, and a hydrogen atom that is covalently linked to another electronegative atom.

hysteresis An apparent lag of an effect with respect to the magnitude of the agency producing the effect.

ideal gas An idealized gas composed of atoms that have a negligible volume and undergo perfectly elastic collisions. Such a gas would obey the gas laws under all conditions.

immunology The study of the body's mechanisms for defense against disease and the various ways in which these can be manipulated or enhanced.

insulin A hormone that is responsible for regulating the level of glucose in the blood, i.e., "blood sugar." It is produced by certain cells in the pancreas; deficiency causes the disease diabetes mellitus.

integrated circuit An electronic circuit made in a single small unit.

interferon Any one of a group of proteins, produced by various cells and tissues in the body, that increase resistance to invading viruses. Some types are synthesized for use in medicine as antiviral drugs.

internal energy The total energy possessed by a system on account of the kinetic and potential energies of its component molecules.

ion An atom or group of atoms with a net positive or negative charge. Positive ions (cations) have a deficiency of electrons and negative ions (anions) have an excess.

ionizing radiation Electromagnetic radiation or particles that cause ionization.

ionosphere A region of ionized air and free electrons around the Earth in the Earth's upper atmosphere, extending from a height of about 31 miles to 621 miles.

isomerism The existence of two or more chemical compounds with the same molecular formula but different arrangements of atoms in their molecules.

isotope Any of a number of forms of an element, all of which differ only in the number of neutrons in their atomic nuclei.

ketone Any of a class of organic compounds with the general formula RCOR′, where R and R′ are usually hydrocarbon groups.

kinetic energy The energy that a system has by

virtue of its motion, determined by the work necessary to bring it to rest.

kinetic theory Any theory for describing the physical properties of a system with reference to the motion of its constituent atoms or molecules.

laser A device for producing intense light or infrared or ultraviolet radiation by stimulated emission.

latent heat The total heat absorbed or produced during a change of phase (fusion, vaporization, etc.) at a constant temperature.

lepton Any of a class of elementary particles that have half-integral spin and take part in weak interactions; they include the electron, the muon, the neutrino, and their antiparticles.

lipid An ester of a fatty acid. Simple lipids include fats and oils; compound lipids include phospholipids and glycolipids; derived lipids include the steroids.

liquid crystal A state of certain molecules that flow like liquids but have an ordered arrangement of molecules.

macromolecule A very large molecule, as found in polymers or in such compounds as proteins.

magnetohydrodynamics The study of the motion of electrically conducting fluids and their behavior in magnetic fields.

meiosis A type of nuclear division, occurring only in certain cells of the reproductive organs, in which a diploid cell produces four haploid sex cells, or gametes.

meson Any member of a class of elementary particles characterized by a mass intermediate between those of the electron and the proton, an integral spin, and participation in strong interactions. They consist of two quarks each.

metabolism The totality of the chemical reactions taking place in a living cell or organism.

mitosis The type of nuclear division occurring in the body cells of most organisms, in which a diploid cell produces two diploid daughter cells.

moderator A substance used in fission reactors to slow down fast neutrons.

monoclonal antibody Any antibody produced by members of a group of genetically identical cells (which thus constitute a "clone"). Such antibodies have identical structures and each combines with the same antigen in precisely the same manner.

morphology The study of the form of organisms, especially their external shape and structure.

muon An elementary particle having a positive or negative charge and a mass equal to 206.77 times the mass of the electron.

mutation Any change in the structure of a gene, which can arise spontaneously or as a result of such agents as x-rays or certain chemicals. It may have a beneficial effect on the organism but most mutations are neutral, harmful, or even lethal. Mutations affecting the germ cells can be passed on to the organism's offspring.

natural selection The process by which the individuals of a population that are best adapted to life in a particular environment tend to enjoy greater reproductive success than members which are less well adapted. Hence, over successive generations, the descendants of the former constitute an increasing proportion of the population.

neutrino An elementary particle with zero rest mass, a velocity equal to that of light, and a spin of one half.

nuclear fission The process in which an atomic nucleus splits into fragment nuclei and one or more neutrons with the emission of energy.

nuclear fusion A nuclear reaction in which two light nuclei join together to form a heavier nucleus with the emission of energy.

nuclear winter The period of darkness and low temperature, predicted to follow a nuclear war, as a result of the obscuring of sunlight by dust and other debris.

nucleic acid Any of a class of large biologically important molecules consisting of one or more chains of nucleotides. There are two types: deoxyribonucleic acid (DNA) and ribonucleic acid (RNA).

nucleotide Any of a class of compounds consisting of a nitrogen-containing base (a purine or pyrimidine) combined with a sugar group (ribose or deoxyribose) bearing a phosphate group. Long chains of nucleotides form the nucleic acids, DNA and RNA.

nucleon A particle that is a constituent of an atomic nucleus; either a proton or a neutron.

nucleus 1. The positively charged part of the atom about which the electrons orbit. The nucleus is composed of neutrons and protons held together by strong interactions. 2. A prominent body found in the cells of animals, plants, and other organisms (but not bacteria) that contains the chromosomes and is bounded by a double membrane.

oncogene A gene, introduced into a living cell by certain viruses, that disrupts normal metabolism and transforms the cell into a cancer cell.

optical activity The property of certain substances of rotating the plane of polarization of plane-polarized light.

osmosis Preferential flow of certain substances in solution through a semipermeable membrane. If the membrane separates a solution from a pure solvent, the solvent will flow through the membrane into the solution.

oxidation A process in which oxygen is combined with a substance or hydrogen is removed from a compound.

ozone layer A layer containing ozone in the Earth's atmosphere. It lies between heights of 9 and 19 miles and absorbs the Sun's higher-energy ultraviolet radiation.

parity A property of elementary particles depending on the symmetry of their wave function with respect to changes in sign of the coordinates.

parthenogenesis A form of reproduction in which a sex cell, usually an egg cell, develops into an embryo without fertilization. It occurs in certain plants and invertebrates and results in offspring that are genetically identical to the parent.

pathology The study of the nature and causes of disease.

peptide A compound formed by two or more amino acids linked together. The amino group ($-NH_2$) of one acid reacts with the carboxyl group ($-COOH$) of another to give the group $-NH-CO-$, known as the "peptide linkage."

periodic table A tabular arrangement of the elements in order of increasing atomic number such that similarities are displayed between groups of elements.

pH A measure of the acidity or alkalinity of a solution, equal to the logarithm to base 10 of the reciprocal of the concentration of hydrogen ions.

photocell Any device for converting light or other electromagnetic radiation directly into an electric current.

photoelectric effect The ejection of electrons from a solid as a result of irradiation by light or other electromagnetic radiation. The number of electrons emitted depends on the intensity of the light and not on its frequency.

photolysis The dissociation of a chemical compound into other compounds, atoms, and free radicals by irradiation with electromagnetic radiation.

photon A quantum of electromagnetic radiation.

photosynthesis The process by which plants, algae, and certain bacteria "fix" inorganic carbon, from carbon dioxide, as organic carbon in the form of carbohydrate using light as a source of energy and, in green plants and algae, water as a source of hydrogen. The light energy is trapped by special pigments, e.g., chlorophyll.

piezoelectric effect An effect observed in certain crystals in which they develop a potential difference across a pair of opposite faces when subjected to a stress.

pion A type of meson having either zero, positive, or negative charge and a mass 264.2 times that of the electron.

plankton The mass of microscopic plants and animals that drift passively at or near the surface of oceans and lakes.

plasma 1. An ionized gas consisting of free electrons and an approximately equal number of ions. **2.** Blood plasma: the liquid component of blood, excluding the blood cells.

plate tectonics The theory that the Earth's surface consists of lithospheric plates, which have moved throughout geological time to their present positions.

polypeptide A chain of amino acids held together by peptide linkages. Polypeptides are found in proteins.

potential energy The energy that a system has by virtue of its position or state, determined by the work necessary to change the system from a reference position to its present state.

probability The likelihood that an event will occur. If an event is certain to occur its probability is 1; if it is certain not to occur the proba-bility is 0. In any other circumstances the probability lies between 0 and 1.

protein Any of a large number of naturally occurring organic compounds found in all living matter. Proteins consist of chains of amino acids joined by peptide linkages.

proton A stable elementary particle with a positive electric charge equal to that of the electron. It is the nucleus of a hydrogen atom and weighs 1,836 times the mass of the electron.

protozoa A large group of minute single-celled organisms found widely in freshwater, marine, and damp terrestrial habitats. Unlike bacteria they possess a definite nucleus and are distinguished from plants in lacking cellulose.

pulsar A star that acts as a source of regularly fluctuating electromagnetic radiation, the period of the pulses usually being very rapid.

quantum electrodynamics The quantum theory of electromagnetic interactions between particles and between particles and electromagnetic radiation.

quantum theory A mathematical theory involving the idea that the energy of a system can change only in discrete amounts (quanta), rather than continuously.

quark Any of six elementary particles and their corresponding antiparticles with fractional charges that are the building blocks of baryons and mesons. Together with leptons they are the basis of all matter.

quasar A class of starlike astronomical objects with large redshifts, many of which emanate strong radio waves.

radioactive labeling The use of radioactive atoms in a compound to trace the path of the compound through a biological or mechanical system.

radioactivity The spontaneous disintegration of the nuclei of certain isotopes with emission of beta rays (electrons), alpha rays (helium nuclei), or gamma rays.

radio astronomy The branch of astronomy involving the use of radio telescopes.

radiocarbon dating A method of dating archeological specimens of wood, cotton, etc., based on the small amount of radioactive carbon (carbon–14) incorporated into the specimen when it was living and the extent to which this isotope has decayed since its death.

radioisotope A radioactive isotope of an element.

recombination The reassortment of maternally derived and paternally derived genes that occurs during meiosis preceding the formation of sex cells. Recombination is an important source of genetic variation.

redox reaction A reaction in which one reactant is oxidized and the other is reduced.

redshift The displacement of the spectral lines emitted by a moving body towards the red end of the visual spectrum. It is caused by the Doppler effect and, when observed in the spectrum of distant stars and galaxies, it indicates that the body is receding from the earth.

reduction A process in which oxygen is removed from or hydrogen is combined with a compound.

reflex An automatic response of an organism or body part to a stimulus, i.e., one that occurs without conscious control.

refractory A solid that has a high melting point and can withstand high temperatures.

relativistic mass The mass of a body as predicted by the theory of relativity. The relativistic mass of a particle moving at velocity v is $m_0(1 - v^2/c^2)^{-1/2}$, where m_0 is the rest mass.

rest mass The mass of a body when it is at rest relative to its observer, as distinguished from its relativistic mass.

retrovirus A type of virus whose genome, consisting of RNA, is transcribed into a DNA version and then inserted into the DNA of its host. The flow of genetic information, from RNA to DNA, is thus the reverse of that found in organisms generally.

RNA Ribonucleic acid: any one of several types of nucleic acid, including messenger RNA, that process the information carried by the genes and use it to direct the assembly of proteins in cells. In certain viruses RNA is the genetic material.

semiconductor A solid with an electrical conductivity that is intermediate between those of insulators and metals and that increases with increasing temperature. Examples are germanium, silicon, and lead telluride.

semipermeable membrane A barrier that permits the passage of some substances but is impermeable to others.

serum The fraction of blood plasma excluding the components of the blood-clotting system.

sex chromosome A chromosome that participates in determining the sex of individuals. Humans have two sex chromosomes, X and Y; females have two X chromosomes (XX) and males have one of each (XY).

sex hormone Any hormone that controls the development of sexual characteristics and regulates reproductive activity. The principal human sex hormones are progesterone and estrogens in females, testosterone and androsterone in males.

simple harmonic motion Motion of a point moving along a path so that its acceleration is directed towards a fixed point on the path and is directly proportional to the displacement from this fixed point.

SI units A system of units used, by international agreement, for all scientific purposes. It is based on the meter-kilogram-second (MKS) system and consists of seven base units and two supplementary units.

soap A salt of a fatty acid.

solar cell Any electrical device for converting solar energy directly into electrical energy.

solar constant The energy per unit area per unit time received from the Sun at a point that is the Earth's mean distance from the Sun away. It has the value 1,400 joules per square meter per second.

solar wind Streams of electrons and protons emitted by the Sun. The solar wind is responsible for the formation of the Van Allen belts and the aurora.

solid-state physics The experimental and theoretical study of the properties of the solid state, in particular the study of energy levels and the electrical and magnetic properties of metals and semiconductors.

speciation The process in which new species evolve from existing populations of organisms.

specific heat capacity The amount of heat required to raise the temperature of unit mass of a substance by unit temperature; it is usually measured in joules per kilogram per kelvin.

spectrometer Any of various instruments used for producing a spectrum (distribution of wavelengths of increasing magnitude) and measuring the wavelengths, energies, etc.

speed of light The speed at which all electromagnetic radiation travels; it is the highest speed attainable in the universe and has the value 2.998×10^8 meters per second in a vacuum.

standing wave A wave in which the wave profile remains stationary in the medium through which it is passing.

state of matter One of the three physical states – solid, liquid, or gas – in which matter may exist.

stereochemistry The arrangement in space of the groups in a molecule and the effect this has on the compound's properties and chemical behavior.

steroid Any of a group of complex lipids that occur widely in plants and animals and include various hormones, such as cortisone and the sex hormones.

stimulated emission The process in which a photon colliding with an excited atom causes emission of a second photon with the same energy as the first. It is the basis of lasers.

stoichiometric Involving chemical combination in exact ratios.

strangeness A property of certain hadrons that causes them to decay more slowly than expected from the energy released.

strong interaction A type of interaction between elementary particles occurring at short range (about 10^{-15} meter) and having a magnitude about 100 times greater than that of the electromagnetic interaction.

sublimation The passage of certain substances from the solid state into the gaseous state and then back into the solid state, without any intermediate liquid state being formed.

substrate A substance that is acted upon in some way, especially the compound acted on by a catalyst or the solid on which a compound is adsorbed.

sugar Any of a group of water-soluble simple carbohydrates, usually having a sweet taste.

sunspot A region of the Sun's surface that is much cooler and therefore darker than the surrounding area, having a temperature of about 4,000°C as opposed to 6,000°C for the rest of the photosphere.

superconductivity A phenomenon occurring

in certain metals and alloys at temperatures close to absolute zero, in which the electrical resistance of the solid vanishes below a certain temperature.

superfluid A fluid that flows without friction and has extremely high thermal conductivity.

supernova A star that suffers an explosion, becoming up to 10^8 times brighter in the process and forming a large cloud of expanding debris (the supernova remnant).

surfactant A substance used to increase the spreading or wetting properties of a liquid. Surfactants are often detergents, which act by lowering the surface tension.

symbiosis A long-term association between members of different species, especially where mutual benefit is derived by the participants.

taxonomy The science of classifying organisms into groups.

tensile strength The applied stress necessary to break a material under tension.

thermal conductivity A measure of the ability of a substance to conduct heat, equal to the rate of flow of heat per unit area resulting from unit temperature gradient.

thermal neutron A neutron with a low kinetic energy, of the same order of magnitude as the kinetic energies of atoms and molecules.

thermionic emission Emission of electrons from a hot solid. The effect occurs when significant numbers of electrons have enough kinetic energy to overcome the solid's work function.

thermodynamics The branch of science concerned with the relationship between heat, work, and other forms of energy.

thermodynamic temperature Temperature measured in kelvins that is a function of the internal energy possessed by a body, having a value of zero at absolute zero.

thixotropy A phenomenon shown by some fluids in which the viscosity decreases as the rate of shear increases, i.e., the fluid becomes less viscous the faster it moves.

transducer A device that is supplied with the energy of one system and converts it into the energy of a different system, so that the output signal is proportional to the input signal but is carried in a different form.

transistor A device made of semiconducting material in which a flow of current between two electrodes can be controlled by a potential applied to a third electrode.

tribology The study of friction between solid surfaces, including the origin of frictional forces and the lubrication of moving parts.

triple point The point at which the solid, liquid, and gas phases of a pure substance can all coexist in equilibrium.

tritiated Denoting a chemical compound containing tritium (^{3}H) atoms in place of hydrogen atoms.

ultracentrifuge A centrifuge designed to work at very high speeds, so that the force produced is large enough to cause sedimentation of colloids.

unified-field theory A theory that seeks to explain gravitational and electromagnetic interactions and the strong and weak nuclear interactions in terms of a single set of equations.

vaccine An antigenic preparation that is administered to a human or other animal to produce immunity against a specific disease-causing agent.

valence The combining power of an element, atom, ion, or radical, equal to the number of hydrogen atoms that the atom, ion, etc., could combine with or displace in forming a compound.

valence band The energy band of a solid that is occupied by the valence electrons of the atoms forming the solid.

valence electron An electron in the outer shell of an atom that participates in the chemical bonding when the atom forms compounds.

vector 1. A quantity that is specified both by its magnitude and its direction. 2. An agent, such as an insect, that harbors disease-causing microorganisms and transmits them to humans, other animals, or plants.

virtual particle A particle thought of as existing for a very brief period in an interaction between two other particles.

virus A noncellular agent that can infect a living animal, plant, or bacterial cell and use the apparatus of the host cell to manufacture new virus particles. In some cases this causes disease in the host organism. Outside the host cell, viruses are totally inert.

viscosity The property of liquids and gases of resisting flow. It is caused by forces between the molecules of the fluid.

water of crystallization Water combined in the form of molecules in definite proportions in the crystals of many substances.

wave equation A partial differential equation relating the displacement of a wave to the time and the three spatial dimensions.

wave function A mathematical expression giving the probability of finding the particle associated with a wave at a specified point according to wave mechanics.

wave mechanics A form of quantum mechanics in which particles (electrons, protons, etc.) are regarded as waves, so that any system of particles can be described by a wave equation.

weak interaction A type of interaction between elementary particles, occurring at short range and having a magnitude about 10^{10} times weaker than the electromagnetic force.

work function The minimum energy necessary to remove an electron from a metal at absolute zero.

x-ray crystallography The determination of the structure of crystals and molecules by use of x-ray diffraction.

zero point energy The energy of vibration of atoms at the absolute zero of temperature.

zwitterion An ion that has both a positive and negative charge.

INDEX

Index • 233